DANTE
SOUNDINGS

PUBLICATIONS OF THE FOUNDATION FOR ITALIAN STUDIES
UNIVERSITY COLLEGE DUBLIN

General editor: David Nolan

1. *Dante Soundings*

DANTE
SOUNDINGS

*Eight Literary
and
Historical Essays*

Edited by DAVID NOLAN

Published for

The Foundation for Italian Studies

University College, Dublin

IRISH ACADEMIC PRESS DUBLIN
ROWMAN AND LITTLEFIELD TOTOWA N.J.

82-444

This book was typeset and printed in the Republic of Ireland for Irish Academic Press Limited, Kill Lane, Blackrock, County Dublin and Rowman and Littlefield, Totowa, N.J.

Irish Academic Press edition ISBN 0 7165 0058 2
Rowman and Littlefield edition ISBN 0 8476 3633 X
©Foundation for Italian Studies University College Dublin 1981

Publication of this book was assisted by grants from
University College Dublin and the Istituto Italiano di Cultura in Dublin

Printed in The Republic of Ireland
by Folens & Co. Dublin

Dedicated to the achievement of
the Directors of the Italian Cultural Institute in Dublin
from the present Director Andrea Tossi
to the first Director a quarter of a century ago
the original inspiration
Enzo Giachino

Contents

Foreword

This collection of Dante studies, like the preceding volume, *Dante Commentaries* (Dublin, 1977), is based on lectures given during the annual Dante series in University College Dublin, and is the first publication of the Foundation for Italian Studies at University College Dublin. The publication has been made possible by generous grants from the Dublin Istituto Italiano di Cultura negotiated by the former Director, Dr. Maria Rosa Maranzano, and from University College Dublin.

As the title suggests, the authors, although they base their soundings on cantos or episodes of the poem, attempt to measure some of the depths of Dante's poetry. In the last essay, however, Michael Richter deals with the *Monarchia* and not with the *Commedia*. In readings of different cantos, Peter Armour discusses allegory and figuralism, Robin Kirkpatrick examines Dante's poetic pragmatism. The role of Virgil in the poem is reviewed by Jennifer Petrie and J.H. Whitfield unfolds the meaning of Statius for Dante; M.B. Crowe puts forward Siger of Brabant as the philosopher in the *Paradiso*; J.C. Barnes performs a minute and revealing anatomy of *Inferno* xiii, while Christopher Ryan examines free will in Dante, both in theory in *Purgatorio* xviii, and in application to Francesca da Rimini and to Guido da Montefeltro, in the *Inferno*.

Of the contributors, three, Miss Petrie, Dr. Crowe and Dr. Richter, are on the staff of University College Dublin in the disciplines of Italian studies, Philosophy and Medieval History respectively; Robin Kirkpatrick, now in Cambridge University, was a member of the University College Italian department when he lectured on *Inferno* vii; Peter Armour formerly at the University of Leicester has moved to Bedford College, University of London; John Barnes, formerly at Hull, is now head of the Italian department in Aberdeen; Christopher Ryan is Fellow and Dean of St. Edmund's College, Cambridge and has been doing research at the Pontifical Institute of Mediaeval Studies in Toronto; J.H. Whitfield, Professor Emeritus at Birmingham University, formerly held the Serena Chair of Italian there.

Texts used in this volume are the *Commedia* edited by G. Petrocchi and the *Monarchia* edited by P.G. Ricci (both Milan, 1965), both by courtesy of the Società Dantesca; for the *Convivio* the edition referred to is that by M. Simonelli (Bologna, 1966); and the *De Vulgari Eloquentia* edition adopted is that by P.V. Mengaldo (Padua, 1968). No specific edition of the *Vita Nuova* is referred to in this volume, and Dante's other works are likewise rarely touched upon. For Dante's Letters, the second Paget Toynbee edition (Oxford, 1966) is used for quotations, although the *Letter to Cangrande*, given as *Epistola* X in Toynbee, is referred to in P. Armour's essay, perhaps more properly, as *Epistola* XIII.

Many well-known editions of the *Divina Commedia* are given in abbreviated form throughout the book. Of ancient commentators, the Anonimo, Benvenuto, Buti, and others are given without further detail. For modern commentators, a particular edition is usually indicated, e.g., N. Sapegno (Florence, 1968); among other editors cited are: G.A. Scartazzini, G. Vandelli, M. Barbi, T. Casini, S.A. Barbi, A. Momigliano, S. Chimenz, G. Giacalone, M. Porena. The usual translations referred to are those by D.L. Sayers and J.D. Sinclair and the dates of the editions used are normally given in the notes. For the classical authors quoted in the text no particular editions are adopted except in the case of the *Aeneid*, where the Loeb Classics edition (London, 1922) and H.R. Fairclough's accompanying translation are used.

Common abbreviations adopted in the notes are ed. for

edited, trans. for translated, comm. for commentary. The abbreviations for Dante's works are: *Inf.*, *Purg.*, *Par.*, *Mon.*, *Conv.*, *VN*, *DVE*; and *Ep.* for *Epistola*. Finally, the *Enciclopedia dantesca*, frequently referred to, is abbreviated as *Enc.d.*

Dublin, September 1980

Dante's Fortuna: Inferno VII

Robin Kirkpatrick

The subject of this essay is the seventh canto of Dante's *Inferno*.[1] In twentieth-century criticism, the canto has not proved to be an especially controversial one. However, in the eyes of the earliest readers, the doctrinal issues which the poet here touches upon raised questions of considerable importance. And remembering this, one may I believe, pay more attention to the poetic character of the passage than has been the case hitherto.

To the fourteenth-century reader, the discourse on Fortune which dominates the second half of *Inferno* vii would seem to have been peculiarly provoking in its implications. So when the poet allows Virgil to assert of Fortuna: "Vostro saver non ha contasto a lei" (*Inf*.vii.85), or immediately afterwards: "necessità la fa esser veloce," (89) it was supposed by certain members of the original audience, notably one, Cecco d'Ascoli, that Dante was sailing dangerously close to determinism and to a denial that the human will was free. In contemporary commentaries the charge was taken quite earnestly.[2] Thus within twenty years of Dante's death, one finds that both Graziolo and the author of the *Ottimo commento* have gone to great lengths to defend the orthodoxy of the poet's position. To Boccaccio as well the canto is for similar reasons of great interest. One would expect this, of course, from the author of the *Decameron,* where the theme of Fortune and its movements plays so significant a part. In Boccaccio's analysis, however, there appears a further emphasis, and that is upon the treatment of avarice provided by Dante in this particular canto. Again, if we think of Boccaccio's interest in the life of commercial society, we might expect this. But a balanced reading of *Inferno* vii does depend, as Boccaccio enables one to see, upon our attending as much to the representation of avarice there as to the representation of Fortuna. I shall return to Boccaccio, particularly to the view he takes of the implications and consequences of avarice.

In the twentieth century, discussion of the themes of Fortune and avarice has largely given way to an assessment of the poetic force and structure of the canto. To Mario Marti, writing in 1957, the figure of Fortuna is nothing more than a "luminous abstraction".[3] But against this position, Giovanni Getto in 1964, argues that Fortuna, so far from being an abstraction, is the focal point imaginatively of the canto, "il momento lirico culminante dell'intero episodio".[4] "La Fortuna", he maintains, "è il vero personaggio, la protagonista autentica del cerchio degli avari". This is a valuable interpretation. Yet it fails perhaps to take account fully of Marti's principal point (a point which latterly critics have been quick to respond to), that in regard to style, the depiction of the avaricious revolves around a vital "componente polemico-grottesca". Marti is particularly concerned to demonstrate the harshness of satirical language which dominates the early part of the canto. As I shall try to show, these observations are important if one is to appreciate not only the structure of *Inferno* vii, but also the wider significance of Dante's poetic procedure there.

More to the point in this respect, however, than any consideration of the canto's critical history, is the significance which *Inferno* vii must have had for the poet Dante himself. It would seem obvious that the canto is one which mattered very greatly to him. The discussion of Fortune which it contains is after all the first sustained piece of doctrinal exposition in the *Commedia.* The only comparable passages to precede it are certain brief references to the Last Judgement and the Resurrection of the Body at the end of *Inferno* vi. Nor is the Fortuna passage finally unconnected with these references to Judgement Day. Let me, however, emphasize for the moment that the theme of Fortune itself is one which for Dante, always conscious of his own misfortunes as an exile and political outcast, is bound to have had a peculiarly personal resonance. In this aspect, the Fortuna passage is the initial statement of a concern which will occupy the poet intermittently throughout the *Commedia* until the moment in *Paradiso* xvii where, from the lips of his ancestor Cacciaguida, he learns how bitter his life as an exile will be, and where he comes to realize how essential it is that in fulfilling his destiny as a poet he should stand:"ben tetragono ai colpi di ventura" (*Par*.xvii.24).

At the same time *Inferno* vii announces a further theme, which, if not related so intimately to the poet's own experience, is none the less expressed at all times with penetrating fervour and zeal. This is the theme of avarice. To Dante, avarice is "una lupa", the She-Wolf, who makes her first appearance after the Dark Wood at *Inferno* i.49. We are reminded of this when in the eighth line of the present canto Pluto is addressed as "maladetto lupo". Somewhat similarly, in the *Purgatorio*, Dante in execration of avarice cries: "Maladetta sie tu, antica lupa" (*Purg*.xx.10). The image of the wolf is of some significance. For it is by this image that Dante expresses the inhumanity and savagery of avarice; the depredations of the sin stand as an abiding threat to civilized existence and to all notions of order. In *Inferno* vii, the poet offers for the first time a close analysis of the vice which in its consequences he considered to be supremely destructive.

Considering then how significant the themes of *Inferno* vii are in regard both to the personal experience of the poet and to his moral vision, it is not surprising to find that in form and style the canto is peculiarly powerful and highly wrought. His imagination as always responds with vigour and with precision to the exigencies of his experience. But in particular I want to suggest that the canto before us is one in which Dante achieved an exceptional coherence of form. That this is so may not at first sight be apparent. For on the face of it the canto seems to divide into three distinct sections: the portrayal of the avaricious (1-60); Virgil's discussion of Fortune (67-96); and at the end (97-130), the punishment of the wrathful and the slothful. These final lines are frequently supposed to be connected in theme rather to *Inferno* viii than vii. Yet even these, I shall argue, have a part to play in the structure of thought and image which the poet creates in *Inferno* vii.

To do justice then to the complexity of the canto, I propose in what follows to consider it under three heads. Firstly, I shall examine the origins and implications of the doctrine of Fortune which Dante here expounds. Secondly, I shall look in detail at the internal consistency of the canto, examining at the same time the place which the canto occupies, in the structure of the whole *Commedia*. Thirdly, albeit briefly, I shall suggest the bearing that the canto has upon our general understanding of Dante's poetic purposes and procedure; the canto is, I believe, both original enough and characteristic enough to tell us something of that.

Turning firstly to the doctrine expressed here, one might suppose that few tasks were easier than to decide the sources of the poet's argument. For in particular the figure of Fortuna must surely be derived, as to its principal features, from the discussions of Fortune which Boethius offers in his *Consolation of Philosophy*. From the first, commentators have drawn attention to this derivation. Indeed Dante's own son, Pietro, insists upon it. And it is demonstrably true that Dante himself makes repeated and respectful reference to Boethius. This is particularly noticeable in the *Convivio*, while in the circle of Paradise devoted to the heavenly philosophers Dante describes Boethius as:

> l'anima santa che 'l mondo fallace
> fa manifesto a chi di lei ben ode.   *Par.*x.125-6

And he goes on to acknowledge an especial kinship with this holy spirit, in that he, like the poet himself, suffered pain and exile, coming to heavenly peace "da martiro/e da essilio" (*Par.*x.128-9).

Moreover, judging from the immediate context of *Inferno* vii, there is reason to suppose that Boethius was clearly present to Dante's mind. Already in *Inferno* v Francesca has adapted to her sentimental purposes a translation of Boethius:[5]

> E quella a me: "Nessun maggior dolore
> che ricordarsi del tempo felice
> ne la miseria."   *Inf.*v.121-3

It is also noticeable that throughout *Inferno* vi and vii the poet makes extensive use of the adjectives "serene", "sweet" and "beautiful" applying them particularly to the loveliness of the actual world. These same adjectives characterize the early *Consolatio*; as for instance in "dulcibus annis" (I *metra* i.13); "serenis . . . diebus" (I *metra* vii.9-10); or "humanae felicitatis dulcedo" (II *prosa* iv.60). Dante, with closely comparable reference, speaks of "dolce mondo" (*Inf*.vi.88); of "la vita serena" (*Inf*.vi.51), meaning temporal life as contrasted with eternal damnation; of "lo mondo pulcro" at *Inferno* vii.58; and in the same canto of "aere dolce" (122).

Now there are, I think, at least two good reasons why Dante should have referred at this point in the *Commedia* to Boethius. Boethius after all is concerned to demonstrate in his *Consolatio* the decisive superiority of the intellect to the bonds of physical imprisonment. Dante likewise realizes in these cantos that sin, specifically carnal sin, entails a condition of eternal imprisonment. To elude that consequence he needs, as Francesca implicitly acknowledges in her reference to Boethius, to pursue a precisely similar lesson in intellectual and spiritual liberty. In *Inferno* vii Virgil by his discourse on Fortune ensures more directly than Francesca that the lesson is one which the poet will attend to.

More particularly, and even more importantly perhaps, it would appear that Boethius and Dante are of like mind in the view they take of avarice. Boccaccio, expounding the allegorical meaning of *Inferno* vii, is of great value in allowing one to recognise this.[6] And the interpretation which, on Boccaccio's authority, one may attribute both to Boethius and to Dante is that avarice radically disturbs the primordial simplicity of the world. For Boethius and Dante there was indeed a time when the world was a sweet and serene place. Both look back to the Golden Age of patriarchal restraint. But both understand that this age has passed. And it is avarice, they agree – above all the avarice which appears in commercial adventure – that wrought the change. For avarice is precisely an offence against the divine order which allotted to man a particular place and a limited portion of the natural dispensation for his use and enjoyment. Thus in the *Consolatio*, Boethius exclaims (II *metra* v.1-7,13-15):

> Felix nimium prior aetas
> contenta fidelibus arvis
> nec inerti perdita luxu,
> facili quae sera solebat

ieiunia solvere glande.
Non bacchica munera norant
liquido confundere melle . . .
Nondum maris alta secabat
nec mercibus undique lectis
nova litora viderat hospes.

(Too blest the former age, their life who in the field contented led, and still by luxury unspoiled, on frugal acorns sparely fed. No skill was theirs the luscious grape with honey's sweetness to confuse . . . Not theirs to cleave the deep, nor seek in strange far lands the spoils of trade.) In the context of the Fortuna passage, evidence of a similar attitude (other than the evidence which Boccaccio gives) is to be found in the impressive imagery of sea-travel which Dante associates with the punishment of the avaricious. Thus Pluto at a word from Virgil collapses like a ruined sail:

Quali dal vento le gonfiate vele
    caggiono avvolte, poi che l'alber fiacca,
    tal cadde a terra la fiera crudele.   13-15

More obvious still, Dante elaborates a sea-image of epic proportions to govern the scene of the avaricious themselves:

Come fa l'onda là sovra Cariddi,
    che si frange con quella in cui s'intoppa,
    così convien che qui la gente riddi.
Qui vid' i' gente più ch'altrove troppa,
    e d'una parte e d'altra, con grand' urli,
    voltando pesi per forza di poppa.   22-7

These images exactly express the nature of avarice. For increasingly in Dante's time the pursuit of gain led men to venture out on the ocean. And while such enterprise may in Boccaccio's *Decameron* have come to seem heroic, for Dante the danger of it, which he evokes here, must surely have stood as an indication of foolhardiness and of disruptively unnatural vanity.[7]

Yet granted that on these two counts the connection between Dante and Boethius is a strong one, it is remarkable to note that Dante nonetheless departs from Boethius on certain quite crucial points.

Thus in the first place the tone of Dante's treatment of Fortuna is altogether different from that which is suggested by

Boethius. In the *Consolatio* Fortune appears as a power which, to unenlightened men at least, is mechanical, predictable and overwhelmingly cruel:

Haec cum superba verterit vices dextra
et aestuantis more fertur Euripi,
dudum tremendos saeva proterit reges
humilemque victi sublevat fallax vultum.
Non illa miseros audit aut curat fletus
ultroque gemitus, dura quos fecit, ridet.
Sic illa ludit, sic suas probat vires
magnumque su[ae v]is monstrat ostentum, si quis
visatur una stratus ac felix hora.   (II *metra* i)

(So with imperious hand she turns the wheel of change this way and that like the ebb and flow of the tide, and pitiless tramples down those once dread kings, raising the lowly face of the conquered, only to mock him in his turn; careless she nor hears nor heeds the cries of miserable men: she laughs at the groans that she herself has mercilessly caused. So she sports, so she proves her power, showing a mighty marvel to her subjects, when the self-same hour sees a man first successful, then cast down.) But in Dante there is no mention of a *wheel* of change. Dante's image is that of the sphere (96), a celestial sphere, with the suggestion that such an image arouses of a wholly satisfying beauty. Dante's emphasis, if anything, falls upon the movements of the sphere, upon the subtlety and dexterity implied in "permutasse" (79) and "permutazion" (88), and upon the lucid and splendid qualities of these changes not upon their cruelty. The movements are traced in the alteration of earthly objects. And it is important to note that these objects are referred to as things of splendour, "splendor mondani" (77), while Fortuna herself is not so much heartless as transcendent and angelic:

ma ella s'è beata e ciò non ode
con l'altre prime creature lieta
volve sua spera e beata si gode.   94-6

Now these differences in tone have in the past frequently been recognized and the last lines which I quote here have led critics to suppose that Dante looked upon Fortune as an aspect of Divine Providence.[8] This view is broadly acceptable although, as will appear, the full consequences of it have not to my mind been realized. Moreover I would emphasize that, apart from any discrepancy of tone between Boethius and Dante, there are two further differences which need to be taken into account.

Firstly, there is a sense in which Dante somewhat extends the notion of Fortune so that, even in discussing it in this canto, the movements of Fortune govern not only the lives of individuals but also the lives of nations: "per ch'una gente impera e l'altra langue" (82). In a rather general way one can argue that Dante here has in mind the notion of destiny as well as that of Fortune.[9] Certainly the poet has from the first in the *Commedia* been deeply concerned with the way in which the very plan and purpose of the Heavens bear upon the life of men. And through the sense that God may elect a particular race to a particular destiny, we also arrive at his awareness of how the individual may be required to receive and respond to the purpose which God has conceived for him. To see this, we have only to recall the coupling of Aeneas and Paul at *Inferno* ii.32, where in a moment of doubt Dante protests: "Io non Enea, io non Paulo sono". Indeed almost the first task which Virgil has to perform on Dante's behalf is to convince him that he has been chosen for a destiny as exalted in its own way as that of Aeneas and of Paul. It is surely true to say that while Dante's sense of his own misfortunes is strong, his sense of his own destiny and of his election in God's eyes is decidedly stronger. Remembering that Dante, so far from reserving a discourse on Fortune for the person of Boethius himself, hands it confidently to Virgil at an early stage of the *Commedia*, it is natural that one should discern in Fortuna the shadow of Destiny.

If however one is to pursue this particular point one must note a further and final difference between Boethius and Dante. This difference lies in the formal presentation of the Fortuna doctrine.

The formal procedure which Boethius adopts in the *Consolatio* is a dialectical one. Lady Philosophy and the Prisoner, proceeding by argumentative discourse, are concerned with the gradual achievement of understanding, and it is upon that understanding that the intellectual, if not the physical, liberty of the Prisoner depends. So Philosophy declares (IV *metra* i.1-8):

> Sunt etenim pennae volucres mihi,
> quae celsa conscendant poli.

> Quas sibi cum velox mens induit,
>   terras perosa despicit,
> aeris immensi superat globum,
>   nubeque postergum videt,
> quique agili motu calet aetheris,
>   transcendit ignis verticem . . .

(Wings are mine; above the pole far aloft I soar. Clothed with these, my nimble soul scorns earth's hated shore, cleaves the skies upon the wind, sees the clouds left far behind. Soon the flowing point she nears, where the heavens rotate . . .) In this flight all things are transcended, even the beauty of the earth. Indeed, "Why rejoice in such inanities", Philosophy asks (II *prosa* v.30-40):

> An vos agrorum pulchritudo delectat? Quidni? Est enim pulcherrimi operis pulchra portio. Sic quondam sereni maris facie gaudemus; sic caelum sidera lunam solemque miramur. Num te horum aliquid attingit? Num audes alicuius talium splendore gloriari? An vernis floribus ipse distingueris, aut tua in aestiuos fructus intumescit ubertas? Quid inanis gaudiis raperis? Quid externa bona pro tuis amplexaris.

(Does the beauty of the fields delight you? Surely, yes; it is a beautiful part of a right beautiful whole. Fitly indeed do we at times enjoy the serene calm of the sea, admire the sky, the stars, the moon, the sun. Yet is any of these thy concern? Dost thou venture to boast thyself of the beauty of any one of them? Art thou decked with spring's flowers? Is it thy fertility that swelleth in the fruits of autumn? Why art thou moved with empty transports? Why embracest thou an alien excellence as thine own?)

But what of this do we find in Dante? That any comparable contempt for the beauty of the natural world should be found in his writing will seem unlikely to any one who bears the *Purgatorio* in mind. Equally, the very procedures of thought, which in the *Consolatio* led to that contempt, are in the Fortuna passage strikingly absent. In fact on the question of Fortune Virgil allows no argument at all to take place between himself and Dante. His words, to be sure, are clearly articulated and forcefully organized. But it is precisely this which denies the possibility of dialogue. Above all one notes the finality with which Virgil, ending his account of Fortuna, moves on to the presentation of a further aspect of Hell:

> con l'altre prime creature lieta
> volve sua spera e beata si gode.
> Or discendiamo omai a maggior pieta.   95-7

The abruptness of this transition positively disallows discussion, and indeed underscores those passages in the Fortuna speech which speak of Fortuna as being unswayed by human argument:

> che permutasse a tempo li ben vani
> di gente in gente e d'uno in altro sangue,
> oltre la difension d'i senni umani   79-81

and: "Vostro saver non ha contasto a lei" (85). In fact, considering the firmness of these lines and of Virgil's attitude, it is not hard to see why the early readers of the canto should have suspected that Dante here might have infringed that very freedom of the rational mind which Boethius fought so vigorously to maintain.

That suspicion, although justified to the extent that Dante does depart from Boethius, is not entirely well-founded. For the finality which is characteristic of Virgil's language does not simply disallow argument, it is also the stylistic function which makes it possible for the poet to delineate the features of Fortuna with such exceptional clarity. The sharpness and incisiveness with which the voice falls in the final lines is reflected at large in the rhymes of the Fortuna passage, giving point and emphasis to each new assertion as it occurs. Thus with solemn intensity Virgil draws the mind of his pupil away from the ignorance which he dismally envisages in the sinners and invites him, in his own words, to "feed" his intellect on the clear image of Fortuna: "Or vo' che tu mia sentenza ne 'mbocche" (72). The mind in short, if not called upon to argue, is nonetheless invited to play with understanding around the confident statements which are offered to it. Indeed so assured is Virgil's grasp of his subject that it appears to encourage a sheer delight in the aesthetic attraction of the vision he holds forth. And when a modern critic such as Getto emphasizes that the Fortuna figure represents the point of aesthetic concentration in the canto, his position is, I think, entirely at one with

Dante's own. Fortuna is to be looked upon with clear-minded understanding but also to be received in some way with admiration and delight.

Man's freedom in regard to Fortuna depends in Dante upon an attitude of considerable complexity. To arrive at a fairly comprehensive explanation of the points upon which Dante has departed from Boethius it is time to turn to a work which will I think help. I have in mind a passage from the Book of Wisdom, where Solomon describes the characteristics of Wisdom herself:

> est enim in illa spiritus intellectus sanctus unicus multiplex subtilis mobilis dissertus incoinquinatus certus suavis amans bonum acutus qui nihil vetat benefacere humanus stabilis certus securus omnem habens virtutem omnia prospiciens et qui capiat omnes spiritus intellegibiles mundos subtiles omnibus enim mobilibus mobilior est sapientia adtingit autem ubique et capit propter suam munditiam vapor est enim virtutis Dei et emanatio quaedam est claritatis omnipotentis Dei sincera et ideo nihil inquinatum in illa incurrit candor est enim lucis aeternae et speculum sine macula Dei maiestatis et imago bonitatis illius.
>
> (*Liber Sapientiae* 7:22-6)

(For in her is the spirit of understanding: holy, one, manifold, subtile, eloquent, active, undefiled, sure, sweet, loving that which is good, quick, which nothing hindereth, beneficent, gentle, kind, steadfast, assured, secure, having all power, overseeing all things, and containing all spirits, intelligible, pure, subtile. For wisdom is more active than all active things: and reacheth everywhere by reason of her purity. For she is a vapour of the power of God, and a certain pure emanation of the glory of the almighty God: and there no defiled thing cometh into her. For she is the brightness of eternal light: and the unspotted mirror of God's majesty, and the image of his goodness). In a general way, there can be little doubt of the importance in Dante's eyes of the Solomon literature. Its significance is especially evident in *Convivio* IV where, as in *Inferno* vii, Dante's subject is in large part the nature of avarice, contrasted in the *Convivio* with the nature of true nobility. One might also mention that the Book of Wisdom is sometimes regarded as an influence even on Boethius's philosophy.

Be that as it may, one may immediately recognize in Solomon's representation of Wisdom similarities between this figure and the figure of Fortuna. The two are comparable in four major respects, in that each is mobile, each is subtle, each is bright and each is perfectly pure. So Wisdom is "mobilis", while Fortuna is "veloce" (89) and "Le sue permutazion non hanno triegue" (88). Each being subtle in the sense, equally, of "penetrating" and of "discriminating", Wisdom appears as "subtilis" and "acutus"; while Fortuna is as cunning as a serpent, "come in erba l'angue" (84), and chooses to act for reasons which no man can understand. The brightness of Wisdom is spoken of in the present passage as "candor . . . lucis aeternae" and, at the end of the same chapter, as "speciosior sole, et super omnem stellarum dispositionem"; while Fortuna is one of the heavenly distributors of light, characterized by "splende" and "splendor" (73-8). Lastly, both Wisdom and Fortuna are immaculate and superior to injury or persuasion, Wisdom being described as "certus", "stabilis", "securus", "quem nihil vetat", "sincera", and "sine macula"; while Fortuna, as one has seen, secure in her beatitude, is in no way touched by the cries of the unfortunate.

What then are the implications of these similarities? Though I have not the space to discuss this question fully, there are, I suggest, certain quite evident conclusions to be drawn. For supposing that Dante did have the Wisdom passage in mind as he wrote *Inferno* vii, can we not say, firstly, that he saw in Fortuna a manifestation of the Wisdom of God, particularly as that Wisdom operates in the lower spheres of Creation? Such an interpretation of course, is consistent with that which would represent Fortuna as a providential power or as distributive justice. Having said this however, one may proceed to explain why it is appropriate to find in Fortuna some of the lineaments of Destiny and also to account for the peculiar attitude of benign acceptance which Dante appears to adopt towards Fortuna.

For in the *Liber Sapientiae* one finds that Solomon, having understood that Wisdom governs the world, considers it a profound privilege to exercise in that sphere the capacity which he possesses for appreciating its nature.[10] Nor indeed is it merely a figure of speech to say that for Dante himself the importance of Solomon was to show that man's destiny lay in his acceptance and willing knowledge of the place which Divine Wisdom had allotted to him in the universal plan. Certainly, when one turns to the appearances of Solomon in the *Paradiso*, we find that the true mark of Solomon's dignity as a king in Dante's eyes was that he should humbly ask only for as much wisdom as would enable him to govern men aright in the natural sphere of their existence:[11]

> acciò che re sufficiente fosse;
> non per sapere il numero in che enno
> li motor di qua sù, o se *necesse*
> con contingente mai *necesse* fenno;
> non, *si est dare primum motum esse*,
> o se del mezzo cerchio far si puote
> triangol sì ch'un retto non avesse.   *Par.*xiii.96-102

Aquinas is speaking here in praise of the modesty of Solomon. And it is not difficult to show from an examination of *Paradiso* xiii that Solomon's modesty, stamped with the approbation of Aquinas, was intended as a paradigm for all men to act upon, whatever their rank or station. For *Paradiso* xiii discusses precisely the conditions under which God's Creation operates, as it moves from the highest spheres of the spirit, which are specific to angelic beings, down to those realms, specific to man, where body and spirit commingle. Solomon, in this context, is important to Dante in that he recognizes fully the place which he, as a king, must agree to accept in Creation. Yet the final lines of the canto issue a warning which applies far more widely, indeed to anyone who might be tempted to challenge the divine dispensation in thought or act:

> Non sien le genti, ancor, troppo sicure
> a giudicar, sì come quei che stima
> le biade in campo pria che sien mature;
> ch'i' ho veduto tutto 'l verno prima
> lo prun mostrarsi rigido e feroce;
> poscia portar la rosa in su la cima;
> e legno vidi già dritto e veloce
> correr lo mar per tutto suo cammino
> perire al fine a l'intrar de la foce.   *Par.*xiii.130-8

The image of merchant adventure in the last *terzina* underlines the bearing of this passage on the discussion of *Inferno* vii. So in the *Paradiso*, Aquinas is made to direct our attention to the conditions of uncertainty which govern the existence of creatures in the physical sphere. These are the conditions which impose modesty upon human beings. In *Inferno* vii these same conditions are represented in the movements of Fortuna. As in *Paradiso* xiii the message which Fortuna embodies, I suggest, is that man must exist in the material world and, like Solomon, accept this destiny with good will and modest intelligence.

A further argument for the view I have adopted here arises when one remembers that in *Paradiso* xiv it is to Solomon that Dante gives the great account of the Resurrection of the Body, which begins at *Paradiso* xiv.37 and ends with the longing assent of all the Christian philosophers to the promise of physical rebirth (60). From this passage we learn that man's true and ultimate end is not to exist in a purely spiritual heaven, be it even Dante's Paradise, but in a sphere of physical nature, redeemed and restored to purity by the Incarnation of Christ and by his Second Coming. The sphere of Fortuna presages man's proper home. And it is no accident, therefore, that the one doctrinal passage to precede the account of Fortuna in the *Commedia* is the discussion of the Resurrection of the Body at the end of *Inferno* vi. The two discourses point to a single end, which is the happy acceptance of one's existential destiny in the physical grade of creation.

It will not now be difficult to appreciate why the formal properties of the Fortuna passage should differ so greatly from those which appear in the arguments of the *Consolatio*. For to Dante's truly Christian consciousness the physical world is not an impediment to be overcome, at least not in the sense that Boethius would overcome it when he counsels blindness to the beauties of the spring flowers or of the calm sea (*Consolatio* II *prosa* v.35). On the contrary, the mark of an appropriate adjustment in one's election to life must be precisely that comprehensive, intelligent and even aesthetic delight which Virgil displays in his attitude to Fortuna. Rightly, we should indeed "praise" Fortuna, as Dante insists we should (*Inf.* vii.92), since she is the very condition of our existing at all.

With this, one is close to the point at which one may consider the extremely significant position which the Fortuna canto occupies in the *Commedia* at large. Before doing so, however, it is important to recognize that while the Solomon literature may suggest the lines along which the imagination of the poet worked in revising the philosophy of Boethius, nonetheless, in explicit doctrine Dante remains close to the letter of Boethius. This is evident especially in *Paradiso* xiii, even though Solomon here plays a vital part in Dante's definition of intellectual propriety. For it is in this canto that Dante demonstrates how the universe, in its structure, descends from the highest ranks of pure spirit down to the material sphere of what he calls "brevi contingenze" (*Par*xiii.63) – the realm precisely of Fortuna. The doctrine, as such, is firmly grounded in Boethius's thought. But we can, I believe, do justice to the influence both of Solomon and of Boethius upon Dante's thinking if we describe the attitude which in both *Paradiso* xiii and *Inferno* vii Dante recommends as one which expressed an "heroic poverty". The phrase, I hope, suggests an awareness equally of the miseries which, as Boethius knew well, man must courageously attempt to conquer, and also of that gladness of spirit in which, learning from Solomon, human beings might undertake to accept these miseries as the natural condition of their existence.

At all events, if one now looks to the place which *Inferno* vii holds in the *Commedia* at large, its importance, I suggest, will be found to lie in that it does introduce in an imaginatively forceful way the notion of heroic poverty. One may add, without attempting to develop the suggestion at great length, that the implications of this notion are not to be found in the *Commedia* alone. In *Convivio* IV for instance, this theme, as in *Inferno* vii, is a cardinal element in the contrast Dante draws between true nobility and the characteristics of avarice. So in the chapter in which Boethius is constantly cited (*Conv*.IV. xiii.12-14), Dante refers to the sequence in the *Pharsalia* where Lucan describes Caesar's importunate visit to the fisherman Amyclas. Dante in fact returns to this story in his account of the poverty of St Francis in *Paradiso* xi. And what especially concerns him is that the fisherman does not bestir himself or panic at all when Caesar comes knocking at his door, even though, in his own good time, he proves generous with what he has to offer. A true nobility lies in the security which his poverty affords him. Indeed this is a passage which shows the two-fold nature of Dante's view of Fortune very clearly. For, interested as he is in Amyclas, he is also interested in Caesar, who in this scene is preparing to pursue his imperial destiny against the adversities of an Adriatic storm. The dignity of mankind appears alike in overt heroism and in the subtleties of the poor. But in the minor works Dante's adherence to such a notion of poverty is expressed perhaps most forcefully in the *Monarchia*. In *Monarchia* III.x or II.xi, not surprisingly, we find that the true destiny of the church is precisely to follow in the footsteps of Christ's poverty. But this is by no means the only expression in that work of the virtues of poverty. For it is a precisely similar virtue which will motivate, in Dante's view, the true Roman in the pursuit of *his* peculiar destiny. Thus when Dante speaks of the exemplary, even miraculous evidence of the divine favour which Rome enjoys, Dante firstly applauds the Romans for putting aside greed, the great enemy of justice, and then goes on to consider particular cases:

> De personis autem singularibus compendiose progrediar. Nunquid non bonum commune intendisse dicendi sunt qui sudore, qui paupertate, qui exilio, qui filiorum orbatione, qui amissione membrorum, qui denique animarum oblatione bonum publicum exaugere conati sunt?   *Mon.*II.v.8

(Now taking Romans individually, I shall be brief. Who can refrain from calling them mindful of the common good when by sweat, by poverty, in exile, in loss of children, limbs, and even in the sacrifice of their very lives, they sought to promote the public weal?) If I have stressed the conception of heroic poverty which emerges in passages of this sort in the minor works, it is partly because in this conception we observe one of those half-expressed themes which, accompanying Dante's orthodox and explicit statements of belief, in some respects express his Christianity more trenchantly than orthodox statement itself could ever do. At the same time, this theme is a counterpart to the poet's understanding of avarice, and significant in one's interpretation of that. Indeed in the *Commedia* one of the final expressions of this theme, stemming from and connected to the Fortuna passage, is the Allegory in *Paradiso* xi of St Francis and Poverty. For Fortuna, in a manner more or less accessible to reason, presents the same truth as Lady Poverty presents mystically in *Paradiso* xi. Both are depicted as loathsome to the ignorant and lovable to those of awakened understanding. And if Fortuna is "posta in croce/pur da color che le dovrien dar lode"

(91-2), Poverty likewise is so close to Christ that "dove Maria rimase giuso,/ella con Cristo pianse in su la croce" (*Par*.xi.71-2). St Francis's action in espousing Poverty is the ultimate and loving recognition of what as a man is his true nature. And the Fortuna passage stands appropriately at the head of Hell to indicate the path which in the temporal world was comprehensibly demonstrated to all men and which the damned have inexcusably failed to take.[12]

However, the most striking extension of this initial point occurs in the Cacciaguida cantos: *Paradiso* xv-xvii, where, as I have said before, Dante finally comes to terms with his own destiny as a political exile and as a poet. It is of course significant that the character who teaches Dante this lesson should be Cacciaguida. For Cacciaguida himself, beatified as a warrior of Christ, sacrificed himself as a crusader, defending the Christian faith. He, one may suppose, knew supremely well the virtue and purposes of the heroic as well as of self-denial and poverty. It is significant too, that the Cacciaguida cantos should follow directly from the sequences in the Heaven of the Sun where Solomon's presence is so strongly apparent. For throughout the Cacciaguida episode there runs the sense that the lesson of Solomon's humility is one which men may translate into the very nerve of their daily lives. Thus in the great picture of Florence in its ancient glory which the poet presents here, one realizes that the harmony which reigned among the patriarchs of Cacciaguida's generation arose from their austerity and self-possession:

> Bellincion Berti vid' io andar cinto
> di cuoio e d'osso, e venir da lo specchio
> la donna sua sanza 'l viso dipinto . . .   *Par*.xv.112-14

Indeed, even the city itself as to its physical form seemed in that age to know the virtue of self-restraint. For,

> Fiorenza dentro da la cerchia antica,
> ond' ella toglie ancora e terza e nona,
> si stava in pace, sobria e pudica.   *Par*.xv.97-9

In this very conformity to ancient – and for Dante presumably natural – limitations, the Florentines showed themselves to be the true heirs of Rome. The poet emphasizes this by speaking of how, in ancient times, the children of Florence were nurtured on the legends "d'i Troiani, di Fiesole e di Roma" (*Par*.xv.126). But if Cacciaguida thus insists in the past the true spirit of civic life depended upon sobriety and self-limitation, he also intends his depiction of old Florence to stand as a satire upon the Florence of the present day. For avarice now leads its inhabitants away from a just recognition of the honour which lies in conforming to the natural dispensation. The city grows in size, the citizens in luxury.

And it is with this understanding that one may return to *Inferno* vii to observe how Dante here brings to bear upon the sinners whom he condemns the principles and standards which are represented in his portrayal of Fortuna.

In this regard, the most significant, if not the most central instance, is the treatment of those who at the end of the canto are condemned for ire and sluggishness to wallow in the slime of the murky Styx:

> Fitti nel limo dicon: "Tristi fummo
> ne l'aere dolce che dal sol s'allegra,
> portando dentro accidioso fummo:
> or ci attristiam ne la belletta negra."   121-4

Now nothing could be more obvious than the contrast in imaginative effect between this passage and the brilliant lucidity of the Fortuna passage. What though, is the significance of this contrast? The answer – which should enable one to see how coherent in structure *Inferno* vii is – follows quite naturally, I think, from the argument I have been presenting. For these sinners, as the lines I have quoted make explicit, are those who at heart have failed to rejoice in the sweetness of the air and the brightness of the sun. Through anger or spiritual laziness, they have ignored precisely the value of the sphere of existence in which they are called to live their lives. This is the sphere which Fortuna governs, offering to the mind which looks upon her with understanding that same splendour which Dante's own description of Fortuna shows him to have understood so well.

But the ignominy to which the wrathful and the sluggish are now condemned is the consummation of a condition which is evident also in the principal sinners of *Inferno* vii, the avaricious. Thus as Dante states:

> la sconoscente vita che i fé sozzi,

ad ogne conoscenza or li fa bruni.   53-4

A state of ignorance (associated in the word "sconoscente" with
a notion of boorishness), with regard particularly to the way
they should conduct themselves in the world, underlies the sin
of the avaricious.[13] And one consequence of this, which is
reflected in the punishment they suffer, is that where the
movements of Fortuna are swift and intelligent, those of the
avaricious in Hell are mechanical and base. Their lives are now
spent, as essentially their temporal lives were spent, in the
wholly material clash of one against another:

> Percoteansi 'ncontro; e poscia pur lì
> si rivolgea ciascun, voltando a retro,
> gridando: "Perché tieni?" "Perché burli?"   28-30

The laws of matter to which they never learned to respond with
delight now master them utterly.

Perhaps the strongest evidence, however, for this view of the
avaricious occurs in the sequence where, as at the end of
Inferno vi, Dante calls to mind the Day of Judgment:

> In etterno verranno a li due cozzi:
> questi resurgeranno del sepulcro
> col pugno chiuso, e questi coi crin mozzi.   55-7

These sinners have so failed to make a true or valuable
impression on the physical sphere that when this sphere is at
last redeemed, they will stand forth in a singularly inhuman,
indeed even ridiculous posture. On that day, finally, they will be
mocked by the laws of physical nature which while they lived
they sought to manipulate to their own ends.

But this, in regard to the structure and style of *Inferno* vii,
brings me to a last point. For the ludicrous, almost cartoon-like
quality of the portrayal here is by no means an isolated feature.
As early as the depiction of Ciacco in *Inferno* vi, where the
principal character is known to us only by his nick-name, Dante
seems deliberately to have introduced a note of caricature into
his style. And this note is heard with especial force at the
beginning of *Inferno* vii where the sheer inanity of Pluto is
brought out by the opening, nonsense line: "*Pape Satàn, pape
Satàn aleppe!*" This line, coupled with the vivid image of Pluto
suddenly windless like a shattered sail, is surely to be taken as
comic. Indeed the opening of the canto is comic even in the

sense which Dante would have given to the word, in that its linguistic register is of the lowest and least dignified level. Nor is it difficult to see that Dante must have intended a contrast between the language associated with Pluto and the language which Virgil is given in the Fortuna sequence. For just as the "tristi fitti nel limo" are contrasted in spirit with the exhilarating brilliance of Fortuna herself, so the comic language of Pluto forms a direct contrast with the controlled and well-formed finality of Virgil's address.

But in fact the Pluto passage is only the beginning of a series of "comic" usages which dominate the whole description of the avaricious. Mario Marti, in his *lectura* of the canto (see note[3]), has given a full account of these. And here I need only draw attention to the harshness and, in Dante's eyes, the evident "baseness" of "chioccia" (2), "insacca" (18); to the realism of " 'Perché tieni' e 'Perché burli?' " (30); to "cozzi" (55) and "crin mozzi" (57).

What purpose though, does this language serve, particularly in contrast to the lucidity of the Fortuna passage? In one respect the answer is clear. The unintelligent and unheroic nature of greed and avarice has led to the loss of all individual merit and dignity so that, in dealing with such sinners, diction of an elevated cast would be wholly out of place. In this realm of eternity, there is no Bellincion Berti, no firmness of feature, no heroic austerity. And indeed this aspect of the style is consistent with a theme which has been developing in the *Inferno* since the moment in *Inferno* vi when Dante speaks of himself as walking over the spirits of the gluttons: "sovra lor vanità che par persona" (*Inf.*vi.36). Here, as in Dante's argument that the avaricious at Judgment Day will be unrecognizable as individuals, we see the irony which is specific to these circles of Hell: the supreme selfishness of carnal sin entails in eternity the loss of individual substance.

But in *Inferno* vii itself the most illuminating expression of this theme occurs when, referring to the punishment that the avaricious sustain, Virgil curtly remarks: "qual ella sia, parole non ci appulcro" (60). Virgil refuses to beautify what he sees with words of dignity. Yet beauty is exactly what he does bestow upon the figure of Fortuna, whom as we know from Boethius he could have treated so grimly. His very ability to do this is a mark of the intelligence which distinguishes him from those of "sconoscente vita".

With this I come to my final point. I suggested at the outset that Dante in this canto reveals a general conception of what he considered poetry should be and should do. And this revelation is principally brought about by the distinction he draws between the style of the Fortuna passage and the style which emerges in his satire upon the avaricious. For in this distinction Dante sets apart not only Virgil from the ignominy of the sinners, but himself too, as the only begetter of the Fortuna passage. Thus the wild and stupid yelling of the avaricious is described as an "ontoso metro" (33), a shameful and insulting chant. But it is the utter opposite of such a "metro" that he himself accomplishes in speaking of Fortuna. His song there is a song of praise and equally, I think, a claim to honour. It is an assertion that the poet is in his own way able, as, say, Bellincion Berti was, to grasp clearly the wisdom of God and to be admired, as Bellincion Berti was, for doing so.

Without exaggeration one may, I think, conclude that in the world of "brevi contingenze", where Dante as a poet must pursue his mission, the proof of his own fibre and intellectual heroism will be found in the very form that his poetry assumes. Thus in *Convivio* I.iii, Dante, recognizing a similarity between himself and Boethius, insists that Boethius wrote his *Consolatio,* as he now writes his own works, as a vindication of honour and worth against the "perpetuale infamia del suo essilio". More importantly, in the Cacciaguida cantos, Cacciaguida emphasizes that the proper course for the poet to take in the face of his coming misfortunes is to speak out boldly, being no "timid friend to the truth" (*Par.*xvii.118). In travail and poverty Dante's task must be to announce with all courage the significance of the vision which God has chosen him to see. And when Dante writes:

> Se mai continga che 'l poema sacro
>   al quale ha posto mano e cielo e terra,
>   sì che m'ha fatto per molti anni macro,
> vinca la crudeltà che fuor mi serra . . .   *Par.*xxv.1-4

going on to speak of the possibility of his triumphant return as laureate to Florence, we see from the first line of the passage how clearly the poet recognizes his place in the world of "contingencies" and equally, how urgently he looks to his own poetry as the means of fulfilling his destiny among men. In conclusion, I would suggest that these observations hint at the need for a certain adjustment in our approach to Dante's poetry. We have learned, rightly, to look for the dramatic interplay between Dante as a character in his own narrative and the characters of that narrative. We have learned also to regard the structure of Dante's writing from canto to canto as peculiarly coherent. What we have now to do, I believe, is to return to Dante the poet, and to consider the ways in which the personality and personal ambitions of the poet are impressed upon the words that he writes. For, in the achievement of clear and definite statement, we may observe the poet's specific attempt to defeat the gross stupidity and the abasement of individual honour which, as *Inferno* vii demonstrates, are consequent upon sin. Against the savagery of the She-Wolf, the absurdity of the "maladetto lupo", and the entangling wilderness of the Dark Wood, Dante holds high his own poetry as a proof of his heroic civility and of his right to be considered a willing citizen of God's providential Creation.

Notes

[1]This paper was originally given as a Dante lecture at University College Dublin in 1978. A number of the issues which the paper raises were probably too large to illustrate satisfactorily in the compass of a *lectura*. Nonetheless there is something to be gained, I think, from stating the issues concisely. And consequently I have followed here the plan of the first reading. I should like to thank the editor very warmly for the opportunity he has given me to present this interpretation of *Inferno* vii and for the constant encouragement which he has offered.
[2]On this controversy see V. Cioffari, *Fortune in Dante's Fourteenth Century Commentators* (Cambridge, Mass., 1944). For Cecco d'Ascoli's censure see Francesco Stabili, *L'Acerba* ed. A. Crespi (Ascoli Piceno, 1927) II,i,p. 172. For the defence of Dante's orthodoxy see *Il commento dantesco di [Ser] Graziolo de' Bambaglioli* ed. A. Fiammazzo (Savona, 1915) and *L'Ottimo commento della Divina Commedia* ed. A. Torri (Pisa, 1827).
[3]M. Marti, *Il canto VII dell'Inferno,* Lectura Dantis Romana (Turin, 1959), "la luminosità astratta . . . di una serena e indifferente beatitudine" (p.23).
[4]G. Getto, "*Inferno* canto VII", *Letture dantesche* ed. G. Getto (Florence, 1962) p. 125.
[5]The Scartazzini-Vandelli commentary, 20th ed. (Milan, 1969), cites the *De consol-*

atione philosophiae II *prosa* iv as one source for these lines, although St Thomas, *Summa theologiae* II, ii, 36, 1, is also cited. For quotations from Boethius's *Consolation* see [Anici Manli Severini Boethi] *De Consolatione Philosophiae* ed. George D. Smith (London, 1925), which has been followed except where "u" is modernized to "v".

[6]So in Boccaccio's comment to *Inf.* vii. 30 in *Tutte le opere*, VI, *Esposizioni sopra la comedia di Dante* ed. G. Padoan (Milan, 1965) p. 420, there occurs the following great lament: "E, non bastando allo 'nsaziabile appetito le cose poste dinanzi agli occhi nostri e nelle nostre mani dalla natura, trovò lo 'ngegno umano nuove ed esquisite vie a recare in publico i nascosi pericoli: e, pertugiati i monti ed eviscerata la terra, del ventre suo l'oro, l'argento e gli altri metalli recarono suso in alto . . .; di che Boezio, nel primo libro De consolatione [in fact II.v.27-30], fortemente dolendosi, dice:

> Heu primus qui fuit ille
> auri qui pondera tecti
> gemmasque latere volentes
> pretiosa pericula fodit?"

[7]See G. Padoan's excellent discussion of Dante's attitude to the mercantile adventures of the period in "Dante di fronte all'umanesimo letterario", *Il pio Enea, l'empio Ulisse* (Ravenna, 1977) p. 14.

[8]See for instance Sinclair's translation (London, 1971) p. 107.

[9]Cristoforo Landino writes on this canto in his *Comento sopra la Comedia de Danthe Alighieri poeta fiorentino* (Florence, 1481): "credo chel poeta in questo luogho voglia indextinctamente confondere el fato et la fortuna", and goes on to quote Virgil: "Fortuna omnipotens: et ineluctabile fatum" (*Aen*.VIII.334).

[10]See for instance *Liber Sapientiae* 7:17-21, "ipse enim mihi dedit horum quae sunt scientiam veram ut sciam dispositionem orbis terrarum et virtutes elementorum initium et consummationem et medietatem temporum et meditationem omnium morum mutationes et divisiones temporum anni cursus et stellarum dispositiones naturas animalium et iras bestiarum vim ventorum et cogitationes hominum differentias arborum et virtutes radicum et quaecumque sunt absconsa et inprovisa didici omnium enim artifex docuit me sapientia" (He himself gave me true understanding of things as they are: a knowledge of the structure of the world and the operation of the elements; the beginning and end of epochs and their middle course; the alternating solstices and changing seasons; the cycles of the years and the constellations; the nature of living creatures and behaviour of wild beasts; the violent force of winds and the thoughts of men; the varieties of plants and the virtues of roots. I learnt it all, hidden or manifest, for I was taught by her whose skill made all things, wisdom). And also, Wisdom 7:1-8, "sum quidem et ego mortalis homo similis omnibus et ex genere terreno illius qui prior finctus est et in ventre matris figuratus sum caro decem mensuum tempore coagulatus in sanguine ex semine hominis et delectamento somni conveniente et ego natus accepi communem aerem et in similiter factam decidia terram . . . propter hoc optavi et datus est mihi sensus et invocavi et venit in me spiritus sapientiae et praeposui illam regnis et sedibus et divitias nihil esse duxi in comparatione illius" (I too am a mortal man like all the rest, descended from the first man, who was made of dust, and in my mother's womb I was wrought into flesh during a ten-months space, compacted in blood from the seed of her husband and the pleasure that is joined with sleep. When I was born, I breathed the common air and was laid on the earth that all men tread; . . . Therefore I prayed, and called for help, and there came to me a spirit of wisdom. I valued her above sceptre and

throne, and reckoned riches as nothing beside her). Latin text from *Biblia sacra* II (Stuttgart, 1969) p. 1011; translation from *The New English Bible: The Apocrypha* (London, 1970).

[11]On "The Wisdom of Solomon", see E. Gilson, *Dante the Philosopher* (London, 1948) pp. 253-7.

[12]One may recall here the poem by Jacopone da Todi, "Povertade ennamorata", also referred to as "De la Santa Poverta Signora De Tutto"; where the domain of, so to say, Imperial Poverty, is shown to extend over all the nations of the known world. See *Poeti del Duecento* ed. G. F. Contini, II (Milan, 1960) pp. 75-7.

[13]Opinions differ as to the force of "sconoscente". G. Giacalone in his commentary (Rome, 1968), accepting a suggestion made in the commentary by S. Chimenz (Turin, 1962), takes the word to indicate the way in which avarice leads men to isolate themselves from social life, wholly dedicating themselves to the pursuit of wealth. The Scartazzini-Vandelli commentary (Milan, 1969) takes it to mean that the avaricious are ignorant of the "vero valore dei beni". Both meanings have their place.

Inferno XIII

John C. Barnes

The thirteenth canto of the *Inferno* is remembered by readers of the *Commedia* as the canto of Pier della Vigna; but, although the bare fact of Piero's prominence is undeniable, this is a very limited view of *Inferno* xiii, which is the canto of two whole groups of souls, the suicides and the squanderers, as well as the setting in which they are encountered: the pathless wood inhabited by the Harpies. Our attention is in fact drawn not to one character but to four: two squanderers, Lano and Iacopo, and two suicides, Piero and the anonymous Florentine. Piero is not even mentioned until line 32, where he is merely "un gran pruno", a large thornbush; Dante's selection of this particular bush to pluck a twig from is quite arbitrary; Piero remains unnamed and completely undistinguished from the crowd of suicide-trees, except by the wound that Dante has arbitrarily inflicted, until the beginning of his first main speech (55); and when he has said his piece he disappears (108) with forty-three lines of the canto still remaining. So, numerically speaking, the most we can say is that half the canto is devoted to Pier della Vigna; and there is even a suggestion, as we shall see, that in comparison with other suicides Piero is relatively insignificant.[1]

The first three lines of the canto serve simultaneously to link the narrative of the present canto to that of its predecessor (through the mention of the Centaur Nessus, who has carried Dante on his back across the Phlegethon), to separate it from *Inferno* xii (Nessus is abruptly abandoned and left to complete his return crossing of the Phlegethon unobserved), and to sketch out the setting of the new "girone" which is the second "girone" of violence, accommodating souls which in life committed violence against themselves. It is a pathless wood: "un bosco /che da neun sentiero era segnato" (2-3); and the fact that it is pathless inaugurates a sense of disorientation which pervades especially the early lines of this canto.

For a medieval Christian in particular, violence against oneself was a bewildering perversion of the moral order, and the bewilderment is powerfully reflected in the second *terzina*, where the physical details of the wood are dwelt upon, and specifically those features (its gloomy colour and its twisted, knotted vegetation with its poisonous fruit) which make it the opposite of a normally pleasant wood:

> Non fronda verde, ma di color fosco;
>   non rami schietti, ma nodosi e 'nvolti;
>   non pomi v'eran, ma stecchi con tòsco.   4-6

The words "nodosi e 'nvolti" (5), together with the phrase "stecchi con tòsco" (6), were picked out by Leo Spitzer as the first in a series of harsh-sounding words and phrases creating a verbal disharmony which he saw as combining with the visual disharmony of the monstrous hybrids of man and plant (which will be revealed shortly) to express the moral disharmony of the souls' wayward condition.[2] This is an attractive and certainly not misguided theory, but on the other hand it could be argued that in the remainder of *Inferno* all the other souls are in a condition of moral disorder, so that a similar treatment would be equally appropriate throughout.

Another conspicuous feature of the second *terzina* is the series of parallel constructions around the strongly antithetical pattern "non . . . ma" in each line, striking, as Spitzer (p.97) put it, an "insistent note of schism", and thus establishing a sinister atmosphere of disunion or severance, which is central to the sins of both suicide and, as Dante sees it, squandering. In actual fact the use of anaphora extends to the first three *terzine* of the canto, all of which begin with the word "non", and this inconspicuous negative particle might therefore be regarded as a key-word in the canto as a whole, since the sins of suicide and, to a lesser extent, squandering represent a negation of one's God-given identity. Both the three-fold antithesis in the second *terzina* and the anaphora running through the first three *terzine* are elements of rhetoric, and rhetoric is to be a particularly prominent feature of this canto, so that one may see in the rhetorical devices of the opening lines a process of acclimatization to rhetorical density. This process is maintained in the third *terzina*, where we again find repetition, in the verbs "han" (7) and "hanno" (8), while with some dexterity it is arranged that both these verbs have the same subject, the "fiere selvagge" (8), but strongly contrasted objects (the "aspri sterpi . . . folti" (7) and (9) the "luoghi cólti"), echoing the kind of antithesis we had in the second *terzina*; in addition we observe the more obvious antithesis between "selvagge" and "cólti":

> Non han sì aspri sterpi né sì folti
> quelle fiere selvagge che 'n odio hanno
> tra Cecina e Corneto i luoghi cólti.   7-9

The area delimited by the River Cecina and the town of Corneto (modern Tarquinia) is the wild, unhealthy marshland along the south-west coast of Tuscany known as the Maremma, and the comparison (7-9) is ostensibly between the vegetation of the Maremma and that of the second "girone" of the seventh circle, which is said to be even harsher. But the *terzina* is more complex than that, since half of it is devoted to the wild beasts which inhabit the Maremma, avoiding cultivated places. This mention of beasts prepares us for another poetic strand in the canto, a fierce animal strand which further complicates Spitzer's monstrous hybrid of human and plant. The hypothetical snakes to which Pier della Vigna refers (39) continue this strand, and so too do the black bitches (125) and the wild boars to which the squanderers are compared (113). But the animal strand is most immediately picked up by the Harpies, who appear in the very next *terzina*. The opening nine lines of the canto, then, besides providing a masterly prelude to the rhetoric, do much in other ways to establish the overall character of the canto.

Then (10-12) another important component of the canto makes its appearance: the *Aeneid*. The most important literary source for *Inferno* xiii is the third book of Virgil's epic, which narrates the eventful travels of Aeneas from Troy, after its fall, as far as Carthage. More precisely, *Aeneid* III contains two sources for this canto: firstly, the episode of Aeneas's first landing, in Thrace, where he encounters his dead compatriot Polydorus through an attempt to uproot a tree(*Aen*.III.13-68); and secondly that of Aeneas's fourth landing, on the Strophades Islands (*Aen*.III.209-69), where the Trojans are attacked by the Harpies. I stress the separateness of these two episodes to show that one of the first things Dante did in composing this canto was to fuse them together, so that the tree-souls, of which Polydorus is the prototype, now appear in the same setting as the Harpies, though originally they were a good 650 miles apart on the route that Aeneas took.

Half human and half bird, the Harpies are another monstrous hybrid. All the physical and historical details concerning them here (10-15) are selected from Virgil's presentation of them on the Strophades:

Ali hanno late, e colli e visi umani,
piè con artigli, e pennuto 'l gran ventre;
fanno lamenti in su li alberi strani.   13-15

They are referred to as "brutte" (10) not because they are ugly (in fact Virgil describes them as *virginei vultus*, having the faces of maidens), but because of the foul droppings with which they constantly assail their Trojan enemies: within only a few lines Virgil describes them with such epithets as *immundus, foedus, taeter* and *obscoenus*, all meaning foul or filthy. The "tristo annunzio di futuro danno" (12) is the prophecy their leader made, to the effect that the Trojans would be punished by a fearful hunger which would force them to gnaw and devour their very tables, for seeking to engage the Harpies in battle. In the context of this canto, however, the phrase "con tristo annunzio" could be taken to modify not "cacciar" (11) but "fanno" (10); "lor nidi fanno . . . con tristo annunzio di futuro danno" would then refer forward with considerable foreboding to the wounds the Harpies inflict here on the souls of the damned.

The first direct speech of the canto (16-21) is a preliminary speech by Virgil, who informs Dante that this is the second "girone". As Virgil has already said in *Inferno* xi.40-5, this is where the suicides and squanderers vainly repent, while the first "girone", already seen in *Inferno* xii, contains the souls of those who were violent against others, and the third, the "sabbione" alluded to here (*Inf.*xiii.19) and extending from the beginning of *Inferno* xiv to the middle of *Inferno* xvii, is occupied by the souls of those who in various ways performed violence against God:

> E 'l buon maestro "Prima che più entre,
> sappi che se' nel secondo girone",
> mi cominciò a dire, "e sarai mentre
> che tu verrai ne l'orribil sabbione."   16-19

The style of Virgil's speech, in striking contrast with the complex rhetorical formulation of much of the canto, is remarkably simple and unadorned, as if he were addressing a child. He seems to know in advance everything that will happen, and dissociates himself from his ignorant protégé through the use of the second person singular rather than of the corresponding "noi" forms.

Virgil continues:

> "Però riguarda ben; sì vederai
> cose che torrien fede al mio sermone."   20-1

The "cose" he here anticipates are the events (28-45) of the plucking of a twig from one of the trees and the tree's startling reaction, consisting of oozing blood and hissing speech which reveal the suffering immortal soul of a former human being, a sequence of events which Dante adapts from the *Aeneid*'s Polydorus episode. In the Virgilian story the keynote is horror: at the point where blood oozes from Polydorus's tree Virgil uses the word *horror* and its derivatives three times in seven lines. On the other hand there is evidence to suggest that Dante wished to attenuate the explicit element of horror, as if the scene was intrinsically horrible enough without direct comment. Significantly, only once in the whole of *Inferno* xiii is a word from the *horror* family used, and then, rather than referring to anything in the second "girone", it looks forward to the third, the "sabbione", which is described precisely at this point as "orribil" (19). I shall suggest later that in Dante's wood, rather than horror, one of the keynotes is "pietà". Perhaps the poet was keeping some dramatic impact in reserve for the episodes of the violent against God.

In referring here to his own "sermone", Virgil could have in mind either his words already written in *Aeneid* III or words which he might have uttered here and now in the wood but refrains from uttering, because Dante would not have believed them. He mentions his own words again at the end of this sequence of events, when he explains to the tree-soul that his seemingly heartless action of inducing Dante to wound it was necessary because Dante would otherwise have been unable to believe what he had read in the *Aeneid*:

> "S'elli avesse potuto creder prima",
> rispuose 'l savio mio, "anima lesa,
> ciò c'ha veduto pur con la mia rima,
> non averebbe in te la man distesa;
> ma la cosa incredibile mi fece
> indurlo ad ovra ch'a me stesso pesa."   46-51

The "cosa" (50) may be "incredibile", unbelievable, in common parlance, but since it is an element of God's universe it has got to be believed, though according to Virgil here, it has to be seen to be believed. Dante has seen this sequence of events before, but only, "pur" (48), in the *Aeneid*, which is neither the Bible nor even the work of a Christian, so that in order to believe this unbelievable thing Dante needs more authoritative evidence, the evidence of his own eyes in some part of God's universe. Owing to the *Aeneid*'s defective authority then, the "cosa" has been hitherto incredible not only in common parlance but absolutely.[3]

Despite Virgil's exhortation, "riguarda", and his promise, "vederai", the first sense-impression reported after his speech is one of hearing: "Io sentia d'ogne parte trarre guai" (22), which must be the cries of the Harpies, like the "lamenti" (15); and the accompanying visual impression is a negative one: "e non vedea persona che 'l facesse" (23), which momentarily seems to break the promise Virgil has made with "vederai". These two sensory data further develop the feeling of bewilderment, and Dante stops in his tracks, "tutto smarrito" (24).

The following line is striking by virtue of its threefold polyptoton involving parts of "credere":

> Cred' io ch'ei credette ch'io credesse . . .   25

Clearly, one of the functions of this ostentatious word-play is to develop the rhetorical network characterizing the canto and already initiated (1-9); and its stammering effect is also

expressive of Dante's confusion at the bizarre surroundings.
But perhaps the most important aspect of the line is the word
itself which is highlighted by the repetition: "credere", which
follows hard on the heels of a remark about the "fede", which
Dante may or may not legitimately place in Virgil's "sermone"
(21). The closely-related concepts of faith and belief are
extremely important in this canto as we shall see later.

What Dante-poet believes that Virgil believed that Dante-
character believed is that the Harpies' cries were uttered by
souls hiding from the two travellers among the bushes,

> che tante voci uscisser, tra quei bronchi,
> da gente che per noi si nascondesse.   26-7

If this had been what Dante-character was believing (and in his
state of confusion he does not know what to believe), it would
have been a false belief, so Virgil sets in motion the process
which resolves Dante's confusion and crisis of belief, suggesting that he pluck a twig from one of the trees:

> Però disse 'l maestro: "Se tu tronchi
> qualche fraschetta d'una d'este piante,
> li pensier c'hai si faran tutti monchi".   28-30

Again Virgil's language is unadorned, until the last word of his
terzina, where he suddenly permits himself an exceptionally
bold metaphor. "Monco" means maimed, but applies almost
solely to the loss of a hand; so Virgil is saying, "the thoughts you
have will all have a hand cut off". His progression from plain
words to rhetoric, and the specific meaning of his chosen
metaphor, may be taken to represent a closer approach to the
theme of the severance of suicide and to the rhetorical extremes
which characterize Dante's treatment of it.

Dante does as he is told, selecting at random a "gran pruno":

> Allor porsi la mano un poco avante
> e colsi un ramicel da un gran pruno.   31-2

The plants in the wood have been referred to by the more
majestic word "alberi" (15), whereas a "pruno" is a blackthorn
bush, which never grows to a height of more than fifteen feet, or
some similar thorny shrub. Apparently then, Dante by no
means chooses the largest of the trees around him. This presumably has a moral dimension. A first reading of the canto is
likely to give the impression that Dante regarded Pier della

Vigna, whose soul this "pruno" later turns out to be, as a great man, perhaps a "magnanimo" like Farinata. On the other hand, as we begin to see here, Dante takes steps to undermine Piero's own implied pretensions to greatness: even if it is a "gran pruno", Piero's soul is far from being the greatest in the "girone".

Dante's action is remarkably gentle, to judge by the words "porsi", "un poco", "colsi" (a verb suggesting the effortlessness of picking a flower rather than the removal of a twig, and much milder than the "troncare" (28) proposed by Virgil) and "ramicel", which, with its diminutive suffix, takes up a device already used by Virgil in his suggestion: "fraschetta" (29). There is, however, a violent contrast between the mildness of Dante's gesture and the extravagance of the response: "e 'l tronco suo gridò: 'Perché mi schiante?'" (33). Dante is careful about the ways he introduces speech and he never uses "gridare" unless he really means it. On the other hand the dramatic shout is attenuated by another factor: we learn in a minute (40-5) that the speech of these tree-souls is nothing but a hiss, so that, for all his verbal violence underlined by the metre of the line, Piero's shout is a mere shadow of a shout. The contradiction inherent in the tree's shouted hiss, like the contradiction inherent in the "gran pruno" itself, besides further building up the disturbing atmosphere, suggests that Piero is not as great as he thought he was.

After Piero's three-word outburst there is a pause, while blood spreads from the wound Dante has inflicted, and Piero calms down somewhat before reiterating his question and developing it into an explanation, in a tone conveyed this time by the verb "dire" rather than "gridare":

> Da che fatto fu poi di sangue bruno,
> ricominciò a dir: "Perché mi scerpi?
> non hai tu spirto di pietade alcuno?
> Uomini fummo, e or siam fatti sterpi:
> ben dovrebb' esser la tua man più pia,
> se state fossimo anime di serpi".   34-9

The two parallel rhetorical questions (33 and 35), linked by anaphora, echo the rhetorical question of Virgil's Polydorus: "Quid miserum, Aenea, laceras?" (*Aen.*III.41; Woe is me! why dost thou tear me, Aeneas?); but here the two rhetorical questions are followed by a third (36), which appeals to the wayfarer's sense of "pietade". I have already suggested that "pietà" is an important word, and the same would appear to be suggested by its involvement in *replicatio* with the adjective "pia" two lines later.

Dante seems to have been well aware of the Roman interpretation of *pietas*, consisting of a threefold attitude of dutiful respect, towards the gods, towards one's fatherland, and towards one's kinsmen, especially one's parents.[4] By Dante's day however, the third element, that of dutiful respect towards one's kinsmen, had so extended its semantic scope as to embrace in the first place comrades (which point it had already reached in Classical Latin) and ultimately the whole race of one's fellow-humans, giving a vernacular meaning of "pity, compassion". However much Sapegno may at times resist this obvious interpretation (see his note to *Inf.*v.72), the word always has in Dante either the ancient Roman connotations or the obvious vernacular sense, even if it does sometimes have more complex overtones as well. Here Piero is again echoing Polydorus (*Aen.*III.42): "parce pias scelerare manus"(spare the pollution of thy pure hands). Since Piero was not Dante's comrade, however, the meaning must have changed in the adaptation, and line 36 must mean "have you no pity?", while 38 must mean "your hand should have been more compassionate". The same meaning is present in line 84, where Dante feels unable to ask Piero any more questions because he is so overcome by "pietà". But the episode also shows Dante as *pius* in the ancient sense: his initial lack of "pietà" in plucking the twig from Piero's tree is reversed and in a sense atoned for in the first three lines of *Inferno* xiv where he gathers up the "fronde" of the other suicide tree-soul, inspired by "la carità del natio loco" (since the soul is Florentine), which is precisely one of the three manifestations of Roman *pietas*. These are some of the circumstances which prompt the suggestion that "pietà" (in all its senses) replaces *horror* as the prevailing emotion in Dante's adaptation of the Polydorus story.

With the following *terzina* Piero's speech broadens out into the explanation Virgil has been anticipating. Line 37 puts it in a nutshell, with an epigrammatic quality created by the twin devices of antithesis (between "uomini" and "sterpi") and chiasmus, which effectively polarizes the two antithetical terms at opposite ends of the line: "Uomini fummo, e or siam fatti sterpi" (37), a line which recalls Virgil's words at *Inferno* i.67: "Non omo, omo già fui". In both these lines there is a second antithesis in the tenses of the verbs. Aquinas had defined humanity as a substantial union of body and soul,[5] so that when the body and soul are separated by death, the human being ceases to exist as such.

The next two lines make what seems to be an absurdly hyperbolic statement, that Dante's hand should have been more compassionate if these had been souls of snakes. Surely, one objects, to broaden the concept of *pietas* so far as to embrace so much more than the whole human race is unthinkable. The idea of "pietà" towards the souls of snakes[6] then, further develops the bizarre atmosphere of the place and, occurring here in Piero's opening speech, warns us that there is something wrong with Piero's own conception of humanity and human morality. Moreover the word "serpi", strongly linked by rhyme and paronomasia with the word "sterpi" (the opposite in this context of "uomini"), consolidates the grotesque, bewildering juxtaposition and intermingling of animal, vegetable and human elements which we have already noted.

Then begins the famous extended simile in which the simultaneous issue of speech and blood from the broken branch is compared to the simultaneous issue of air and sap from one end of a green branch which is burnt at the other end:

> Come d'un stizzo verde ch'arso sia
>   da l'un de' capi, che da l'altro geme
>   e cigola per vento che va via,
> sì de la scheggia rotta usciva insieme
>   parole e sangue; . . .   40-4

The simultaneity of this production of blood and hissing words is effectively expressed by the application of a singular verb, "usciva", to a plural subject, "parole e sangue", a type of calculated solecism for which Dante shows a predilection at several points in the *Commedia*. The phrase "va via" may seem rather a weak rendering of the escape of the hissing air, but in combination with the word "vento" it does offer a most expressive sequence of "v" alliteration in which the movement of air, and perhaps also the flickering of the flames, are translated into audible terms; "cigola", too, is almost onomatopoeic. The extended simile was, of course, a set piece, a bravura figure, and few people would deny that Dante here creates a little masterpiece of the genre. Not only are the explicit terms of the comparison perfectly appropriate, but there is also a less obvious allusion, in "ch'arso sia", to the state of Piero's soul; the background fire which causes the oozing and hissing in the unreal term of the comparison is an image of the cause of the oozing and hissing in the real term. In other words it alludes both to Piero's inner suffering and to the extreme emotional intensity which has occasioned his shout (33).[7]

The sequence of events is completed by Dante's dropping the twig and being immobilized by fear: "ond' io lasciai la cima/cadere, e stetti come l'uom che teme" (44-5). The phrase "come l'uom che teme" is a little pseudo-simile of a type which Dante uses frequently, where the particular experience is subsumed in a general type: Dante does not merely resemble a man afraid, he is one.[8]

At the immobilization of Dante, it is Virgil who steps into the breach, explaining to Piero that the apparent cruelty he suggested to Dante was necessary. These lines (46-51) have already been commented on in discussing the "cose che torrien fede al mio sermone" (21). It may now be added however, that while maintaining a basically direct style of speech, Virgil indulges in an elegant and expressive word-play, between once again that important word "creder" (46) and "incredibile" (50); also these two words together are in antithesis at a secondary level with "ha veduto" (48), underlining the inherent tension between two modes of cognition, seeing and believing.

Then Virgil changes the subject and, still in his unadorned style, asks Piero to reveal his identity to Dante. But once again, although the language is simple, it would seem that the thoughts in Virgil's mind are less so: he still appears to know everything that is to come. As a means of persuading Piero to say who he is, Virgil refers to the envisaged report about him that Dante will carry back to the land of the living:

> Ma dilli chi tu fosti, sì che 'n vece
> d'alcun' ammenda tua fama rinfreschi
> nel mondo sù, dove tornar li lece.   52-4

In particular Dante will be able to put the record straight on the question of treachery: whereas the world believes that Piero betrayed his lord, one of the things that happen further on in the canto is that Piero acquits·himself of this charge, evidently to the satisfaction of Dante-character, and this satisfaction is transmitted to the reader. But Virgil actually avoids saying that Dante will necessarily say anything good about Piero. In fact his proposal to Piero is double-edged: although Dante will be able to clear Piero of the charge of treason, that is the only good news he will be able to deliver, since he will also have to say that Piero is in Hell. In addition, as we shall see, he will have some quite damning things to say about the state of Piero's soul. Virgil's promise that Piero's fame will be refreshed is then a trap.

Pier della Vigna lived in the first half of the thirteenth century and died in 1249, sixteen years before Dante was born. He was an accomplished jurist and worked in Sicily at the court of the Emperor, Frederick II. So talented was he that during the 1220's he quickly became Frederick's right-hand man and occupied that position for more than twenty years. As Frederick's principal adviser in government, Piero exercised considerable power: it was he who worded the laws of the Kingdom of Sicily, wrote the Emperor's speeches and drafted the imperial correspondence with the pope and other contemporary heads of state. Since these communications were often polemical or propagandistic in character it was important that they should be ably and persuasively written. In this respect Piero was unrivalled: the various documents composed by Piero were in Latin, and Piero has been called "the last creative writer of living Latin", as well as the "greatest Latin stylist of the Middle Ages".[9] I emphasize the literary facet of Piero's expertise because, together with the juridical facet, this was one of the main aspects Dante had in mind when he portrayed Piero in *Inferno* xiii.

The events of the closing months of Piero's life were more or less as Piero relates them in this canto: having been accused of treason against the Emperor, he was imprisoned; whereupon he committed suicide in order to, in Dante's words, "fuggir disdegno" (71), to evade scorn or to escape humiliating punishment.[10] Whether or not the charge of treason was justified we shall probably never know, but Dante was clearly convinced that it was false, that the other courtiers' reports to the Emperor had been trumped up out of envy of Piero's exalted position.

Reading between the lines here, one can see an additional implied reason for Dante's interest in Piero. Dante had been exiled from Florence in 1302 on a charge of corruption in public office similarly concocted by his political adversaries (at least, it is generally assumed that the charge was unfounded). His love for Florence was great and his inability to return there for the last nineteen years of his life was one of his greatest sadnesses. He thus had good reason to sympathize with Piero, whom he saw as having been driven to suicide by the same kind of false accusation as that which had resulted in his own exile. What, then, does Dante make of this interesting figure? In the first place, he dwells extensively on the story of envious slander and ignoble suicide of Piero's last months; this is the theme throughout the central section of Piero's first main speech (63-72). But equally important is the way in which Dante has Piero speak in the style of his own Latin letters. Piero's style was a complex and highly artificial rhetorical one, in which he strove to achieve all sorts of tricks of language which are not altogether to the taste of the modern reader. Such devices as alliteration, periphrasis, antithesis, figurative vocabulary and various forms of word-play were the stock-in-trade of this style. Not only was Piero a past-master of it, so too was Dante when he chose to be, and accordingly we find that most of Piero's first main speech is a dazzling display of verbal virtuosity, for which the rhetoric earlier in the canto is presumably, in part, a preparation.

Piero begins to speak again:

> E 'l tronco: "Sì col dolce dir m'adeschi,
> ch'i' non posso tacere; e voi non gravi
> perch' io un poco a ragionar m'inveschi."	55-7

The rhetoric begins immediately with the alliteration of "dolce dir"; but the principal *recherché* ingredients of this first *terzina* are the two rhyme-words "adeschi" and "inveschi", which are both precious metaphors. The first is a fishing term and derives from the root-word "esca", meaning bait, so that here Piero says he is being allured as a fish by the bait with which Virgil has primed his fish-hook, namely the promise which he has just made in the preceding *terzina* and which we have recognized as a trap. In "m'inveschi" Piero momentarily casts himself as a bird, because "invescarsi" is borrowed from the language of bird-catching and means to be caught in a snare. In both these metaphors, then, Piero appears to be aware that he is falling into Virgil's trap.

Piero thinks, however, that his own guile is a match for Virgil's, and intends to turn the trap to his own advantage. This is already suggested by the verb "ragionar" (57). As three words would have answered Virgil's "dilli chi tu fosti" (52), he politely apologizes in advance (56-7) for saying more than has been asked of him,[11] thus announcing his intention to "ragionar", which in this context basically means to talk, to discourse. More subtly though, in modern Italian as well as in Dante, the verb "ragionare" can be used to indicate discursive if informal speech with the purpose of justifying something, such as oneself, a personal viewpoint or a political creed, using "ragione" or rational argument in so far as it can be manipulated to support the underlying conviction. Right at the beginning of this speech, then, Piero gives us a concealed hint at its concealed purpose.

Piero's concealed purpose is one which is not only cunning but malicious: it is to overwhelm Dante's intelligence and distort the truth that he is to carry back to the land of the living. Dante's envisaged report is more important than it might appear at first sight, in fact it is no exaggeration to state that Piero's dominant passion throughout this speech is a passion for earthly fame. Only the first and last *terzine* of the speech (55-7 and 76-8) actually allude to Dante's report, but Piero does refer to Virgil's promise as "dolce" and as a bait, a motive inducing him to speak. The whole of the eighteen-line passage between those two *terzine* is subordinate to the desire to create a favourable impression, and consists of a carefully calculated handling of language (of which Piero was such a master in his mortal life), designed to delude Dante in the first place and the world at large in the second.

Piero begins his answer, but it is anything but straightforward:

> Io son colui che tenni ambo le chiavi
>   del cor di Federigo, e che le volsi,
>   serrando e diserrando, sì soavi,
> che dal secreto suo quasi ogn' uom tolsi.   58-61

Instead of saying "I am Pier della Vigna", he launches into a periphrasis which occupies almost four lines, and in the course of which we notice more alliteration in "secreto suo" and word-play in "serrando e diserrando". These lines also contain a veiled play on Piero's own name: by referring to the keys of Frederick's heart, Dante is reminding us of another Piero and another pair of keys, the keys of St Peter, which are a means of humanity to enter the Kingdom of Heaven. But whereas St Peter was entrusted with the propagation of the Christian faith, the use to which Pier della Vigna put his keys, as he says in these four lines, was that of excluding other men from his lord's affairs, an intention in which he achieved more or less complete success. The frequent "s" sounds in these lines, especially when we remember that the whole speech is one long hiss, powerfully suggest the meanness and subterfuge involved in the effective discharge of this function.[12] So Dante-poet counter-acts Piero's attempt to whitewash himself in the eyes of Dante-character and of the reader by hinting, in the mention of the keys, at a contrast between Piero as he was and Piero as he might have been. (Paradoxically, St Peter denied his Lord three times, while his namesake, it appears, never broke his allegiance to Frederick).

We should not ignore the rhythm of these four lines: the strong *enjambement* at the end of 58, the pauses in the middle of 59 and 60, and the fact that the statement overflows into a fourth line rather than being contained in a *terzina*. The majority of Piero's Latin letters were in prose, and Dante here momentarily allows the tense rhythm of the hendecasyllable to slump, thus characterizing Piero with a verse utterance that sounds like prose. He does exactly the same thing again farther on:

> La meretrice che mai da l'ospizio
>   di Cesare non torse li occhi putti,
>   morte comune e de le corti vizio,
> infiammò contra me li animi tutti.   64-7

Meanwhile, though, he says (and notice the important word "fede" again):

> fede portai al glorioso offizio,
>   tanto ch'i' ne perde' li sonni e ' polsi.   62-3

What he means when he says he lost his wrists is that he lost his life: life = blood = pulse = wrist. This is a good example of metonymy and of the kind of artifice for which Piero was renowned, as is also the whole phrase "perde' li sonni e ' polsi", a case of syllepsis, where one verb governs two objects which are in rather surprising juxtaposition. Piero is warming to his theme and the rhetoric too is gathering momentum. The next four lines contain another complex periphrasis since the prostitute, "meretrice", is Envy; in fact not only periphrasis but personification (Envy has eyes: 65), and almost allegory. In line 66, "morte" is a metaphor, since envy is not literally death, and the whole line is structured as a case of chiasmus (noun+adjective: adjectival phrase+noun), the parallelism being all the stronger for the fact that both expressions are in apposition to "meretrice".

It was considered good style by writers of Piero's type to delay the name of characters who were being introduced (*retardatio nominis*), and accordingly Piero withholds this prostitute's name, "'nvidia", until line 78, the last line of this speech. It was also considered good style to vary the ways in which a single entity was referred to when it was mentioned more than once (*variatio*), so he refers to the imperial court as the "ospizio" (64) and reserves the more obvious "corti" (66) for a general reference. More importantly, he varies the ways in which he refers to the Emperor: first he refers to him simply as "Federigo" (59)[13] then as "Cesare" (65), Frederick being Caesar metonymically as a successor of Julius Caesar, ideally the first emperor; he is "Augusto" (68) for much the same reason; and then finally he becomes "il mio segnor". The first three of these designations increase progressively in grandeur as part of the growing momentum of Piero's speech; there is a reason, as we shall see, for the fourth one dropping to a much less colourful register.

"Infiammò" (67) is another metaphor when its object is "animi", and it prepares for the ever-increasing verbal dexterity of the next two lines:

> e li 'nfiammati infiammar sì Augusto,
> che ' lieti onor tornaro in tristi lutti.   68-9

The three-fold word-play on this verb "infiammare" answers the three-fold play on "credere" (25) and suggests the way in which hostility towards Piero spread along the links of the chain connecting the courtiers and ultimately reaching the Emperor himself. The sentence culminates in a double antithesis involving two nouns and two adjectives ("lieti onor . . . tristi lutti"). But the rhetorical climax, coinciding with the moral crux of the whole story, comes in the following *terzina*:

> L'animo mio, per disdegnoso gusto,
> credendo col morir fuggir disdegno,
> ingiusto fece me contra me giusto.   70-2

"L'animo mio" is in opposition to "li animi tutti" (67), while "contra me" (67) is repeated here (72), where, however, it is compounded with a repetition of "me", and the resulting phrase "me contra me" forcefully represents the outrage committed by one half of the human being against the other in the act of suicide. The linguistic artifice of the *terzina* is completed by two further word-plays, "disdegnoso":"disdegno" and "ingiusto":"giusto"; the latter emphatically arranged at the two ends of the line, and both underlining the contradiction in Piero's motivation. The concern with justice at this climactic moment is particularly appropriate on the lips of one who was, among other things, a High Court judge.

Very suddenly, however, with the next *terzina* (in which we notice the word "fede" once again) all the verbal artifice is abandoned. Piero is here changing the subject slightly, from the tortuous, involuted and somewhat specious examination of conscience, expressed in tortuous, involuted and somewhat specious language, to the sincere statement, indeed the swearing, of a single, simple fact — that he was innocent, not of suicide but of treason:

> Per le nove radici d'esto legno
> vi giuro che già mai non ruppi fede
> al mio segnor, che fu d'onor sì degno.   73-5

What could be more straightforward? And what could be more persuasive, especially when uttered by a man who has just shown such a marked propensity for playing with words? By this contrast of styles, Dante is not only allowing Piero to assert his innocence but subtly playing on the reader's sensibilities to make him accept Piero's oath at face-value. Such acceptance is doubtless Dante's intention, but, given that an oath is a guarantee of faith ("fede" again) in the form of an appeal to God or some other revered or dreaded entity, Piero's oath is formally invalid and a guarantee of nothing. It is made "per le nove radici d'esto legno". And what is "esto legno"? Nothing more than the pitiful, monstrous form assumed by Piero's own perverted soul. It is a far cry from that other tree on which men have been known to base their oaths, the Cross on which Jesus Christ was crucified. Like the earlier veiled comparison with St Peter, the oath serves to point the contrast between Piero as he was and Piero as he might have been.

The final *terzina* of Piero's first main speech is in the same straightforward register as his oath; it is a direct plea for Dante to rehabilitate his reputation on earth:

> E se di voi alcun nel mondo riede,
>   conforti la memoria mia, che giace
>   ancor del colpo che 'nvidia le diede.   76-8

He does speak politely, with the iussive subjunctive "conforti" and the optative subjunctive "riede", which is answered, as so often in Dante, by a second optative subjunctive on the lips of the interlocutor (here, Virgil in lines 85-6); and he does employ the elegant personification of "invidia" and his "memoria" together with the extended metaphor of "colpo" and "giace". But there is nothing particularly striking about these figures: as far as Piero is concerned, the ostentatious rhetoric has disappeared for good.

Piero speaks, then, in two distinct styles, which must be expressions of two sides of his character. The simple, direct style of the last six lines of his speech seems to be an expression of sincerity, and the complex, indirect style of his earlier lines, an expression of insincerity. There is, in fact, a parallel between Piero's use of rhetoric in talking here about the motives behind his suicide and his use of rhetoric in the Latin letters he wrote in life to the political leaders of his day. In both cases Piero is a propagandist. His propaganda here consists of an attempt to divert our attention from the naked fact of his suicide, with all its inescapable moral implications, and he attempts this partly by dwelling on the exalted position he held in life and on his political downfall (both of which are essentially irrelevant to his suicide), partly by emphasizing the role of other people in his political *démise*, partly by trying to blind Dante with words, partly by twisting language; when he eventually does talk about his suicide, he devotes to it only one three-line sentence (70-2), and casts that sentence in such a complicated form that the casual reader would have very little idea of what he is talking about. Instead of making himself, "io", the subject of the sentence, he has as subject "l'animo mio", which sounds like something external to himself, yet another third party; he continues the syntax with a third-person verb, "fece", and casts himself as the object of the sentence, "me", as if his wilful self-destruction were an action inflicted by some external entity on an unwilling victim. Such are the ways of propaganda.

After line 78 there is a pause and the tension is relieved for a few moments while the two wayfarers debate their next move. Virgil exhorts Dante to make use of the pause, if he so desires, to extract further information from Piero:

> Un poco attese, e poi "Da ch'el si tace",
> disse 'l poeta a me, "non perder l'ora;
> ma parla, e chiedi a lui, se più ti piace".
> Ond' io a lui: "Domandal tu ancora
> di quel che credi ch'a me satisfaccia;
> ch'i' non potrei, tanta pietà m'accora".   79-84

Dante-character, in his only utterance in the canto, speaks only to say that he cannot speak: he is too overwhelmed by that "pietà" which Piero has been seeking to instil into him since his rhetorical question on the subject: "non hai tu spirto di pietade alcuno?" (36).

Virgil's second address to Piero is still rhetorically elegant and impeccably polite:

> Perciò ricominciò: "Se l'om ti faccia
> liberamente ciò che 'l tuo dir priega,
> spirito incarcerato, ancor ti piaccia
> di dirne come l'anima si lega
> in questi nocchi; e dinne, se tu puoi,
> s'alcuna mai di tai membra si spiega".   85-90

Besides capping Piero's optative subjunctive, in combination with a iussive subjunctive, "ti piaccia", he also indulges in three-fold polyptoton: "dir-dirne-dinne" and answers Dante's "i' non potrei" (84) with "se tu puoi", as well as his own "ti piace" (81) in "ti piaccia". He asks how the soul comes to be fixed in these gnarled trunks, and whether any of the souls is ever freed from them. The first of these questions is answered in lines 94-102, while the second is indirectly answered in lines 103-8. Thus Piero's final speech falls clearly into two sections.

Virgil's second question, relating to the liberation of the soul from its present "membra", receives an alternative, ironic reply in lines 109-29.

Piero's second main speech is introduced by a reminder of the peculiar process of the suicides' speech-production, with the words "soffiò" and more alliterative "v" sounds, "convertì -vento-voce":

> Allor soffiò il tronco forte, e poi
> si convertì quel vento in cotal voce.   91-2

The speech itself begins with a programmatic declaration invoking the stylistic principle of plain, direct expression (*brevitas*): "Brievemente sarà risposto a voi" (93). Here Piero is submerging his individual identity and speaking only of what he shares with all his fellow-suicides. It is therefore fitting that his language should become unremarkable. The line is also cast in the passive voice, preparing us for what will be a highly impersonal recitation. The following nine lines, answering Virgil's first question, are in fact formulated in the third person singular, "l'anima feroce" being the generic subject:

> Quando si parte l'anima feroce
>   dal corpo ond' ella stessa s'è disvelta,
>   Minòs la manda a la settima foce.
> Cade in la selva, e non l'è parte scelta;
>   ma là dove fortuna la balestra,
>   quivi germoglia come gran di spelta.
> Surge in vermena e in pianta silvestra:
>   l'Arpie, pascendo poi de le sue foglie,
>   fanno dolore, e al dolor fenestra.   94-104

The answer is that, despatched by Minos to the seventh circle, the soul of the suicide falls at random in the wood [14] and assumes the functions of a seed, growing eventually into a "pianta silvestra", at which point the Harpies begin their two-fold assault: in line 102 *traductio* and syllepsis combine very effectively to give a condensed expression of tension. The Harpies hurt the souls physically by plucking their leaves and emotionally by providing in the wound where each leaf is plucked, an outlet for the expression of their grief: it seems that lamenting speech increases the torment. These lines, relatively businesslike and dispassionate though they are, do contain two colourful metaphors: "disvelta", uprooted, evinces the violence of the act of suicide (violence being the basic characteristic of the whole of circle seven), and at the same time neatly suggests arboreal characteristics in anticipation of the soul's transformation into a tree; "balestra" (literally meaning shoots with a cross-bow) conveys the violence with which the soul's own violence is punished.

The change of subject (to Virgil's second question) is marked by a change from the third person singular of the present tense to the first person plural of the future:

> Come l'altre verrem per nostre spoglie,
> ma non però ch'alcuna sen rivesta,
> Ché non è giusto aver ciò ch'om si toglie.
> Qui le strascineremo, e per la mesta
> selva saranno i nostri corpi appesi,
> ciascuno al prun de l'ombra sua molesta.   103-8

Here the answer is that none of the souls will ever free itself from its arboreal form, not even at the Last Judgment, when, in common with other souls, they might have expected to return to the physical form they had in life. Rather, although they will fetch and drag their former bodies back from the Valley of Jehoshaphat (*Inf.* x.10-12), these will hang from the branches of their present tree-forms for all eternity. In line 105 Piero is still concerned with justice, and this time he appears to make no mistake, sententiously accepting the justice of the *contrapasso*. His closing *terzina* makes a final emotive appeal to Dante's already-awakened "pietà": the five syllables of "strascineremo" suggest wearisome, fruitless labour; the melancholy of the elegiac strand is evoked phonically in "mesta/selva. . . appesi"; and "ombra . . . molesta", ending the speech, is a meditative variation on the "anima feroce" with which the speech opened.

The twenty-one lines following the end of Piero's speech, although doctrinally essential in that without them we should know nothing about the squanderers, is poetically a passage of light, and indeed comic, relief. The most intense moments of the canto are now past, but grave matters remain to be discussed in the last seven *terzine*. It is therefore appropriate that a lively, realistic episode should intervene as a contrast to the overall immobility and solemnity:

> Noi eravamo ancora al tronco attesi,

credendo ch'altro ne volesse dire,
quando noi fummo d'un romor sorpresi,
similemente a colui che venire
sente 'l porco e la caccia a la sua posta,
ch'ode le bestie, e le frasche stormire.   109-14

The travellers are surprised by a commotion which retro-
spectively reminds the poet of a boar-hunt, another image
fusing the human and the non-human, since the part of the boar
is in fact played by the souls of two squanderers, Lano of Siena
and Iacopo of Sant'Andrea, near Padua. The realism of the
simile is heightened by the addition of the strictly unnecessary
line 114, with its sharper focus on the specifically animal and
vegetable components in the uproar. In addition, as is so often
the case with Dante's animal imagery, the emphasis on
"bestie" underlines the point that sin makes a man less than a
man, in fact nothing more than a beast, because it consists of the
misuse of reason and free will, the faculties of the intellect,
which alone distinguishes man from the animals.

From this point to the end of the comic interlude, all is
movement, animation, relative informality and relative in-
dignity. There is no question of compassion this time because
the pace of the episode precludes any insight into the individual
personalities of the two squanderers. The mood is signalled by
the informal construction with which the hunted souls become
visible:

Ed ecco due da la sinistra costa,
nudi e graffiati, fuggendo sì forte,
che de la selva rompieno ogne rosta.   115-17

The details "nudi e graffiati" are intimately physical ones,
while the drama of the scene is heightened by the alliteration of
"fuggendo . . . forte" and "rompieno . . . rosta". More
excitement is generated by Lano's appeal to death, expressed in
broken speech with intensifying *conduplicatio* and a four-fold
insistence on the *or* syllable: "Or accorri, accorri, morte!"
(118).[15] The impression of speed is sustained by more alliteration in "tardar troppo" (119), and the sense of exasperating
delay (it is Iacopo who finds himself excessively slow) is neatly
rendered by the pause after "l'altro", while the next line
contains another use of "gridare", a verb which, as we have

seen, was a particularly dramatic one for Dante:

> E l'altro, cui pareva tardar troppo,
> gridava: "Lano, sì non furo accorte
> le gambe tue a le giostre dal Toppo!"   119-21

The ford at the Pieve al Toppo was the scene of an ambush in 1288 at which the Guelph army of Siena was massacred by the Ghibellines of Arezzo under the command of Bonconte da Montefeltro, and Lano was one of those slain. In the circumstances then, the words Iacopo here shouts to Lano express both admiration and envious malevolence. Unable to keep up with Lano, Iacopo feels that, although at the Pieve al Toppo Lano was not quick enough to escape death, he might on this occasion be more successful.[16] At the same time, whatever might be the outcome here and now, Iacopo will not let Lano forget that his legs have on a previous occasion proved insufficient to keep him alive. The compliment is thus also a sarcastic taunt worthy of Maestro Adamo or Sinon. What is more, it is a waste of precious breath, especially for one who has been running flat out and is still falling behind: Iacopo's breathless state is effectively evinced by the "f" alliteration in line 122. In desperation he changes tack and seeks to evade his fate not by flight but by crouching behind a bush:

> E poi che forse li fallia la lena,
> di sé e d'un cespuglio fece un groppo.   122-3

The comic interlude is promptly brought to a close with the appearance of a host of black bitches, as keen and swift as hounds newly released from the chain:

> Di rietro a loro era la selva piena
> di nere cagne, bramose e correnti
> come veltri ch'uscisser di catena.
> In quel che s'appiattò miser li denti,
> e quel dilaceraro a brano a brano;
> poi sen portar quelle membra dolenti.   124-9

The periphrasis "quel che s'appiattò" seems to correspond to a desire to name the souls only in the direct speech of their fellows. It perhaps corresponds, too, to a desire to place an oxytonic verb, "s'appiattò", with its air of finality, immediately before the intensely realistic, "miser li denti". The realism becomes still more savage when *conduplicatio* (128) powerfully expresses the remorselessly methodical manner of the unfortunate soul's dismemberment.[17] With the word "membra" we are reminded of a previous occurrence (90) of the word when Virgil was asking Piero whether any "anima" which "si lega in questi nocchi" is ever freed from "tai membra". As far as the suicides are concerned the answer remains unchanged, but we have just seen a squanderer make "un groppo . . . di sé e d'un cespuglio". The answer in cases such as his is that the soul *is* freed from such limbs (incidentally causing damage and pain to the bush in question) and is freed from his own quasi-human limbs at the same time.

The final part of the canto, together with the first three lines of *Inferno* xiv, contains the episode of the second suicide, an anonymous Florentine who brings Dante back home. The twelve cantos from *Inferno* vi to *Inferno* xvii are sometimes referred to as the "Florentine" cantos because, from the encounter with Ciacco, through those with Filippo Argenti, Farinata degli Uberti, Cavalcante dei Cavalcanti, Ser Brunetto Latini and Bishop Andrea dei Mozzi, to the appearance of the noble Florentines of *Inferno* xvi and the representatives of the Gianfigliazzi and Ubriachi families among the usurers, Florence is never far from Dante's thoughts. Even in *Inferno* xiii, dominated as it is by a drama from Federician Sicily, the Florentine *leitmotiv* is not suppressed. Commentators have made their suggestions as to the historical identity of the anonymous Florentine, but it seems to me that the reader is intended to find the character's anonymity impenetrable, that Dante had no historical individual in mind at this point, or that if he had he deliberately emptied that figure of its individual historical identity, to present us with an emblem of Florence *tout court*. Florence is the suicide here, as is borne out by comments made in the other Florentine cantos, where the specific instruments of suicide are shown to be factionalism, indiscriminate immigration, opportunistic territorial expansion, and ultimately "superbia, invidia e avarizia" (*Inf.*vi.74; see also *Inf.*xv.68).

The episode of the second suicide in many ways parallels that of the first. Again the action is firmly set in motion by Virgil, and again it is prefaced by an allusion to the bush's bleeding wounds (though this time the aggressors are Iacopo and the bitches rather than Dante):

> Presemi allor la mia scorta per mano,
> e menommi al cespuglio che piangea
> per le rotture sanguinenti in vano.   130-2

Again the suffering soul expresses anger against the aggressor and again, as in lines 33-5, this is done with anaphora and rhetorical questions, not to mention *retardatio nominis*:

> "O Iacopo", dicea, "da Santo Andrea,
> che t'è giovato di me fare schermo?
> che colpa ho io de la tua vita rea?"   133-5

Again the bush is asked by Virgil to give its identity, again using the words "Chi fosti" (as in 52), and again the amalgam of oozing blood and grieving, hissing speech is alluded to (as it was at 43-4 and also 91-2):

> Quando 'l maestro fu sovr' esso fermo,
> disse: "Chi fosti, che per tante punte
> soffi con sangue doloroso sermo?"   136-8

Again the damned soul is happy to oblige because it hopes for a specified reward; again the reply is preceded by an allusion to the favour envisaged (139-42) and then begun with "I' fui" and continued with a periphrasis (as in 58-61); again the speaker attacks those who surrounded him in life, again adopting an ornate style for the purpose.

The anonymous Florentine then, parallels Piero not only in his crime and punishment but also in his language, though the degree of his rhetorical virtuosity is no match for that of Piero. If we look at the main speech in this last section, we see in the first place a rhyming word-play, "giunte: disgiunte", which to some may appear forced but is in keeping with the artifice of the canto as a whole:

> Ed elli a noi: "O anime che giunte
> siete a veder lo strazio disonesto
> c'ha le mie fronde sì da me disgiunte,
> raccoglietele al piè del tristo cesto".   139-42

The strong *enjambement* (139), the weaker one (140) and the overspill of the sentence into a fourth line are also reminiscent of Piero, though this is not to suggest that the anonymous Florentine is another writer of rhetorical Latin prose.

The speech continues with a series of circumlocutions still in the mould of Piero's:

I' fui de la città che nel Batista
 mutò 'l primo padrone; ond' ei per questo
 sempre con l'arte sua la farà trista;
 e se non fosse che 'n sul passo d'Arno
 rimane ancor di lui alcuna vista,
 que' cittadin che poi la rifondarno
 sovra 'l cener che d'Attila rimase,
 avrebber fatto lavorare indarno.   143-50

The city that changed its first patron for the Baptist is
Florence, and within that periphrasis the first patron himself is
Mars, the god of war, to whom Florence was dedicated before
becoming a Christian city. "L'arte sua" then, the art of Mars, is
war, and the speaker is referring to the civil strife which Dante
deplored as endemic in his native city. The phrase "alcuna
vista" (some semblance) is a periphrasis for the statue of Mars
which in Dante's day still stood at the north end of Florence's
Ponte Vecchio. Lines 148-9 contain a historical reference to
the supposed rebuilding of the city in the eighth century A.D.
after its supposed destruction by Attila the Hun, while the
following line sarcastically implies that it is only civil dissension
that keeps Florence going.[18] In this sentence the speaker has
also used two conspicuous verbal repetitions: "trista", picked
up from line 42, and "rimase", derived from "rimane" (147).
Like Piero before him, however, this speaker reserves the
climax of his rhetoric for the climax of his speech, with a three-
fold play on the first-person pronoun: "Io fei gibetto a me de le
mie case" (151), where the pronouns and also the verb "fei"
remind us strongly of Piero's "fece me contra me giusto" (72).

   If we have provisionally assumed that the purpose of the
rhetoric in this canto is to characterize Piero (though Piero
himself speaks in two contrasting styles), then it must seem odd
that the second suicide should affect similar mannerisms. In
fact the canto as a whole, of which Piero occupies only half, is
highly rhetorical for much of its length and, although we have
suggested that the rhetoric in the early lines may serve to
prepare the reader for Piero's rhetoric, nevertheless we must
now feel that the rhetoric in the canto has not been properly
accounted for. Leo Spitzer (pp. 93-9) felt the same, and saw this
involuted, twisted, perverse language as connected with the
high incidence of harsh-sounding words, thinking it had the

function of representing the involuted, twisted, perverse mentality which leads a man to take his own life. There are, however, further possibilities.

I have already hinted at the uneasy relationship between truth (represented by Piero's simple style) and propaganda (represented by Piero's complex style), between truth, then, and rhetoric, and we can recognize that rhetoric is associated with a form of untruth, a distorted version of the truth. Which version of the truth are we to believe? Belief is clearly a problem. And it seems to me to be no accident that two of the rhetorical word-plays outside Piero's speeches are built out of variations on the verb "credere". "Credere" and its derivatives in fact occur eight times in this canto,[19] which is far more than in any other canto of the *Commedia*. Faith is another concept very closely related to truth and belief, and, sure enough, the word "fede" turns up in lines 21, 62, and 74, and also in "*Fede*rigo" (59). "Fede" and "credere" then may be regarded as key-words.

Of the uses of "credere", some clearly denote mistaken belief, warning us that belief pure and simple is worth nothing: for example the "credesse" (25) indicates that Dante might have been believing that the voices from among the trees came from people who were hidden from view, which would have been false. The play with "credere" in the first third of the canto prepares for the "credendo" (71), which is one of the hinges on which the episode turns. It indicates another mistaken belief, though rather less clearly at first sight, since Piero is here touching on a much more complex subject-matter, namely the whole essence of Christian morality. By seeking to achieve, through suicide, the immediate object of escaping the scorn of his fellow-courtiers, Piero was closing his eyes to the more profound implications of his self-destruction, and incurring the far deeper and more lasting scorn of, potentially at least, the whole of Christendom, a scorn which can only be increased by Dante's returning to the world and refreshing Piero's memory in the pages of his *Inferno*.

The same shortsightedness characterizes Piero's two uses of the word "fede": "fede portai al glorioso offizio" (62), and "già mai non ruppi fede al mio segnor" (74-5). In both cases Piero is talking about Frederick's faith in him, the position of trust of which he is so proud.[20] This trust marks the outer limit of Piero's moral universe, and, by comparison with the much vaster moral responsibilities Dante has in mind in the *Commedia*, this is an extremely severe limitation. That Piero is thus blinkered is underlined by the extravagant terms in which he refers to the Emperor: "Cesare", "Augusto", and even the simpler "mio segnor"; it is perhaps not too much to say that for Piero the Emperor has taken the place of God. What a paltry, immoral creature Piero looks now! The process of belittling him, which began with his taking the form of a mere "pruno" among "alberi", has been gathering momentum throughout the episode.[21]

It would seem that the subject of truth acts as a keystone in the conceptual structure of the canto, relating rhetoric and propaganda, on the one hand, to belief and faith, on the other. I should like to propose the view that, whatever else it may be, *Inferno* xiii is a canto about truth, and that rhetoric is here used as a vital instrument for the unmasking of false semblances of truth. The problem of truth is central to the Pier della Vigna episode, and it is also central to another conspicuous aspect of the canto, the presence in it of the *Aeneid*. Just as we have seen Pier della Vigna cut down to size by the contrast with St Peter and the Christian moral order St Peter represents, so the *Aeneid*, and with it all pagan literature, is, I feel, deflated by a contrast with that same Christian moral order. This helps to explain why no special recognition is accorded by God to Virgil or to any pagan writer, as it is to Trajan and Ripheus, who have places in Heaven. If *Inferno* xiii embodies a message about pagan literature, it seems to me that it must be one which is consistent with the confinement of the pagan authors to Limbo: that, rather than an authority on the divine, non-Christian literature is in this area another false semblance of the truth and therefore unworthy of the ultimate faith.

Inferno xiii is about faith, belief and ultimately truth, the nature of truth and the masking and unmasking of truth; by focusing our attention primarily on Piero and his fellow-sufferers, Dante makes a broader and deeper comment on the illusion, the non-truth, of sin in general. As a canto about truth, then, *Inferno* xiii says a lot of things we knew before, or at least things we feel we should have known before. But this is precisely Dante's strategy: he is constantly reminding us of things we ought to know. His interest in this canto is not confined to Pier della Vigna, nor is it confined to the four souls he isolates, nor even to the souls of suicides and squanderers at large. He consistently has his mind on the overall themes of the *Comedy*, the themes of God's universe and the Christian moral order applying to man in this life. In expecting the reader to realize this, Dante makes enormous demands. But he was not writing for the average reader: he challenges the reader to exercise all his intelligence and acumen, and in so doing he exhibits one of the hallmarks of genius.

Notes

[1] For studies of this canto see "Pietro della Vigna" by E. Bigi, *Enc. d.* IV, 515-16. Further studies are: G. Güntert, "Pier delle Vigne e l'unità del canto (*Inferno* XIII)", *Lettere italiane* 23 (1971) 548-55; J. D. Levenson, "The Grundworte of Pier delle Vigne", *Forum Italicum* 5 (1971) 449-513; A. Jacomuzzi, *Il palinsesto della retorica e altri saggi danteschi* (Florence, 1972) pp. 43-77, the title essay originally appeared in *L'approdo letterario* 17 (1972); V. Presta, "In margine al canto XIII dell' *Inferno*", *Dante Studies* 90 (1972) 13-24; D. Sheehan, "The Control of Feeling: a Rhetorical Analysis of *Inferno* XIII", *Italica* 51 (1974) 193-206; D. H. Higgins, "Cicero, Aquinas, and St. Matthew in *Inferno* XIII", *Dante Studies* 93 (1975) 61-94. D. Rolfs, however, "Dante, Petrarch, Boccaccio and the Problem of Suicide", *Romanic Review* 67 (1976) 200-25, deals almost exclusively with Cato and other pagan suicides (pp.201-9). The present commentary owes most to the Jacomuzzi article (above) and to E. Paratore, "Analisi 'retorica' del canto di Pier della Vigna", *Studi danteschi* 42 (1965) 281-336, also in his *Tradizione e struttura in Dante* (Florence, 1968) pp. 178-220. Further references to these studies and to Spitzer (note [2] below) are by author only.

[2] Pp. 92-3 of L. Spitzer, "Speech and language in *Inferno* XIII", *Italica* 19 (1942) 77-104, later in Italian: see G. Getto ed., *Letture dantesche* (Florence, 1962) pp.221-48. Spitzer's series continues with "aspri sterpi" (7), the rhyme words "bronchi-tronchi-monchi" (26-30), "schiante" and "scerpi" (33-5), "stizzo" (40), "scheggia rotta" (43).

[3] The converse may be argued that the credibility of the *Aeneid* is not undermined but vindicated here. To this end one would point to *Purg*.xxii.64ff., where Virgil's fourth eclogue is cited for Statius's conversion to Christianity, suggesting that, although written by a pagan, Virgil's works, at least, had a function in a divine plan. A passage of the *Aeneid* is found to be true in *Purg*.vi.28-42, and "se fede merta nostra maggior musa" (*Par*.xv.26) has only marginally less force than a plain statement. Indeed P. Damon sees that this line suggests that the *Commedia* "embodies, in its full manifestation, the 'fede' of which Virgil, when he sang of Aeneas's journey to the 'immortale secolo', had only the shadowiest intimations" in "Geryon, Cacciaguida, and the Y of Pythagoras", *Dante Studies* 85 (1967) 15-32 (p.30). So Dante, finding in *Inf*.xiii that Virgil was right, learns

to recognize in the word of Virgil the authority of the word of God.

[4]See W. C. Greene, "Pietas", *The Oxford Classical Dictionary* (Oxford, 1949) and A. Lanci, "pietà", *Enc. d.* IV, 496. And see *Conv.*II.x.6: "pietade . . . è una nobile disposizione d'animo, apparecchiata di ricevere amore, misericordia e altre caritative passioni".

[5]"Homo . . . est aliquid compositum ex anima et corpore"; "nulla alia forma substantialis est in homine, nisi sola anima intellectiva" (*Summa theologiae,* I,q.75,4 and q.76,4).

[6]A. Medin, *Due letture dantesche* (Padua, 1906), says (p. 54) "e il serpe è qui designato come animale tipico della bestialità vile e orribile".

[7]The "scheggia rotta" (43) might wrongly be taken as the twig in Dante's hand, especially as the emission of speech and blood startles him into dropping it (44-5). But clearly the tree's trunk speaks (33) and "tronco" is still the subject of "ricominciò a dir" (35). The focus in the simile is on the aperture in the tree itself, though the total soul of which the tree is the form is present in the background.

[8]See p. 7 of J. C. Barnes, "Dante's Matelda: Fact or Fiction?", *Italian Studies* 28 (1973) 1-9.

[9]E. H. Kantorowicz, *Frederick the Second, 1194-1250,* (London, 1931) pp. 299-300.

[10]Higgins pp. 73-4, argues persuasively in favour of the latter interpretation.

[11]This apology, "e voi non gravi" echoes the form of Virgil's apology to him: "ovra ch'a me stesso pesa" (51).

[12]Piero's speeches have many *s*'s. In the first (33-9), every alternate rhyme-word begins with *s*: "schiante, scerpi, serpi", and line 39 has several.

[13]For those with a taste for the extremes of nominalism, the name *Federigo* contains the key-word *fede*, just as *Piero* contains the word *pio*.

[14]The absolutely arbitrary character of these events is poetically very effective. An inversion of the Thomistic: "Natura nihil facit frustra" (Nature does nothing without a purpose), is noted by Güntert, pp.552-3, in the useless flight of the squanderers and the *in vano* sufferings (132), combined with the region's overall literal fruitlessness (6); whereas God's created order is necessary and just, the sad realm of those who have committed violence against themselves is abandoned to chaos.

[15]Unless it is ironically absurd (not unthinkable in a comic passage such as this), Lano's invocation of death means the "seconda morte" (*Inf.*i.117), the Last Judgement, still fresh in the reader's mind from Piero's speech (103-8).

[16]In Dante's comic scenes all the souls are not constantly subject to their punishment: here Lano may temporarily get away, just as in the fifth *bolgia* (*Inf.*xxii) souls momentarily outwit the Malebranche.

[17]". . . quel *dilaceraro* è in sommo grado rappresentativo, e per la lunghezza e per i suoni e per l'uguaglianza delle sue sillabe;" and "nella forma avverbiale *a brano a brano* si sente lo squarciarsi delle carni", L. Pietrobono, *Il canto XIII dell'Inferno,* Lectura Dantis Romana (Turin, 1962) p. 22.

[18]Or, it implies that without the power of the statue Florence would have been razed to the ground again (e.g. Pietrobono p. 24, see note 17 above).

[19]Lines 25 (three times), 46, 50, 71, 83, 110.

[20]"Vow" best translates "fede" (74), a specific reference to Piero's oath of allegiance to the Emperor. Similarly in "ruppe fede al cener di Sicheo" (*Inf.*v.62), "fede", again the object of "rompere", is perhaps "vow".

[21]Dante is examined on faith in *Par.*xxiv by that *alter Petrus*, St Peter, the greatest exponent of faith and the great spearhead of *the* faith, "l'alto primipilo" (*Par.*xxiv.59).

It may also be no coincidence that St Peter is indicated as "colui che tien le chiavi di tal gloria" (*Par*.xxiii.139) closely reflecting: "colui che tenni ambo le chiavi del cor di Federigo" (*Inf*.xiii.58-9). And it may even be no coincidence that Dante, replying to Peter, refers to the Christian faith as "la buona pianta che fu già vite e ora è fatta pruno" (*Par*.xxiv.110-1), the plant which was once a vine and is now a thorny shrub. Piero, too, was once "della Vigna", a name commentators suggest gave Dante the idea of the arboreal form of the suicides.

The Theme of Exodus in the First Two Cantos of the Purgatorio

Peter Armour

Some years ago T. G. Bergin adapted the old phrase, *quot homines tot sententiae*, to the field of Dante studies: *quot homines tot poemata*;[1] and indeed there may sometimes seem to be almost as many interpretations of the *Commedia* as there are critics interpreting it. This statement both expresses an important truth, that Dante's subject, range and technique in the poem necessarily and intentionally require that the reader should have considerable liberty in his appreciation and assimilation of it, and describes a resulting, perhaps rather confusing, state of affairs. The modern reader, especially one who is approaching the poem for the first time, may feel the need for a few signposts to help him find his way through the innumerable and often conflicting analyses of it to its central inspiration, its principal aims and the basic elements on which its narrative technique, its significance and maybe even its relevance are founded. For such a reader, therefore, it may be useful to consider three ways of interpreting the poem as a whole before proceeding to a study of the first two cantos of the *Purgatorio* in the light of these approaches. These three ways are not mutually exclusive but co-existent and closely connected and, since they are all traceable in *Epistola* XIII (to Cangrande), they all originate in the fourteenth century, that is, in the world of Dante himself and of his earliest readers. It is to be hoped that these general introductory principles will help to define the *Commedia* more clearly as a great and important poetic achievement in its creation of a realistic fictional world and in its presentation of an all-containing system of truths and aspirations, whilst at the same time showing the limitations of the tradition which sees the poem as some sort of text for a theological or moral sermon. Moreover, these three basic approaches by no means exclude further elaborations and interpretations, perhaps more suited to modern taste and aesthetic theory, but already present in the rich polysemy and allusiveness of the work itself.

Many of the complications in interpreting the *Commedia* go back to Dante himself, in his distinction between the "allegory of theologians" and the "allegory of poets" and in his definitions of poetry as "truth hidden beneath a beautiful lie" and as "a fiction fashioned with rhetoric and music". *Epistola* XIII, whether it is by Dante, as seems most likely, or by some exceptionally acute commentator, actually says: "It should be known that the sense of the work is not simple but indeed can be called polysemous, that is, of many senses". After describing the relationship of the literal to the allegorical senses, *Epistola* XIII talks of "other" or "alternative" or perhaps even "alternating" senses which flow or revolve around the subject of the poem.[2] So the possibility of co-existing multiple solutions goes back to the very earliest times.

It is in the complex relationship between the literal sense, the narrative of a fictional but realistically described journey, and the "other", allegorical meanings that the fundamental problem resides, and here it is probably necessary to elucidate for the modern reader the distinction, described in Auerbach's famous article, "Figura", between the two traditions of allegory in Judeo-Christian, patristic and medieval culture.[3] On the concept of "figural allegory" depends the important modern view of the poem as a work of "figural realism", a view which provides an essential bridge between the fourteenth-century context of the poem and our twentieth-century appreciation of it as a poem. The question has been complicated by the loose use, by some critics, of the key-word "figure", when they mean "symbol" or "image" or even just "metaphor" or "figure of speech". When used without qualification the word has in fact a highly technical meaning. It requires that we cast aside our modern view of history as a succession of distinct events which occur either casually or by identifiable but to a large extent blind political, social, or economic forces. Instead, we must put the imprint of mind upon history, the mind of God in planning the history of the human race and the mind of the theologian in interpreting his plan. History has a "schema" or "typos", a scheme or imprint, for which the most common Latin words were *figura* and *typus*.

Figural allegory or typology is that allegory of the theologians which interprets history as significance, as the plan of the Divine Mind, by explaining the strange, primitive, or even unedifying events of the Old Testament as prefigurations ("figures" or "types") of New Testament events and doctrines. Similarly, many of the events in Christ's life and aspects of his teaching, including, in a slightly looser but still real sense, his parables,[4] are themselves figures of the establishment of the Kingdom of Heaven, which is the Church on earth first and then, after the Second Coming, the Church of the redeemed in Paradise for all eternity.

The basis of figural allegory is in the relationship of the Old Testament to the New. Examples include Adam as a figure of Christ and Eve as a figure of the Church, born from Christ's side, or Solomon and his temple as figures of Christ and the Church, with the Queen of Sheba as the Gentiles who come to hear Christ's word. The curious story of Abraham's willingness to sacrifice his only son, Isaac, is a type or figure of God's plan for the Redemption, and Isaac carrying the sacrificial wood up the mountain for his own immolation prefigured and acquired significance in Christ, the Son, carrying the wood of the cross up Mount Calvary for his own crucifixion.[5] So two real events were related in the divine scheme of history: the Old Testament event prefigured the New Testament event, and the New Testament event fulfilled and explained the Old Testament story.

Some characters and events in the New Testament were also considered as figures of a real event, the establishment of the Church. Lazarus prefigured the Church itself, led out with Christ from the tomb, whilst Martha and Mary, themselves fulfilments of the sisters Leah and Rachel, prefigured respectively the active Church Militant on earth and the contemplative Church Triumphant in the world to come. Christ's miracles, for instance the feeding of the five thousand, prefigured the ministry of the Church and its sacraments, including the Eucharist. His parables, designed to reveal to the apostles truths unknown to the people of the Old Law (Matthew 13:10 ff.) were also interpreted as prophetic, if metaphorical, types insofar as they referred to a real event, the establishment of the Kingdom of Heaven, the Church, on earth. Thus, in the parable of the prodigal son, the father welcomes back his errant son, the Gentiles, together with the son who never strayed, the Jews, and a great feast is prepared to celebrate the homecoming of the Gentiles. The parable expresses in vivid human terms a future, indeed imminent, real event, the foundation of the Christian Church, which will fulfil and supersede the law of Moses and the synagogue, and which will include the Gentiles as well as the Jews. Another parable expresses in even closer allegorical detail the same truth: a king (God) invites to the wedding-feast (the Kingdom of Heaven) some guests, the Jews, who refuse and who maltreat his servants (the prophets); so he invites other guests (the Gentiles). But in this case, the episode of the man who turns up without a wedding-garment and who is cast into the darkness where there is weeping and gnashing of teeth shows that the allegory of the wedding-feast refers not just to the Church on earth but is to have a further fulfilment in the future, at the Second Coming, when, as in the parable of the wheat and the tares or that of the Church as a net containing good and bad fishes, Christ will receive the saved into the "kingdom prepared for them since the beginning of the world" and cast the wicked into the everlasting fire "which was prepared for the devil and his angels". Moreover, the King's destruction of the recalcitrant guests was seen as foretelling the definitive superseding of the Old Law with the destruction of Jerusalem in 70 A.D., an event which, when associated with Christ's other apocalyptic parables and eschatological pronouncements, itself prefigured the day of the universal judgment.[6]

Thus, there are three aspects of figural allegorical reference: real Old Testament events related to future real events, the life and death of Christ; New Testament events and parables related to the foundation of the Church through and after

Christ's death; and the future fulfilment of all this on the Last Day. Moreover, some figures have more than one stage of fulfilment and an example such as that of Leah and Rachel, Martha and Mary, described above, runs through the whole series from the Old Testament to the life of Christ to the Church on earth and to Paradise after death. As readers of the *Purgatorio* will know, Leah and Rachel have also a moral allegorical meaning, as active and contemplative life, which, as will be seen, does not entirely conflict with their strict typological significance.

It is now time to turn to the other main tradition of allegory, moral or tropological allegory. Auerbach describes how this co-existed with true figural allegory and how it is in fact more abstract and learned and so less suitable for the early Church's missionary aims in converting pagan tribes. In this allegory, Old Testament events and New Testament events and parables are seen not as references to historical events to be realized and fulfilled in the future but as vivid stories to be used as images, symbols, or a code of rules for the individual Christian's moral journey through life.

In this mode of allegory, the story of Isaac would be interpreted not just as a prefiguration of a real event, Christ's carrying of his cross, but as a "figure" in a more abstract, non-historical sense, as a model for any Christian to make him live obedient to God as Abraham was, prepared for total self-sacrifice like Isaac. Now in certain cases this moral allegory is also figural in the proper sense of the word. A.C. Charity notes that the figure of Job has both a typological and a dependent moral sense,[7] and the same is true of that of Isaac. The story of Isaac was fulfilled first by Christ and is then fulfilled, through Christ, by any good Christian who takes up his cross and follows Christ (*Par.* xiv.106). Charity sees such a Christian as a "sub-fulfilment" of Christ and makes the reasonable proviso that, strictly speaking, the imitation of Christ is typological only when it is in action, that is, realized in history, and not if it remains solely an ethical imperative.[8] So, in a truly historical and theologically real sense, Christ is the *figura* of the perfect Christian, who is called, especially by dying to sin and rising to life by baptism and in his moral life, to be "another Christ". So the typology of Christ is fulfilled continuously in history in the Church, both in the conduct of individual Christians and insofar as the Church as a whole, the Mystical Body of Christ, reforms itself and moves towards conformity with the person of its founder.[9] The most important of such Old Testament figures which like Isaac were fulfilled in Christ and so became figures also for the Christian and the whole Church was the story of Moses and the Exodus, to which we shall return. Suffice it to note here that some moral allegory does not conflict with but actually depends upon the figural allegory and fulfils it in its turn. One relevant example, referred to above, affords a sort of intermediate stage between the two sorts of allegory: Martha and Mary, who fulfil the figures of Leah and Rachel, at the same time adopted modes of behaviour, approved by Christ, which defined the essential elements of the active and the contemplative lives to be imitated by Christians. Clearly, in practical terms, the imitation and fulfilment of Christ's life required some investigation of patterns and of "ethical imperatives".

It is in an abstruse and frequently pedantic seeking of patterns that moral allegorization has acquired its largely unfavourable reputation. No doubt, however, it was useful in sermons to reinterpret such figural parables as that of the prodigal son, depriving it of its historical significance and using it a a symbolic story of a sinner who strays from God, but who repents and returns to him and is welcomed by the merciful and forgiving Father. The parable of the wedding-feast, like the other parables with an eschatological conclusion, was much more difficult to allegorize in this way, but in general it could be presented as referring to all the good, who accept God's word, the king's invitation, and live good lives on earth so that at their death they are taken up to the eternal wedding-feast of Heaven. Typological and moral interpretations of the same events and parables co-existed, but, apart from all the small but important category mentioned above, they may be regarded as different approaches and different traditions. Nor was this sort of allegory confined to the Bible. The classics too were allegorized in this way in the Middle Ages. Even Ovid, by later commentators, was so "moralized"; similarly, voyagers such as Aeneas or Ulysses could be seen as symbols of man sailing through life, with a mission like Aeneas, or beset by many perils like Ulysses, distracted perhaps by the pleasures of love which must be overcome, as Aeneas was by Dido, or lured by sirens or turned into pigs by lust, as was Ulysses's crew. Man must sail through the perils and temptations of life in order to arrive at the harbour of Heaven.

Also in this wide category of moral allegory we can include the personification of abstracts, at least when they are used as a series of symbols with connected meanings. Such allegories can be of events (Spring, Time, Death), virtues or vices (Hope, Despair; Justice, Mercy; Peace, War), or ideals (Beauty, the "Patria", St Francis's Lady Poverty, Ambrogio Lorenzetti's "Good Government"). Artists, of course, frequently used this visualized portrayal of abstractions. Medieval literature abounds in it, as is shown by C. S. Lewis's analysis of *The Allegory of Love* or by Brunetto Latini's description, in the *Tesoretto,* of the realm of the Empress Virtù with her four daughters, the cardinal virtues. Similar is the use of allegory on the model of Prudentius's *Psychomachia* to dramatize the struggle of thoughts or emotions within or for possession of a man; for example, of Anger and Mercy within a king's soul as he considers a judgment. In some of the earlier poems of the *Vita nuova*, Dante takes over from Cavalcanti the device of the interior drama or struggle in the soul; he personifies Lady Pity and "superbia" and "ira"; for poetic reasons, he describes an accident, Love, as a substance, a separate person. In the *Commedia,* he has Pier della Vigna personify Envy as a harlot of Emperors' courts (*Inf.*xii.64-6), and Virgil describes Geryon as the personification of fraud (*Inf.*xvii.1-3, 7).[10] He uses dream allegory in the *Purgatorio*, although it should be noted that none of the three morning dreams is simple moral allegory; apart from their importance in the structure of the *cantica*, each of them explores new possibilities: mystical allusiveness in the dream of the eagle; a psychological and moral struggle interpreted through contrasting feminine characters in the dream of the Siren; and biblical and figural moral allegory in the dream of Leah, who literally prefigures a real, or apparently real character, Matelda. In the *Purgatorio* especially, Dante also uses the moral *exemplum*; the "whips" and "bridles", contrasting examples of virtues and vices, provide a constant pattern of moral reference and instruction in their presentation of biblical and classical models of behaviour to be imitated or avoided. Even here, however, not only is there enormous variety, but Dante's references deliberately eschew the purely mechanical in favour of a more general, sometimes even rather distant, allusiveness.[11]

These instances of moral allegory in the *Commedia*, however, all pertain to details and not to the basic structure of the poem; the device of the "whips" and "bridles" as a whole needs to be seen in a somewhat different light. The essential difference between the two methods of allegorization is admirably summarized by Auerbach in these terms: "The figural interpretation establishes between two facts or persons a connection by which one of them does not merely signify itself, but it signifies also the other, while the other includes or fulfils the first . . . Figural prophecy includes the interpretation of one earthly process by means of another: the first signifies the second, and the second fulfils the first. Both remain events within history; but in this conception both contain something provisory and incomplete; each refers to the other, and both refer to a future still to come which will be the real, true process, the full, real, definitive event. This is valid not only for the prefiguration of the Old Testament which announces the Incarnation and the proclamation of the Gospel, but also for these latter, which are in fact not yet the final fulfilment but are in their turn the promise of the end of time and of the true kingdom of God". The other tradition of purely moralizing allegory stems largely from Philo, who interpreted the various facts of the Scriptures "as different phases in the stage of the soul and in its relationship to the intelligible world; in the destiny of Israel, in its totality and in its individual figures, he saw contained allegorically the motions of the guilty soul, which needs salvation, in its fall, in its hope, and in its final redemption. As one can see, this is a purely spiritual and extra-historical interpretation". Real figural allegory must be distinguished not only from moral allegory on the one side but also from primitive myths and symbols on the other: the figure must always be historical, the symbol not; "real prophecy refers to historical interpretation and is in essence the interpretation of a text, while the symbol is the immediate interpretation of life and originally, above all, of nature".[12]

Having made this essential distinction, we can now turn to the three basic approaches to the *Commedia*: the tradition which tends to see it as pure moral allegory; the poem as realistic figural allegory with, as I see it, a vital figural-moral component; and the poem as *exemplum* in a special sense which depends upon its figural realism. We will examine these with particular reference to the *Purgatorio*. The treatment of the poem as moral allegory is the oldest method of interpreting the *Commedia*. It seems to have preoccupied all the early commentators, who wanted, quite rightly, especially in the guilt-ridden aftermath of the Black Death, to trace in Dante's poem the means and methods by which the individual soul might turn from sin to God in this life and so go to Heaven in the next. Dante's journey describes the passage of a representative living man from darkness, despair, ignorance, sin, to light, knowledge, grace, salvation, love of and union with God. In this approach, Dante "personaggio" becomes a forerunner of Bunyan's Christian, who travels through the Slough of Despond, Vanity Fair, Doubting Castle, and so on, meeting on the way such personages as Mr. Worldly Wiseman, Faithful, Hopeful, and the giant Despair, and finally reaches the Celestial City. Now it is clear to any reader of the *Commedia* that this is just what Dante does not do.[13] The essential innovation of his poetry is to abandon this scheme of personified abstractions of the sort which led Brunetto Latini from his lost way in his dark wood to the realm of the Lady Natura and the kingdom of the Empress Virtù. Nevertheless, from the earliest times, there has been the tradition of interpreting the poem as this sort of allegory. Virgil, who rescues and guides Dante, represents Human Reason, which has been dumb in the sinful Dante for a long time: "per lungo silenzio parea fioco" (*Inf.*i.63); Beatrice, who supersedes Virgil, is therefore Supernatural Knowledge, Revealed Truth, Grace and so on: "il cui bell'occhio tutto vede" (*Inf.*x.131). So Dante becomes a preacher and the *Commedia* a skilful sermon and a text for further sermons, exhortations, and instructions.

The purely moral interpretation does not explain satisfactorily any of the major episodes or characters. Virgil is not "Ratio" in a white robe, carrying a lantern and perhaps a copy of Aristotle under his arm, but he is the shade of a real Roman poet who once lived and his voice is "fioco" because of the 1300 years' gap between Roman civilization and Dante's own age. Francesca is not "Adulterina", dressed in gaudy and seductive robes, holding a flaming torch of lust and perhaps a sword, for adultery is an act of injustice and often, as here, leads to violence, but she is a real woman who once lived in a minor

Italian court and was killed in adultery. Farinata is not Heresy but a dead Ghibelline leader; Brunetto is not Sodomy but a dead teacher and father-figure. Beatrice's fair eye sees everything, not because she is a symbol of Theology, but because she is a real woman whom Dante loved and loves and who is now in Paradise where she sees everything in the mind of God who is infinite Love.

So, following Auerbach, some critics today put forward a figural view. Firstly, one must establish the literal sense of the poem around which the allegorical "other" meanings flow and this literal sense is, of course, a journey through the afterlife, described as absolutely real, as having really taken place. Virgil, Beatrice, Francesca, Farinata, Cato, Casella, and all the others are real people whose earthly lives, now over, prefigured and determined their eternal destiny and are now being fulfilled in the afterlife: for Virgil in Limbo, for Francesca and Farinata in different parts of Hell, for Cato and Casella on a given date in the year 1300 in Purgatory, for Beatrice in Paradise. Strictly speaking, the use of the word "figural" in this respect is merely modelled on biblical typology and is something of an analogy, for the souls are not distinct people related in history, but each is an individual who has had an existence in history and is now seen in the next phase of existence, which fulfils the first. However, the whole impetus of Christian typology towards the afterlife justifies our use of the term by which earthly life becomes the prefiguration and the afterlife the fulfilment. It is certainly the basis of Dante's realism, for as a result of this the souls have taken with them into the afterlife their earthly lives, their tendencies and preoccupations, their choice at the moment of death, and many of their qualities as individuals in terms both of personal moral responsibility and of the historical, political, or social environment in which they lived their now completed earthly lives. Francesca's views on love and her passionate sin at the moment of death continue on into Hell and do not abandon her; in Hell Farinata keeps his pride and obsession with Florentine party politics, Brunetto his paternal interest in Dante, and so on. The characters in the *Commedia* are real people, projected by death and by Dante's poetic imagination into the afterlife, where they fulfil their evil deeds in Hell or their choice of good in Heaven for all eternity. Their earthly lives adumbrated their state in the afterlife; the afterlife is the eternal fulfilment of their earthly lives. Dante visits the afterlife at a certain time in history in 1300, and, for accuracy's sake, one should remember that the world he visits has not yet reached its final, eternal, definitive fulfilment; this will only be attained at the Second Coming, the Last Day, when the body rises. Then the sufferings of the souls in Hell will be increased, but the bodies of those in Paradise will be glorified and glow brightly like coals in the light of the souls' spiritual vision, love, and joy (*Inf.*vi.103-11; *Par.*xiv.37-66). When Dante meets them, however, the souls have already received their personal judgment. Some souls are already fixed in Hell or Paradise, as they will be for eternity after the universal judgment; others, however, at this historical moment in earthly time are still travelling from this world to the next through Purgatory. Purgatory alone of the three realms is not eternal, for the ultimate destiny of all the souls whom Dante meets there is to be the eternal bliss of Paradise (*Purg.*x.109-11).

Nevertheless, the souls in Purgatory must be considered, in the fiction of the poem, to be just as real as those in Hell or Paradise. Otherwise, this *cantica* is perilously liable to interpretation as a mere moral allegory of this life.[14] This not only leaves a central gap in the narrative unity of the whole poem, but it also weakens the special beauty, the dynamics, and the lessons of the *Purgatorio*, which appears pale and even essentially abstract in comparison with the vivid, flamboyant colours and spectacular dynamics of the other two *cantiche*. Cato, Casella, Manfred, Belacqua, and so on, are as real as Virgil and Beatrice, as real, though dead, as Dante himself in the poem.

There are two important differences between Purgatory and the other two realms. In the first place, the souls whom Dante meets have not yet reached their final place of fulfilment. They have died in a state of grace, and their destiny is assured in Paradise, but Purgatory is the realm of transition and pilgrimage towards this destination. Auerbach, who sees Cato as a *figura* of Christ, a pagan prefiguration chosen with exceptional imagination or even unorthodoxy by Dante, is right in describing the Cato whom Dante meets as "the figure revealed and fulfilled", at least in the sense that this is the real Cato met in the afterlife, fulfilling his earthly life in a unique way for a pagan and a suicide, as guardian of the base of the mountain. But

Raimondi's objection is also valid, when he points out that Dante's Cato is not yet the final fulfilment. Like all the souls in Purgatory Cato too is *in statu viae,* not yet *in statu termini.* [15] This applies not merely to the case of all the souls in the *Commedia* as they await the definitive eschatological fulfilment upon the resurrection of their bodies, but it also concerns Cato's eventual home in the afterlife, whether he is to return to Limbo or go to Paradise. There are several theories on these points, but it seems to me that Dante answers them all in *Purgatorio* i. Cato has been taken from Limbo and separated irrevocably from Marcia, his wife; therefore, he is not to return there. In one extraordinary line (*Purg.* i.75), which solves the problem, Virgil shows his knowledge that Cato, although a pagan like Virgil himself and unlike the suicides of *Inferno* xiii, will in fact regain the garment of his body at the Last Day and it will be glorified in Paradise for ever. Certainly from Casella, who has only just arrived, to Statius, who has performed all the centuries of purification required of him for his sloth and prodigality, all the souls in Purgatory are at different stages in their journey to Paradise and God. This is why Dante's Purgatory, especially above the Door (*Purg.* ix), is not negative but positive, why the souls are content in their torments, which indeed are not torments but a joy: "io dico pena e dovria dir sollazzo" (*Purg.* xxiii.72). So the souls in Purgatory are not yet fulfilled but travelling to fulfilment, being fulfilled, and on this crucial concept depends Dante's whole optimistic, dynamic, and forward-looking presentation of Purgatory.

The second main difference between the souls in Purgatory and those in Hell (fixed unchangingly in the evil in which they died) or Paradise (already fulfilled according to their appropriate degree of beatitude), arises from their situation as travellers to Paradise. They have died in a state of grace, some of them only in the nick of time, and they are assured of salvation, but in Purgatory, they can, indeed they must and will, develop. They can look back to their earthly lives and to the moment of their deaths and can see them in a new perspective; Manfred acknowledges the heinousness of his sins and at the same time is experiencing the results of his excommunication. They can also look forward to the moment, when, like Statius, they will rise to travel to God. Between their deaths in a state of grace and their final release from Purgatory, they too are fulfilling the results of their earthly lives, "reaping the harvest of sin" (*Purg.* xiv.85), paying off the debt of temporal punishment due to sins committed and being purified from their earthly tendencies to and habits of those sins. In Antepurgatory this is a negative process: unless helped by the prayers of the living, Manfred must "relive" his excommunication thirty times over, whilst Belacqua and the others must also "live" a whole second lifetime of sloth, failure to repent, and other forms of negligence, before they can even begin the positive process of purification on the cornices. Inside Purgatory the souls are doing penance for their besetting sins of pride, envy, and so on; they are praying or singing; and they study the "whips" and "bridles". So as they mature "quel sanza 'l quale a Dio tornar non pòssi" (*Purg.* xix.92), as the seven wounds are healed up, and as they receive moral nourishment from meditating upon examples of virtue and vice (*Purg.* xxvi.138-9), they are aware of their position as trainees for Paradise. Although, with the exception of Statius, Dante sees them confined to their cornices, they can judge their past sins, use the present to suffer and learn, and look forward to their inevitable future salvation. Purgatory is a place of development and progress towards freedom of the will, the purification of love, original innocence and God himself, Supreme Good.

Thus the whole poem, including the *Purgatorio*, describes a real journey through a real world inhabited by real people. In Dante's presentation of this life in the light of the next, we can see an enormous step forward in the treatment of "character" in western literature, but we should be careful not to attribute this to Dante's conscious intentions without some imporant qualif- ications. His characters are not fully-rounded individuals mixed up in the complexities and vicissitudes of this life but the fulfilment, outside history, of their earthly selves and, in particular, of the moral choice in which they died.

In *Convivio* II.i, Dante distinguishes between the literal sense of a text and three other senses: the allegorical, the moral, and the anagogical. He explains the allegorical with the example of the myth of Orpheus as the allegory of poets and not that of theologians. In analysing his *canzoni* which look back to the personification techniques of the *Vita nuova* but forward towards an exposition in terms of philosophical and moral truths, Dante was right to choose the allegory of poets to act as the link. But in *Epistola* XIII the word "allegoria" is first used in its strict theological, that is figural sense, before the author points out that it is also used with a wider meaning, as referring to all the other senses apart from the literal. The example of the text, *In exitu Israel de Aegypto*, used also in the *Convivio*, is here applied to all the senses and illustrates quite clearly this development in Dante's technique, a development which necessitated different methods of expounding the *Commedia* compared with the poems of the *Convivio*. In *Epistola* XIII, the literal event described in the text, the Exodus of the Israelites from Egypt at the time of Moses, is analysed according to three "other" senses.

The first sense is the allegorical, that is the figural, and we may perhaps clarify this for the modern reader by calling it also "christological". In this sense the Exodus refers figurally to the Redemption, when Christ led all mankind from the slavery of sin, the Old Law and paganism to the new era of grace and salvation and the freedom of the children of God. Moses in particular, the founder of the Old Law, the leader of the Exodus and feeder of the children of Israel, was the most important *figura Christi* of all. So the historical event, the Old Testament Exodus, prefigured and was fulfilled first and foremost by the events of the New Testament, the life, death, and resurrection of Christ.

The second sense is the moral or tropological sense. The Exodus refers to the individual Christian soul, who realizes the fruits of the Redemption in his own earthly life, travelling from the grief and misery of sin to a state of grace. In this sense, the strict figural meaning and the moral allegorical system do not conflict, but the latter depends upon the former. Christ, himself the fulfilment of the Old Testament figures, is the essential precondition and model for the moral dying to sin and rising to grace of all those who follow him. Just as the figure of Isaac was fulfilled by Christ and is then fulfilled in the lives of those who shoulder their crosses and follow Christ, so too the Exodus was fulfilled first by the Redemption of all mankind and is again and continuously being fulfilled by each Christian who makes his personal exodus from sin to grace in his earthly life.

The third sense of the Exodus is the anagogical, or we may call it the eschatological in its reference to the "last things", death and judgment, Hell and Heaven. This Exodus is the

journey of the individual Christian *after death* from the slavery
of this corruptible life to the liberty of eternal glory, the
Promised Land, the heavenly city of the New Jerusalem. In
other words, the saved Christian fulfils the event of the Exodus
definitively when, having made his moral exodus in life and died
in a state of grace, he travels to Heaven. Purgatory, therefore, is
the realm of the anagogical exodus of the saved souls precisely
as it is defined in *Epistola* XIII. Moreover, the word "anagogical", glossed in the *Convivio* as "sovrasenso" and sometimes
defined as "mystical", does in fact originally mean "leading
up".[16]

The analysis of the story of the Exodus in *Epistola* XIII is
provided for two reasons: firstly, to indicate, as is stated, how
the allegorical "other" meanings and polysemy of the poem can
co-exist, not excluding but depending on each other, and be
identified using the techniques of theologians in their interpretations of the Old Testament;[17] and secondly, to invite the
reader to connect the theme of the Exodus with the journey-
poem itself in its progress from damnation to redemption,
slavery to freedom, sin to grace, Hell to Heaven.

On the first point two misunderstandings have perhaps
confused the issue. Some critics seem to feel that these three are
the only possible allegorical or other senses in the *Commedia*.
In fact Dante does not use merely christological, moral and
anagogical senses, but also levels of allegory which are not
directly covered by the theologians' figural explanations of the
Bible. His literal narrative includes, for instance, philosophical
lessons presented as part of a continual process of learning with
its dialectic of question and answer; it includes political and
ecclesiastical allegory and imagery, as in the *Monarchia*,
where biblical texts are analysed in a way similar to, but not the
same as, figural moral allegory; he uses *exempla*, prophecies,
and images which are calls for reform; he uses a wide variety of
allusion, biblical, liturgical, literary, and of course, especially in
the presentation of Beatrice, personal; as we have seen, he also
includes in the *Purgatorio* the older technique which ultimately
he did so much to demolish, the device of the dream-allegory.

The second misunderstanding is that the three allegorical
senses are not only basic and exclusive, but are also all present
equally in the poem. This is not true. The christological sense is
not directly present at all, but it is stated as the precondition of

the whole journey in that Dante descends into Hell and rises on the third day during that season of the centenary year which commemorated the death and resurrection of Christ and the exodus of all mankind with him to the era of grace. Christ's journey prefigures that of Dante; Dante's fulfils that of Christ. He is "another Christ", as ideally all Christians should be.

The moral sense, which in every definition of it applies specifically and exclusively to living men, is present only in the character of Dante himself, the only living man in the poem, as is stressed on innumerable occasions. Dante's journey from the dark wood to Paradise describes, and in the fiction of the poem actually is, his own moral exodus from sin to grace in his own life. This aspect too has its figural consequences, for, with the help of Beatrice and Mary, Dante trusts that this journey will prefigure his own definitive anagogical journey to salvation after his death. Moreover, the moral theme is also universalized in that Dante, following Christ, acts as an *exemplum* to all men to make the same moral journey in their earthly lives and the same anagogical journey after death.[18]

The anagogical sense of the Exodus, as illustrated in *Epistola* XIII, is relevant to the figural realism of the whole poem and directly present in the *Purgatorio*. Dante is visiting the three worlds where the souls are fulfilling or reaping the results of their earthly lives: some are already suffering eternal punishment in Hell; others are actually in the process of making their anagogical exodus in Purgatory; others have already reached the Promised Land and are citizens of the heavenly Jerusalem. As *Epistola* XIII states: "The subject of the entire work according to the literal sense is the state of the souls after death". We must take the word "subject" here in a restricted sense; otherwise the statement is not quite true. The entire literal sense of the poem is not the state of the souls after death but the story of Dante's visit to them. In this sense, they are the "subjects", to put it in simple terms, of his exploration and enquiry.

The extraordinary fact about *Epistola* XIII, which is often dismissed as spoiling the poem's beauties for the modern reader, is the great subtlety and yet simplified clarity with which it sees how the poem's polysemy can be analysed using scriptural techniques, whilst at the same time providing us with the necessary distinctions and with an open invitation to continue our investigations on similar lines. The author is not saying that this is a biblical work about events to be fulfilled in the future, but that it is a polysemous poem, written after the Redemption and with a literal sense which inextricably involves moral allegory (Dante "personaggio") and anagogical realities, present now and related to eternity in the future (the three realms).[19]

If we are to appreciate the *Commedia* on its own terms, therefore, we must first of all be ever conscious of its total narrative realism as a description of the way this life is fulfilled in the next. Dante, following Christ in the timing of his journey (the first allegorical fulfilment of the Exodus), passes as a living man from sin to grace (and as a living man he is the only moral allegorical character in the poem) by visiting the world which this world prefigures and determines.[20] In a sense this is not realism but super-realism, for not only are the souls real human individuals projected into an eternal setting, but in Dante's terms his world is the ultimate reality. The three realms of the afterlife, constructed by God's justice, are in fact more real than this life, which is but a brief adumbration, a pilgrimage to death and the life beyond.

The chief difference between this interpretation of the poem and that of others, who also use the concept of figuralism, is that the limitation of the moral allegory to the story of the living Dante has allowed the moral allegory to be re-integrated into the figural scheme, both christological and anagogical, and indeed to depend upon it. But it is also obvious that the poem does have moral reference to this life and it can be shown that this too depends first and foremost on the figural realism of the narrative. It involves regarding the poem as an *exemplum* in a wide but precise sense. Obviously, the *Commedia* contains *exempla*: the "whips" and "bridles" are details which certainly come into this category; the souls frequently have an exemplary function, as do some of the lessons and analogies, the prophecies and passages dealing with key concepts such as love and knowledge; Dante as a representative living man is an *exemplum* of the Christian's moral exodus. But the poem as a totality can also be considered as an *exemplum* and specifically as an *exemplum* of God's justice. *Epistola* XIII, after defining the subject of the literal sense as "the state of the souls after death", actually goes on to say: "If, however, the work is taken allegorically, its subject is man inasmuch as, by his merits or demerits according to his use of his free will, he is subject to the justice which gives rewards and punishments". In other words, Dante's visit to the anagogical world is a visit to a world where God's justice *already* operates finally and infallibly. The word "allegorical" may have its wide sense here, but the context makes the meaning quite clear: the poem describes how God's justice punishes sin and rewards good after death, and thus it shows how man is subject to a punishing or rewarding justice according to whether he uses his free will for good or evil in this life in relation to his eternal destiny in the next. Dante, the only living man in the poem, is to return from the eternal world in which he has seen the state of the souls after death and how their earthly lives are being fulfilled according to the infallible justice of God. His journey is not just his own moral journey, it is a journey of discovery too: the souls he meets in the afterlife show the eternal requirements and decrees of absolute Justice. The poem which he writes after his return from this journey is designed to teach men who are still living their earthly lives the horrifying personal and social results of evil, the path of purification by which souls travel to God, and the eternal rewards of good. As *Epistola* XIII says later on, putting things briefly and simply: "The purpose of the whole and of the part is to remove men living in this life from a state of misery and lead them to a state of happiness"; the poem has an ethical and practical aspect.[21] It is intended to bear fruit for the reader to pick. "Se Dio ti lasci, lettor, prender frutto/di tua lezione" (*Inf.*xx.19-20). The *Inferno* is, of course, a horrible warning; in the *Purgatorio* Dante constantly stresses the theme of turning away from the earth and aspiring towards Heaven; the *Paradiso* promises those who follow the poem's message experience of the inexpressible rewards of good. By describing this journey to the next life, Dante wants to persuade living men to turn from evil to good in this life, to reform themselves and all human society through the general affirmation of the will towards good, through the cultivation of true moral values and of private and, more especially, public standards of conduct in commercial and civil life, through the re-establishment of a just empire co-existing with a reformed Church and papacy, a Church and papacy shorn of temporal ambitions, a purely spiritual institution which has returned to the principles of its founder. In the year 1300 and as he wrote the poem in later years, Dante looked to and yearned for the imminent advent of God's punishment and reform of the world, to the dawning of a new age in a new century. The poem both expresses and embodies this vision and desire. As Cacciaguida tells Dante, it will disturb the conscience of the guilty; it will be a bitter but nourishing food for man; and it is addressed above all to the leaders of society (*Par*.xvii.124-42). So the poem, in its parts and in its entirety, is an *exemplum* and call for personal and universal reform, expressed in terms of the journey of a representative living man from sin to grace, from the terrible city of Dis through the "true city" of Purgatory to the heavenly Jerusalem which is also that Rome "where Christ is the Roman" (*Purg*.xiii.94-5; xxxii.100-2).

So *Epistola* XIII, especially the analysis of the Exodus, helps us to define the poem quite clearly in its Christian basis, in its moral allegorical function, in its figural realism concerning the afterlife, and in its purpose as an *exemplum* and call for reform. All these aspects apply in a unique way to the *Purgatorio*, indeed in a way which it is impossible to trace directly and without adaptation in the other two *cantiche*. After all, the *Inferno* and the *Paradiso* do not actually refer to the Exodus, for the souls there are not going anywhere. They may be seen as representing the two terms, slavery and freedom, but not the actual journey or exodus between them. In the *Purgatorio*, however, the three allegorical senses of the Exodus are all present in the ways in which we have defined them.

The christological sense is present in that the Redemption is the precondition for access to Purgatory by Dante and by the souls. The rhyme-words at the end of *Purgatorio* i, in referring back to *Inferno* xxvi, show that Ulysses as a pagan could not visit it and return, though Dante as a Christian can; Virgil too was buried before Purgatory was made available to mankind (*Purg*.vii.4-6). But Christ's death and resurrection, which led mankind from slavery to freedom in the first fulfilment of the Exodus, opened up the era of baptism (itself a descent into waters and an exodus from original sin) and of Christian faith denied to Virgil. Through the priceless merits of Christ's infinite act of expiation, his followers in the new dispensation were given the possibility of paying their debts to God and expiating their personal sins first in life in the Church Militant, and then after death in Purgatory. For the payment of the debt which still remains after death, Purgatory was opened to mankind; the souls of the redeemed and saved arrive under the sign of the Redemption, the cross, and then ascend through Purgatory to the garden of original innocence, the Earthly Paradise, and then to the heavenly Paradise. To emphasize this parallelism between the redemption of all men and Purgatory as the realm where the individual finally redeems his soul by paying off his debt to God, Dante reminds us that Purgatory is diametrically opposite Jerusalem (*Purg.*ii.1-3); as the antipodean Mount Sion, it is the way to the true heavenly Jerusalem, and the tree of the Fall in the Earthly Paradise is opposite the site of the tree of Calvary, the cross, which it prefigured and made necessary and which the cross then fulfilled and made fruitful again, a process which Dante, in his journey back from the world redeemed by the cross, to the garden lost by the tree, will see represented in the Earthly Paradise (*Purg.*xxxii.37-60). So the first allegorical, the figural, sense of the Exodus is presupposed and underlies the whole *cantica* in its universal application. It also underlies the figural moral function of Dante himself in the poem, for he descends into Hell during Passiontide and then, like Christ at the resurrection, emerges on the third day.

Dante the living man visits Purgatory in order to find out how the Christian, following Christ, can make his exodus from sin to grace anagogically after death and, therefore, morally in this life. In describing it he instructs his reader also in this path. The horrors of Hell have persuaded him to turn away from sin; Antepurgatory demonstrates the necessity of dying contrite and warns against the dangers of excommunication, negligence, relying on last-minute repentance, not living a life of penance here and now; then the seven cornices show him the positive process of expiation, which consists in doing penance, accepting suffering contentedly, praying, meditating upon examples of how sin is punished and virtue rewarded. This is the process which Dante explores and the lesson which he learns, for his own and his reader's moral purification, and it is a process which, if started in this life, will be completed and fulfilled in the next on the final journey to God.

All these aspects depend upon the essential fact about Purgatory, that it is first and foremost the realm of the anagogical sense of the Exodus. The literal sense of the *cantica* is the visit of a living man, making his moral exodus, to the world where souls make their anagogical exodus after death; from slavery in the Egypt of this corrupt world to the liberty of eternal glory in the heavenly Jerusalem. There has long been a tendency to see in the penances and the ritual and liturgical elements in the *Purgatorio* a purely moral allegory, a representation of *this* life within a poetic fiction concerning the next. *Epistola* XIII proves that Purgatory is just as much part of the anagogical world of the afterlife as the other two realms. The souls Dante meets, the landscapes and settings, the penances and rituals are all part of the afterlife, the fulfilment of this life in the next, although in the case of Purgatory this fulfilment is not yet definitive and eternal but a way of being fulfilled by purification and preparation for ascent to the stars. Dante visits this world and makes his journey through it as a living man to prefigure his own exodus after death and as an *exemplum* to his readers to make their moral exodus now and their own anagogical exodus too hereafter. The process of purification belongs to the afterlife, the world where good and evil are subject to divine justice, but its messages are to be read back to men still living their earthly lives. Moreover, the examples and messages of the *Purgatorio* are related back to this life in a way which is excluded in the other two *cantiche*. This is because the path of purification is a single, continuous road to be started in this life and completed in the next. Purgatory, in showing how what was left at death to be achieved is in fact achieved after death, is the real continuation of the process in the afterlife and the model for its commencement in this. Purgatory completes the process of remission after death; penances performed in this life will reduce the debt to be paid in the next (*Purg.*xi.72). So the typological concepts of prefiguration and fulfilment, the figural realism of the poem, which I am more and more tempted to call "fulfilled realism", and the resultant pattern of the *exemplum* are not only present in the *Purgatorio* but fundamental to it.

The *Purgatorio* describes the only way to God through a life of penance with hope, the study of virtue and avoiding of vice, prayer and adherence to a truly spiritual community; in this way alone is human love purified and redirected and man reacquires full freedom of the will which is the automatic choice of God, Supreme Good. This is the only path to God in life and therefore after death, or better, vice versa, for the divine process decreed for the souls after death is the true reality, of which this life is but a brief prelude and preparation. The frequent references to Dante's breathing, his shadow and the weight of his body emphasize not only the uniqueness of his divinely-willed journey but also the fundamental distinction and connections, in the literal sense of the *cantica*, between the moral exodus of the living man and the anagogical exodus of the saved souls. The innumerable requests from the souls for prayers by the living, by relatives or by Dante himself, underline the same truth: that Dante is to return as a messenger to this life, with particular as well as his more general messages. There is an element of the *exemplum* here too, in the imposition of a general duty to pray for the dead (II Maccabees 12:46; *Purg*.xi.31-6; *Par*.xv.91-6). The constant use of the device of the appeal for prayers would be totally illogical if the *Purgatorio* were merely a moral allegory, for they can only ever apply to the dead. It therefore confirms our explanation of the true relationship between the moral, anagogical and exemplary aspects of the *Purgatorio*. Moreover, since the *suffragia mortuorum* were considered to be the chief link between the Church Militant and the Church Suffering, they are not only more useful in a real sense than the promises of fame made to the souls in Hell, but they also reveal the important redemptive link and, ideally, community of interests between the pilgrim Church on earth and the pilgrim Church of Purgatory. All these elements in Purgatory are combined with the certain hope of eternal reward. Thus it is that Dante's Purgatory, though the passages which contrast it with this life are gloomy, is a world permeated with optimism, for the souls making their exodus there represent saved humanity travelling, despite all their failings, on the sure path of God.

All these levels of allegory and multiple meaning are present at the very beginning of the *cantica* and the theme of the Exodus in particular, as we have interpreted it, is the canvas on which Dante has woven the rich and varied tapestry of *Purgatorio* i and ii. Let us examine their five chief elements: the time of day together with the day itself; the figure of Cato; the ritual of cleansing and the reed; the arrival of the boat; and the episode of Casella.

The *Purgatorio* opens with an exordium in which Dante raises the sails of the boat of his mind to embark on his voyage across the calmer waters of a new stage in his journey-poem.

The cruel sea of Hell is behind him and his dead poetry must also rise again with the help of Muses so that he may sing of this new realm of renewal and ascent. The sky, the colour of an eastern sapphire, and the pure atmosphere bring joy back to his eyes after the terrible sights of Hell. In the constellation Pisces, the morning-star, Venus, which strengthens the power of love in man, makes the whole east smile. Turning to the south Dante sees the four stars from the sight of which fallen and degenerate man has been banished. It is just before dawn. As Cato speaks, the sun, which they must follow, begins to rise and Dante sees "il tremolar de la marina". By the beginning of *Purgatorio* ii the sun had reached the horizon of this place, which stands at the antipodes of Jerusalem, when Dante sees another light which swiftly approaches, the shining angel who brings to the shores of Purgatory a boat with more than a hundred souls travelling to salvation.

In *Inferno* i, in the early morning and at the season when God created the sun and the other stars, Dante had tried to climb a sunlit hill but had been impeded by the three beasts. On the 1266th anniversary of Christ's crucifixion he too had had to descend into Hell. Now like Christ he and his poetry rise again from a cruel sea. He starts this new stage of his journey at dawn on the day of the Passover and the resurrection. Of all the nights in the year, this night has the fullest figural and moral importance for mankind, as is shown by the *Exsultet*, the hymn sung at the blessing of the paschal candle during the Easter vigil:

> This is the night on which first you led our fathers the children of Israel out of Egypt and made them cross the Red Sea dryshod. This, therefore, is the night which purged the darkness of sins with the light of the column (of fire). This is the night which today throughout the whole world serves those who believe in Christ from the vices of the world and the darkness of sin, returns them to grace and makes them participants in sanctity. This is the night in which, having destroyed the chains of death, Christ ascended victorious from hell . . . O truly blessed night, which alone was worthy to see the time and the hour when Christ rose from the depths! This is the night of which it was written: And the night shall be illuminated as the day; and

the night is my illumination in my delights. Therefore, the holiness of this night puts evil acts to
flight, washes away guilt, and restores innocence
to the fallen and joy to the sad . . . O truly blessed
night, which despoiled the Egyptians and enriched
the Hebrews! The night in which heavenly things
are joined to earthly and divine things to human.
We pray to you, therefore, Lord, that this candle,
consecrated to the honour of your name, may
continue unfailingly to destroy the darkness of this
night. May it be accepted with sweet fragrance,
and may it mix with the heavenly lights on high.
May the morning-star behold its flames – that
morning-star, I mean, which knows no setting: he
who, returning from the depths, cast his serene
light upon the human race.[22]

The Israelites held their paschal sacrifice and then were led
by Moses through the Red Sea to freedom. For Christians
Christ is both the paschal lamb, sacrificed for the whole human
race, and the fulfilment of the figure of Moses, leading the
human race from slavery to freedom through his resurrection.
Christians too must first descend into the baptismal waters and
rise again to grace; thereafter, they must follow Christ through
the desert of this life to the Promised Land and so to the eternal
fulfilment of the Redemption of the Last Day. The anniversary
of the Jewish Exodus and of Christ's resurrection in the year of
the new century is the day when Dante too, and ideally the whole
of mankind, rises from the depths of sin to begin the exodus
towards grace and the light of eternal glory.

These various levels of figural reference, describing daybreak on a day which will in fact close with the souls singing
hymns from compline, may also be illustrated by an interesting
passage from Honorius of Autun, on the special meaning of
morning and of the morning lauds sung to God, "for the word
matutina comes from *manes*, as praise given to God for light".
According to Honorius, there are four reasons for singing these
morning praises:

1. We sing this hour because we believe the world
was created at this hour; at this hour the morning
stars shone with their beauty and with sweet

harmony praised God who made them, that is, the angels were created at this hour, the angels who are also called sons of God and who with great voice and in sweet unison at once sang to the creator a song of exultation for the creation of the world. By singing at this hour, we imitate them, we who are called evening stars, in that if with our praises we follow Christ as the sun who sets for us, we may at the rising of the sun, that is, at the resurrection, be led through him to the morning stars.

2. In this hour God led his people through the Red Sea and drowned their enemies, as it is written: "it happened that in the morning vigil God looked from the cloud and killed the Egyptians" (Exodus 14). This is the hour in which the former were baptized in the sea and the cloud, and the latter were hurled into the waves.

3. In this hour Christ rose victorious from death, brought day back to us from the underworld, led the people he had redeemed with his blood out of the kingdom of the tyrant, and submerged their enemies in the abyss.

4. In this hour at the end of the world the just will wake up from the sleep of death, when they will travel from the night of this world to the light of eternal brightness. Thus, the time of the night which precedes the nocturn stands for the time of death which preceded the law. The nocturn itself expresses the time when the people worshipped God according to the law. But the morning hour, when the light approaches, symbolizes the time from the resurrection of Christ to the end of the world, when the Church sings her hymn to her beloved. For the psalms which are sung here intend to express both the time of the law, which was a shade and prefiguration, and the time of grace, which like light then came to the world and shone.[23]

At the hour and on the day when the figures of the Exodus and the law of Moses were fulfilled and superseded by the resurrection of Christ, with the promise of the final fulfilment of the whole divine plan at the end of time, Dante rises from the pit, the kingdom of the tyrant Satan, to visit the world of the anagogical exodus and to begin his own moral journey to acquire that freedom won for mankind by Christ. In the poem which describes that journey, his dead poetry must also rise again as Dante the character and Dante the poet rejoice in the pure sky, the sight of the planet of love and in the four stars of the virtues.

But in *Purgatorio* i the sun has not yet risen. It is in the mysterious and tenuous pre-dawn light and in an atmosphere of expectation of the rising of the sun that Dante sees the venerable bearded man whose face is illuminated by the four stars. This is, astonishingly, the soul of Cato, a pagan, who lived in the light of classical civilization, illuminated by the four cardinal virtues alone, like sunlight but destined to give way to the full daylight of Christ and the shining of three new stars, the theological virtues, in the firmament at night (*Purg*.viii.88-93). There is no need to repeat here all the theories concerning the problem of Cato's salvation or his function as a symbol of God, a figure of Christ's self-sacrifice for all mankind and a prefiguration of Christian liberty.[24] Suffice it to note that his duty is to guard Purgatory which is now being invaded from Hell, either by souls with special guidance or, contrary to all the laws of Hell, by escapees from Satan's eternal prison; he then instructs Virgil and Dante on the first rituals of purification and tells them to follow the guidance of the rising sun; at the end of *Purgatorio* ii he reappears to rebuke the souls who, enraptured by Casella's song, are neglecting to continue their journey up the mountain.

As has often been noted, Cato is described in the *Aeneid* as a lawgiver in the underworld, whilst Dante's presentation of Cato also reminds one of medieval representations of a biblical patriarch. Indeed Dante's Cato was delivered from Limbo with Moses and the other patriarchs and his duties here are to prevent invasion and to act as the first guide and spur to Dante's moral exodus and the souls' anagogical exodus. As the lawgiver of this exodus, he is the pagan counterpart to Moses and his face shines like the face of Moses when he received the law on the mountain; or like the face of Christ when he was transfigured between Moses and Elijah on the mountain "and his face shone like the sun".[25] Moses, who led the Exodus and stopped the

Egyptians following, who founded the Old Law and guided the ungrateful, fickle and backsliding Jewish people through the desert (*Par*.xxxii.131-2), was the principal figure of Christ to come; he is of course already in Paradise, seated next to Adam in the half of the Rose occupied by the Jews who believed in Christ to come. Here in Purgatory by a master-stroke Dante presents us with another lawgiver and guide to an exodus and his choice is taken from that other great tradition which preceded and helped to prepare for the coming of Christianity, the civilization of ancient Rome.

The startling choice of Cato is of course connected with fundamental themes and allusions in the *Commedia*, with Dante's whole approach to the ethical system and other achievements of pre-Christian antiquity, with his presentation of Virgil, with the episode of Limbo and the general problem of all those who lived according to the four virtues but did not know the three, with his conception of the foundation of the Roman Empire, and so on. The fact that Cato opposed Caesar and the Empire, two traitors to which Dante has just seen in Hell, reflects Dante's source, Lucan, who contrasts the rather unpleasant Caesar and the wholly noble Cato;[26] Caesar is still in Limbo from where Cato has been delivered; so for Dante, Cato stood for higher ideals even than the Empire, ideals which anticipated and remained valid even after the advent of Christianity. So in looking for a counterpart to Moses Dante turned to the noble Roman patriot who also led his men through the desert (*Inf*.xiv.13-15); and in a sense one could argue that he chose Cato not in spite of the fact that he was a suicide but precisely because he was a suicide[27] who for high ideals of pure patriotism and his own political and moral integrity made the supreme sacrifice on behalf of freedom. For the theme of freedom is the essential aspect of Dante's Cato. Dante is seeking a freedom, political as well as moral and spiritual, prefigured in the actions of Moses and Cato. So important is this freedom that even its pagan prefiguration, Cato's suicide, has earned for the noble Roman, exceptionally, eternal salvation and the reacquisition of his body. It was Christ, prefigured by Moses and Cato, who made available that supreme freedom which Dante now seeks, the restoration of the freedom of the will which, as we shall learn, is the essence of the process of purification. The reappearance of Cato at the end of *Purgatorio*

ii not only recalls Moses's many rebukes to the backsliding
Hebrews but also stresses the great urgency with which Dante
morally, and the souls anagogically, should abandon earthly
pleasures and travel upwards to God.

The three specific instructions which Cato gives are that
Virgil should cleanse Dante's face and gird him with a reed and
that they should then follow the guidance of the sun. Here
Dante is using a more allusive symbolism than strict allegory;
he enriches the figural polysemy of the poem with details which
begin the definition of the journey and the freedom which is its
goal, as well as establishing that pattern of objective symbols
and rituals which is so important a feature of his description of
the realm of Purgatory. Here they apply to the person of Dante
alone, in his moral exodus, but they have wider implications in
the definition of the journey and its function as *exemplum*. The
cleansing of Dante's face may be seen to refer to baptism, itself
a descent and an exodus, but this would be necessarily very
indirect. Dante does not need baptizing; nor can any unbaptized
soul enter Purgatory except for Cato and here, exceptionally
and temporarily, Virgil; nor is baptism a washing of the face.
The ritual here is intimately connected with the narrative of the
journey: it is a washing away of the colour of Hell, its darkness
and the tears of grief which Dante has shed; it is also a ritual
which clears his sight and makes him worthy to go before the
angel (*Purg*.i.97-9); the dew which cleanses and refreshes may
well be associated with hope. Purgatory is thus going to be a
journey away from Hell and its effects, a journey of cleansing,
of being made worthy of hope. It anticipates the final cleansing
of Dante in the Earthly Paradise. Similarly the reed, usually
interpreted as a symbol of humility or sincerity, is described as
the only plant on the shore which can bear leaves and survive
because it is pliant. Purgatory is to be a place of moulding of the
will; and the girding of Dante is a replacing of the girdle he left
behind in Hell. The reed when plucked renews itself and so the
whole ritual involves also the theme of renewal in Purgatory
and looks forward to the moment when Dante will return from
other waters "renewed like new plants with new leaves, pure
and prepared to ascend to the stars" (*Purg*.xxxiii.142-5).[28] As
for the guidance of the rising sun, the meaning of this is clear,
both in relation to *Inferno* i and as regards the theme of
resurrection, light and grace in the rest of the *cantica* and

beyond. In fact Dante and the souls will linger over Casella's music and Dante and Virgil will also need help from the souls in their ascent up the mountain. Clearly, these elements can be considered as associated with moral allegory, but once the fundamentally realistic principles of Dante's poem are grasped, as has been our task so far, then only do we see in the range and the accumulation of such elements the true originality of Dante's technique, which is never dry, pedantic allegory but always rich, subtle and surprising.

The dramatic description of the arrival of the angel's boat adds further dimensions to the themes of redemption and salvation and introduces the first of those beings from Paradise who are to form a vital element in the process of purification and the ascent to the heavenly light which shines in their faces. The souls arrive singing *In exitu Israel de Aegypto* (Psalms 113) in its entirety: that is, with its themes of liberation, praise of God, the emptiness of earthly idols, and hope, up to its concluding verses: "The dead, O Lord, will not praise you, nor will all those who descend into hell. But we who live bless the Lord, from henceforward and for ever." The dead in Hell are truly dead; these souls, now freed from the slavery of earthly life, are in fact travelling to a new and more real life. It will be clear from all that has been said that the primary reference here is not to the moral exodus of Dante, nor to some sort of moralizing allegory of this life, but to the real anagogical exodus of the saved souls to liberty after death. All that follows describes this path and the lessons to be learnt from it by men still living their earthly lives on this side of the globe, where darkness is at this very moment spreading (*Purg*.ii.4-6).

We soon learn that the souls of the saved gather at the mouth of the Tiber; and this adds to the theme of exodus the theme of Rome to which we shall return. For the time being, it should be noted that the message is that salvation is through the earthly Church, however imperfect it is and however corrupt its leaders. This small community of more than a hundred psalm-singing souls travelling from Rome to Purgatory is an example of the link between the earthly Church, the gateway to salvation, the Church Suffering, which is the path of salvation and the model for the reform of the Church on earth, and the final fulfilment of the Redemption in the Church Triumphant in Paradise.[29]

Our use of the psalm, *In exitu*, as a basic model for interpreting the whole scheme of the *Purgatorio* is confirmed by another, less direct and less frequently noticed reference to the same psalm much later on in the *cantica*. While Dante is on the cornice of the avaricious, there is a tremendous earthquake and the mountain shakes (*Purg*.xx.124-32). The souls sing *Gloria in excelsis Deo* and Dante and Virgil are as astonished as the shepherds who first heard those words on the night Christ was born. Then, just as after his resurrection Christ appeared unrecognized to the two disciples on the road to Emmaus, a soul comes up alongside them. He explains to them that when a soul's penance is complete, his will to reach God is infused with the power to carry on with the journey; when the soul senses this freedom, he is released from that cornice to move up the mountain; the mountain shakes and the other souls sing the *Gloria*. This soul is Statius, rising from among the avaricious and prodigals and in fact not destined to spend any length of time on the last two cornices. He is about to complete definitively his anagogical exodus: "When Israel went out of Egypt . . . the mountains skipped like rams and the hills like the lambs of the flock" (Psalms 113:1,4). Moreover the *Gloria*, first sung at Christ's birth, recalls the first stage in the history of the Redemption, whilst the elevated and rather daring simile comparing Statius to the risen Christ refers to the final stage in Christ's own exodus, rising from the grave and leading all mankind to freedom. The expiatory penances of Purgatory were made available to man and are modelled on Christ's infinite act of expiation and satisfaction: his death on the cross (*Purg*.xxiii.73-5). To rise from those penances is to fulfil his resurrection. So Statius, risen and released, is not a figure of Christ but is fulfilling in himself the final stage of Christ's exodus, which is his own anagogical exodus, the resurrection to eternal freedom and glory with Christ in Heaven.[30]

The episode of Casella introduces additional themes of friendship, music, Dante's earlier love of Lady Philosophy and the way in which the path to God through Purgatory requires that all these things be superseded. But it also brings in another theme which underlies the general structure of Purgatory as Dante's moral exodus and the souls' anagogical exodus to salvation. The poem is set not only in the season of the year when Christ redeemed man, but in the year of the great Pardon or, as it came to be called, the Jubilee. The Jubilee, a spontaneous popular movement which arose in Rome on New Year's Day in 1300 because of the belief that special indulgences were available in the centenary year to those who visited the basilicas of the Apostles, was sanctioned by the Pope's proclamation of it on 22 February. This decree granted a plenary indulgence to all those who made a pilgrimage to Rome and the Apostles' shrines in that year, and it back-dates the opening of the year of Pardon to Christmas Day 1299. An indulgence was the commutation by prayers, almsgiving, pilgrimages, and so on, of temporal punishment due to sin after it had been forgiven. Purgatory is the realm where the temporal punishment not paid off in life must be finally remitted after death. In other words, it is the place where, by a sevenfold process, the soul completes the earthly process of remission and finally receives full pardon or plenary indulgence after death.

The term "Jubilee", which soon came to be used for the special centenary pardon of 1300, refers to the Jewish Jubilee year, every fiftieth year, when debts were remitted, slaves freed and men were returned to their possessions and their true homes. In these respects the journey through Purgatory is also a Jubilee pilgrimage, for through it the debt of temporal punishment is remitted, liberty is acquired and men return to their lost possessions and their true home, Paradise. Moreover, while later Jubilees were decreed at fifty-year and then twenty-five-year intervals, the first was specifically a centenary occasion when men such as Dante must have been filled with millenarian hopes for reform and the coming of a new age in the new century. So the *Purgatorio*, as an *exemplum* of the centenary Jubilee, offers not only the model for the reform of the individual but also for the reform of human society as a whole, culminating in Beatrice's prophecy of the coming of a deliverer, the DXV, who will punish the harlot and the giant, the corrupt leadership of the Church in its adulterous exile in Avignon. Dante's poem, from the dark wood and the sunlit hill of *Inferno* i, is permeated with such hopes for universal reform, and Purgatory, the mountain which he begins to climb at daybreak on the day of the resurrection in the centenary year, is the description of the way to achieve this ideal of universal pardon and full liberty in a true Church and true city being purified in love.

Casella alludes to this theme when he tells Dante that the special indulgence of 1300 has helped souls to speedier access to Purgatory for the last three months. This is not only an acceptance of Boniface VIII's retroactive decree, making it valid from the previous Christmas, but also, more importantly, a direct association of the doctrine of remission in Purgatory and the ideal of universal pardon.[31] The exodus of Dante and the souls through Purgatory, set in the context of the year 1300, is thus a journey, both personal and universal, for plenary indulgence (the Pardon), for the remission of debts (the Jubilee) and for moral reform as a pattern for the regeneration of man and of society (the Centenary). So the theme of exodus and the theme of a Jubilee pilgrimage for plenary indulgence come together. Dante's exodus as a living man and the souls' anagogical exodus mean that they are all pilgrims through Purgatory (*Purg.*ii.63) and references to this pilgrimage will occur at two important points later on in the journey: on the evening of the first day and at daybreak on the last (*Purg.*viii.1-6; xxvii.109-11). Paradoxically in this second case, the pilgrim who is nearing the goal of his journey is returning home, for he is about to enter the Earthly Paradise, man's original home on earth, from which he will ascend to his final goal, the heavenly Paradise.

In order to escape from the dark wood, Dante has had to make the journey by another way, through the pit of Hell; when he rises up to the shore of Purgatory, he has found the right path again (*Purg.*i.119) and is on his way to the goal of his pilgrimage. Purgatory, which leads inevitably to Paradise, is a true, supranational city, which pilgrim Italy, on the other side of the world, has not yet reached (*Purg.*xiii.94-6). But what is the name of this city? The fundamental theme of the Exodus indicates that Dante is travelling to the heavenly Jerusalem, that he is a palmer through the afterlife. Indeed Beatrice will later describe his journey as an exodus of a living man from Egypt to Jerusalem and its purpose is for him to see (*Par.* xxv.55-7). Dante's return journey from this pilgrimage is his coming back to earth to tell us all about it in his reforming poem. He too, like medieval pilgrims to the Holy Land, will return bearing proof of his visit, a palm-branch circling his staff, and this proof will be the knowledge he has acquired in the afterlife and particularly the foreknowledge of God's vengeance and reform of the world (*Purg*.xxxiii.73-8). What he has seen and learnt he must write down "in pro del mondo che mal vive", as an *exemplum*, warning and call for reform "a' vivi/del viver ch'è un correr a la morte" (*Purg*.xxxii.103; xxxiii.53-4). Mortal life, which is but a race towards death and the afterlife, must be reformed; the readers of the poem must be led from the corruption of this Egypt to a new Jerusalem on earth, which is a figure of the heavenly Jerusalem. The message is urgent, and even eschatological; for the palm Dante acquires on his pilgrimage is in fact the promise of God's imminent victory over the corruption of this life.

There is, however, another strand woven in with the theme of exodus and pilgrimage to Jerusalem. Casella, in the Jubilee year, has travelled first to Rome and then to Purgatory, and all the souls who congregate at the mouth of the Tiber are travellers from the corrupt Church in the earthly Rome to its authentic fulfilment in the afterlife, in the Church Suffering and then the Church Triumphant. In the Middle Ages, a pilgrimage to Rome, which contained many of the most important relics from the Holy Land, could be seen as similar to a pilgrimage to Jerusalem; indeed in 1300, due to Boniface's neglect (*Inf*. xxvii.85-7; *Par*.ix.124 ff.; xv.143-4), Rome would probably have had to replace Jerusalem as the goal of pilgrims, as it did anyway because of the Jubilee.[32]

Dante's journey up the sevenfold mountain of full pardon, a true city and a true penitential and spiritual Church, is thus also a centenary Jubilee pilgrimage to the heavenly Rome, perhaps a replacement for a pilgrimage he really made to corrupt earthly Rome. In the Earthly Paradise Beatrice tells Dante that he is soon to ascend to that true Rome "where Christ is the Roman" (*Purg*.xxxii.102) and when Dante reaches this goal, the Rose of the blessed in Paradise, he describes it in terms of a pilgrimage from the human to the divine, from time to eternity, from Florence to a true nation restored to justice and free from all contamination; like a pilgrim coming from afar to Rome, he is struck with wonder and drinks in the sight of the goal of his pilgrimage, for he already looks forward to telling others about it on his return (*Par*.xxxi.31-48; 103-8).

Paradise contains both Jews and Christians; it is the final eschatological fulfilment of both Jerusalem and Rome. Purgatory is the pilgrim's road to this eternal city and the Dante who travels it is both a palmer and a romer. When, in a poem which presents a fiction as an absolutely true experience, he and his poetry rise from death and darkness on Resurrection Day, when he encounters Cato and is washed and girded with a reed, when he meets Casella and the other souls who arrive from Rome singing *In exitu Israel de Aegypto*, it is the start of an exodus to liberty and a pilgrimage for full pardon, cleansing, and renewal, for Dante morally, for the souls definitively, and, he hopes, also for the attentive reader who sees how to apply the lessons of the afterlife to the reform and renewal of this life, which prefigures, determines, and is eventually fulfilled in the realities of Dante's world.

Notes

[1] T. G. Bergin, *Perspectives on the "Divine Comedy"* (New Brunswick, 1967) p.84.

[2] *Conv*.II.i and *Letter to Cangrande*, 7-8, otherwise *Epistola* XIII (or *Epistola* X in the Toynbee edition). The verb in the key phrase there, *circa quod currant alterni sensus*, is generally translated as "play", but a primary meaning of *currere* is "to flow", with a possible reference to the course of the heavens (so "to revolve"), as in Lucretius's *sol currens* and Psalms 18:6 (where the sun exults like a giant *ad currendam viam*).

[3] E. Auerbach, "Figura" in *Studi su Dante* (Milan, 1967) pp. 174-221; and also his "Typological Symbolism in Medieval Literature" in *American Critical Essays on the "Divine Comedy"* ed. R. J. Clements (New York, 1967) pp. 104-13. The aim of this study is to elucidate and illustrate Auerbach's concept of figural realism, to develop it on the lines indicated in *Ep.* XIII (to Cangrande) and to apply it to the theme of the Exodus in *Purg*.i-ii. On typological allegory see J. Chydenius, *The Typological Problem in Dante: A Study in the History of Medieval Ideas, Commentationes Humanarum Litterarum*, Vol. XXV, No. 1 (Helsingfors, 1960) pp. 1-159, and A.C. Charity, *Events and their Afterlife: The Dialectics of Christian Typology in the Bible and Dante* (Cambridge, 1966). Dante criticism in Italy seems not to have assimilated Auerbach significantly, perhaps because Croce's theories provoked definitions of Dante's allegory that were closer to symbolism; see B. Nardi, "Sull'interpretazione allegorica e sulla struttura della *Commedia* di Dante", *Saggi e note di critica dantesca* (Milan, 1966) pp. 110-65; A. Pagliaro, "Simbolo e allegoria", *Ulisse: Ricerche semantiche sulla "Divina Commedia"* 2 vols (Messina, 1967) II, 467-527; P. Giannantonio, *Dante e l'allegorismo* (Florence, 1969). Other studies of the four senses include: D. L. Sayers, "The Fourfold Interpretation of the *Comedy*", *Introductory Papers on Dante* (New York, 1954) pp. 101-26 (which ignores figural allegory completely); C. S. Singleton, *Dante's "Commedia": Elements of Structure* (Cambridge, Mass., 1954); R. Hollander, *Allegory in Dante's "Commedia"* (Princeton, 1969). See also D. Thompson, "Figure and Allegory in the *Commedia*", *Dante Studies* 90 (1972) 1-11; J.

Pépin, "Allegoria", *Enc. d.* I, 151-65; and J. Pépin, *Dante et la tradition de l'allegorie* (Montreal, 1970); G. R. Sarolli, *Prolegomena alla "Divina Commedia"* (Florence, 1971); J. A. Scott, "Dante's Allegory", *Romance Philology* 26 (1973) 558-91; R. Hollander, "Dante *Theologus-Poeta*", *Dante Studies* 94 (1976) 91-136. Further references to the above are by author only or by author and short-title. There are enormous problems in reconciling these approaches to the basic structure of the *Comedy* and yet without this groundwork it is impossible to proceed to analyse the relationship between structure and poetry, or Dante's further use of allegory and symbol, or his style. The following preliminary remarks may help to clarify the situation: (*i*) The words "figure", "type" and "typology" will be used here with their theological sense (i.e. in the context of a relationship between realities) and not in ways adopted since by literary critics (see Charity, p.4). The word "figure", which has now even wider senses, will sometimes be replaced by "prefiguration". An attempt will be made to preserve the distinction between this "figuralism" and "figurative" modes of thought and speech — a distinction not always observed by Dante scholars. (*ii*) The vocabulary of typology and allegory was not absolutely clear in Dante's time (nor before or since). Some simplification and use of analogy will therefore be necessary from time to time. Thus, in comparison with Charity's use of sophisticated modern theological terminology, the terms will be used here in ways which, whilst excluding their non-theological usage, are nevertheless fairly broad in their openness to allegorization and polysemy – an approach which, it is hoped, will reflect the patristic and medieval tradition behind *Ep.* XIII (to Cangrande). Charity's "post-figurations" and "typological back-references" will be called "fulfilments", which is what they really are. However, the principal figures which we shall use (the Exodus and Jerusalem) will need no analogies, as their different but interdependent levels of reference are comparatively clear-cut. (*iii*) *Ep.*XIII.7 uses the word "allegory" in two meanings; firstly, with the strict typological sense and then in a wider sense which includes the typological, the moral, and the anagogical. Charity (p.171, n.2) notes that the words "type" and "allegory" were not fully distinguished until after the Reformation. Generally speaking, Sayers, Singleton and Giannantonio tend to interpret "allegory" in the wider definition, thus seeing the *Comedy* as having a literal sense and a single, if many-layered, allegorical sense; see Singleton's famous phrase: the *Comedy* signifies both this *and* that (*Dante's "Commedia"*, p.89). So the poem becomes a fusion of literal and allegorical (Singleton, Giannantonio, Pépin), leading perhaps to a definition of it as an elevation of allegory itself into symbol (Pagliaro), with the souls as symbolic personages (D. L. Sayers, *The Divine Comedy: Hell* (London, 1949) p.12) and the whole as a unified statement of Dante as man and poet (Nardi). In practice this approach will often bias the interpretation of the poem, especially the *Purgatorio*, towards the moral allegorical. This study will attempt to build upon *Ep.* XIII's first distinctions, preserving all the senses and dividing the moral allegory into two elements: Dante *personaggio* and the poem as *exemplum.* (*iv*) Thompson objects that Auerbach's definition of typology is inaccurately applied to the *Comedy* in that the relationship between the historical Virgil and Dante's Virgil is between two aspects of the same person and not between two distinct historical persons or events. The objection is technically valid as regards the souls in the *Comedy*. Nevertheless, the relationship between Virgil in his real earthly life and Virgil in his real afterlife is one between prefiguration and fulfilment and so can justifiably, if slightly loosely, be called "figural". Moreover, it should be noted that insofar as Auerbach defines Dante's Cato as the figural fulfilment of the earthly Cato, he is using the typology in this slightly loose sense, but when he interprets Cato's suicide as a figure of Christian liberty or Rahab as a figure of the Church, he is in each case linking two separate earthly realities, and this is true typology; Auerbach's discussion of Cato ("Figura" pp.212-5) in fact shows the indissoluble link between the strict typology of Cato and its fulfilment in the afterlife. Auerbach's use of figuralism in relation to the Christian souls whom Dante meets is supported by the important concept of the earthly Church to be fulfilled, ideally, in the afterlife. In the case of strictly typological events such as the Exodus, Thompson's objection does not apply. (*v*) Chydenius's main conclusion (that Dante's vision of Beatrice in the Earthly Paradise is a typological prefiguration of his visions at the end of the *Paradiso*) and two of Auerbach's examples of figures (the eagle of *Purg*.ix as a figure of Christ and Beatrice's appearance to Dante as a figure of Christ's – *Studi* pp.241,245-7) are misleading. They are partially valid in that they rest upon the typological tradition which runs through the whole poem, as Chydenius's analysis of the typology of Jerusalem, the Church, the Paradise, and the Bride shows. Nevertheless, as presented, they really refer to relationships within the poem and lead to what Pépin calls the theory of an "internal typology" of the *Comedy*. This is close to a literary critic's use of typological terms when referring to an anticipation or even merely an association of themes and symbols within a work. These indubitably exist within the *Comedy*, but it would be better not to call them typological. The typological relationships between the concluding scenes of the *Purgatorio* and those of the *Paradiso* are not poetic inventions of Dante's systematic mind but a pre-existent tradition which he takes over, transforms and enormously enriches.

⁴The two distinct ways of interpreting the parables are very close to the general distinction between figural and moral allegory and so it seems legitimate to use them as examples of multiple meaning in scriptural texts. Chydenius (pp.17,25) shows how for St Paul and Justin Martyr *parable* and *typos* were closely connected or even inter-changeable, whilst Charity (p.147) also indicates that the parables go beyond Old Testament typology when they are activated in Jesus's life and predicate God's future dealings with man. Since the foundation of the Church was the fulfilment of many of the parables, this sense can perhaps be described as typological; it certainly comes under the same heading of "real prophecy" as does typology. This approach is not excluded by medieval definitions of the parabolic sense of the Scriptures, but other conclusions have also been drawn which have some bearing on Dante studies. For St Thomas the parabolic sense is part of the literal sense; the literal sense of biblical parables and metaphors is not what they say (which is "false") but what the author intends, not the *figura* but the *figuratum*; since the parables must be true, the "other" meaning is in fact the literal sense (see Giannantonio pp.154-7,218-9). So it is that St Thomas's analysis of the parabolic sense and its figurativeness comes to be associated with the allegory of the poets and the allegorization of the poems of the *Convivio*; see Pagliaro pp.474-80; see also M. Picchio Simonelli, "Vernacular Poetic Sources for Dante's Use of Allegory", *Dante Studies* 93 (1975) 131-42. "Christ spoke in parables, hence in a form related to poetry": E.R. Curtius, *European Literature and the Latin Middle Ages* (London, 1953) p.216. Those who see the *Comedy* as fundamentally what the *Convivio* calls the "allegory of poets", especially if they also interpret the word "allegory" in *Ep*.XIII in its wider sense, will tend to see the allegory of the poem as most closely resembling the parabolic sense of the Scriptures; those who accept the triple distinction of allegory as the basis for viewing the *Comedy* in the light of the "allegory of theologians" will treat it realistically and interpret it according to typology. However, the *Comedy* is not Scripture and there is truth in both approaches: insofar as the poem is Dante's own invention and pure fiction, a truth hidden beneath a beautiful lie, it is like parabolic

allegory; insofar as its technique is realistic it is like typological allegory. This distinction between a "realistic parable" and a "parabolic reality", however, will not affect discussion of such themes as the Exodus, which as a historical event is a figure in the strict sense and illustrates the true typology underlying the poem. The parables are used here as illustrations of scriptural, not poetic, analysis by which a "fiction" was often interpreted in two ways: on the one hand as having a literal sense beneath the parabolic sense and referring to a reality, the Church, with further eschatological implications; and on the other, the quite distinct and purely moral interpretation of the parables.

⁵For these and other examples, typological and moral, see the "Indices figurarum" and the "Index exegeticus parabolarum" in *Patr. lat.* 219 *Indices* cols 241-74. Chydenius (p. 19) and Auerbach ("Typological Symbolism" p. 108) use the example of Isaac. For the Passover and the crucifixion, see Chydenius (pp. 14-15); see also his account of Marian typology, which links up Eve, Mary, and the Church.

⁶See *Patr. lat.* 219 col. 267 (Parable XIII); see also Chydenius (pp. 51-86) on the typology of Jerusalem. On the eschatological significance of the destruction of Jerusalem, see Matthew 24:1-31; Mark 13:1-4 and 14-27; Luke 21:5-7 and 20-8; and Apocalypse 3:12 and 21:2,10.

⁷Charity pp. 176-7.

⁸Charity pp. 90-4, 150-62, 174.

⁹For St Thomas (*Quodlibet*. 7:6:15, ad 5) Christ's body was a *figura* of the Church in the senses expounded in *Ep.* XIII: "In Christ future glory has been shown to us in advance; thus the things which are said literally about Christ, the head, can be expounded allegorically too, with reference to his mystical body; and morally, with reference to our actions, which must be reformed according to him; and anagogically inasmuch as in Christ the path to glory has been shown to us." On the concept of the Church as Christ's mystical body depend the moral and anagogical senses. (See also the famous tag: "Littera gesta docet, quid credas allegoria, Moralis quid agas, quo tendas anagogia").

¹⁰On Geryon as a real demon and not mere allegory, see Nardi, *Saggi* p. 157. See also A. Vallone, "La personificazione, il simbolo e l'allegoria", *Studi su Dante medievale* (Florence, 1965) pp. 23-61. On Dante and Brunetto, see L. Ricci Battaglia, "Tradizione e struttura narrativa nella *Commedia*", *GSLI* 153 (1976), 500 ff. On Dante and allegories of Ulysses and Aeneas, see D. Thompson, *Dante's Epic Journeys* (Baltimore, 1974) with M. Mills Chiarenza, "Bypassing the Bible: New Approaches to Dante's Allegory", *Dante Studies* 93 (1975) 215-21.

¹¹Two examples of this allusiveness must suffice. The example of David's humility (*Purg.*x.55-72) takes on wider, even political significance, because he was a king; the Madonna's words, "vinum non habent", as a model of charity to remedy envy (*Purg.*xiii.29), are an appropriate example of "courteous invitations to the table of love" but turn the emphasis in the episode away from the miracle of Cana towards the human, loving Madonna (*Purg.*xxii.142-4). By omitting the main link, Christ, between the Old and New Testament, this is moral allegory without typological reference. Nevertheless, the Madonna was the second most important New Testament type, as the "whips" and "bridles" show throughout the *Purgatorio*; and the "whips" and "bridles", though themselves moral *exempla*, are presented as essential elements in the structure of an anagogical world.

¹²Auerbach, "Figura", *Studi* pp. 204-7; see also Pagliaro's distinction (p. 489) between symbol and allegory.

¹³See Sayers, *Introductory Papers* p. 106.

¹⁴However, the early commentators' apparent preference for moral rather than

anagogical interpretations of the *Purgatorio* is perhaps not so obvious. Believing already in the reality of the afterlife they may have chosen to concentrate on the moral allegory rather than Dante's literal presentation of the afterlife as real. Pietro di Dante distinguishes between Dante's "essential Purgatory" (the mountain) and "moral Purgatory" (those who turn from vice, Egypt, to virtue, Jerusalem, like the Hebrews who died in their desert journey). Buti also separates the literal and moral senses to some extent. Benvenuto, however, perhaps shocked by the fiction of Cato ("it seems to smack of heresy"), turns away from the real Purgatory and treats Dante's Purgatory as consisting entirely *in moribus* with Cato as the *pater morum.* The Anonimo for the same reason chooses to see Cato as a symbol of the virtuous man. For the continuing interpretation of the *Purgatorio* as principally moral allegory, though with qualifications, three examples in the opening cantos may suffice: typical of *Purgatorio* i is "il suo costruirsi in una serie di invenzioni allegoriche" in Sapegno's ed. (1968) p.2; "The abstract moral symbols are the framework; the whole is a profoundly imagined experience", in Sinclair, *Purgatory* p. 30; "Dei tre regni, il Purgatorio è certamente quello che meglio si adegua alla condizione terrena del buon cristiano", in V. Russo's *"Purgatorio* Canto II", *Nuove letture dantesche* III (Florence, 1969) p. 243 (also p. 259). C. S. Singleton, *"In exitu Israel de Aegypto"* in *Dante: A Collection of Critical Essays* ed. J. Freccero (Englewood Cliffs, 1965) pp. 102-21, correctly presents the Exodus as a figure of the Redemption and of *conversio,* but then emphasizes the moral allegory in Dante's pilgrimage as the story of such a *conversio.* See also L. Ricci Battaglia, "Polisemanticità e struttura della *Commedia", GSLI* 152 (1975), 161-98. Hence Thompson's dilemma (p. 9): "Auerbach is concerned with what Dante sees, what the souls *are*; Singleton, with what Dante himself *becomes".* Charity (p.251) discusses Singleton, but also makes the strange statement: "It is Dante's life which is the literal sense, not the figurative journey into eternity" (p. 254). Thus arises a problem the poem does not answer: Is the poem an elaboration of a real spiritual conversion which Dante underwent before he wrote it? Or is the poem itself the description of a process of conversion for Dante personally as a character and, through Dante as an *exemplum,* for all mankind? In this respect we can only analyse the poem as presented in its figural references and polysemy and in its universal rather than personal application.

[15] Auerbach, "Figura" p. 213; E. Raimondi, "Canto I", *Lectura Dantis Scaligera: Purgatorio* pp. 1-37, and "Rito e storia nel I canto del *Purgatorio",* in *Metafora e storia* (Turin, 1970) pp. 65-94. For Cato see M. Fubini, "Catone l'Uticense", *Enc. d.* I, 876-82; S. Pasquazi, "Catone", *Cultura e scuola* 13-14 (1965) 528-39; F. Ulivi, "Il canto I del *Purgatorio",* *Nuove letture dantesche* III (Florence, 1969) pp. 209-27; Hollander, *Allegory* pp. 123 ff.; C. V. Kaske, "Mount Sinai and Dante's Mount Purgatory", *Dante Studies* 89 (1971) 1-18; E. Sanguineti, "Dante, *Purgatorio* I", *Letture classensi* III (Ravenna, 1970) pp. 255-82; and G. Rizzo, "Dante and the Virtuous Pagans", *A Dante Symposium* ed. W. De Sua and G. Rizzo (Chapel Hill, 1965) pp. 115-39.

[16] On *anagoge* as *ad superiora ducens* in Cassian, Hugh of St Victor and others: see Chydenius, pp. 36-8; J. S. Carroll, *Prisoners of Hope: An Exposition of Dante's "Purgatorio"* (London, 1906) p. 26.

[17] This is not to say with Singleton (*Dante's "Commedia"* p.15) that Dante is imitating God's way of writing but that the polysemy of the poem can be analysed like the Scriptures (Chydenius p. 49). The *In exitu* is given as the most famous illustration of this (already present in inchoate form in I Corinthians 10:1-11) and as one of the few to have an Old Testament, a figural, a moral-figural and an anagogical sense simultaneously. To

say that the *Commedia* may be analysed like the Bible is quite different from saying that it imitates the Bible, or even that it has the stature of the Bible, an untenable view, rejected by Charity (p. 257), although he also suggests it is gospel-like (p. 277).
[18]Charity says that "Dante's journey is a type of his future" (p. 247); Dante is also the reader's representative (p. 228); and, quoting from Auerbach's "Dante's Address to the Reader", *Romance Philology* VII (1953-4) 268-78, the reader is his disciple (p. 233). Dante is a universal *exemplum* (Giannantonio pp. 299-30). Hollander, *Allegory* p.134, maintains that Dante *personaggio* has all four senses (though his anagogical sense needs clarifying as regards the personal and universal aspects of Dante's visit to the anagogical world). This is the polysemy which underlies what Pépin calls Dante's "autoallegoresis".
[19]See Charity (p. 249) on C. G. Hardie's difficulties in accepting the evidence of *Ep.* XIII because of these problems in "The Epistle to Cangrande again", *Deutsches Dante-Jahrbuch* 38 (1960) 56-8. That *Ep.* XIII simplifies and uses analogies is true, but how else could the poem's complex network of relationships be explained? As *Ep.* XIII helps define the polysemy of the poem, we can hardly quibble if the literal sense of the poem (unlike the divinely-planned Exodus) involves the others as well. Strictly speaking, the poem is throughout the allegory of a poet, not as this is defined in the *Conv.*, but as it is explained in *Ep.* XIII with the allegory of theologians providing an interpretative model and a fundamental theme.
[20]To be valid this untangling of the four senses must not contradict *Inf.*ix.61-3 and *Purg.*viii.19-21 where Dante tells the reader of the hidden allegory. Each time he points to an especially important moral lesson that might be missed: at *Inferno* ix by the reader who is inattentive or without an "intelletto sano"; in *Purgatorio* viii the apparent meaning is that the allegory is quite clear (Pagliaro pp. 480-4). Much could be said about the polysemy of these episodes, but in general the four senses can be seen to underlie them too. In *Inferno* ix, in the literal sense, the devils oppose Dante, defy Virgil and are forced by the heavenly messenger to allow Dante to enter. The presupposed christological sense is that, at the time of Christ's breaking and entering of the upper gate on behalf of all mankind, an angel opens the inner gates on Dante's behalf. Dante's entry is based on Christ's conquest of Hell (just as his entry into Purgatory is based on the resurrection). Moreover, in the Middle Ages, since the gate of Heaven was interpreted as the true Church, the gates of Hell were identified as heretics, Jews and infidels; (so the first souls Dante meets inside are the heretics, not included in the moral scheme of Hell in *Inferno* xi). Given this image, the angel's opening of the gate for a representative living Christian fulfils Christ's prophecy that "the gates of Hell shall not prevail against" his Church and its members. Thus the figural basis of the episode leads to its moral message: when the Christian faces evil, temptations and despair, human reason and wisdom, even the greatest, are insufficient; divine help, made available by Christ, is necessary and will be given. The anagogical is the literal sense in its eternal setting: Dante, a living man on a moral journey to conquer sin and temptation, is with God's help entering a place where the great divide between sins of *incontinenza* and sins of *malizia* is reflected in the eternal structure of Hell, created by God's justice to punish sinners. In resisting Dante, the devils are also blocking his mission as a poet destined to return to describe how the horrifying results of evil in this world are punished eternally in the next; so the angel's intervention confirms Dante's mission as an *exemplum* of divine grace. In *Purgatorio* viii, the literal sense (heavenly protection for Dante and the princes against the snake) presupposes a mariological not a christological sense: Mary, appealed to in the *Salve regina*, sends two angels to drive out the serpent, maybe the one which tempted Eve (*Purg.*vii.82;viii.37,99); Mary, the new Eve, who crushed the serpent's head, now

protects the Church of which she too is a figure (note⁵). The moral message is similar to that of *Inferno* ix, the theme of heavenly help against temptation. The anagogical sense is mysterious, because of the situation of the souls in Antepurgatory. As they certainly cannot sin in Purgatory, it is unlikely that they can be tempted, but in any case Mary's protection is guaranteed. More probably, the episode of the snake serves as a specific reminder and part of the soul's purification, especially of these souls who, having lived in courts among temptations, were spiritually negligent and are now temporarily excluded from Purgatory proper. They are learning the lesson of temptation and Mary's help in the afterlife, and Dante, who experiences the fear and witnesses the snake's defeat, describes the scene as an *exemplum* to be read back into this life. See F. Forti, "Il dramma sacro della 'mala striscia': Grazia e magnanimità", earlier in *GSLI* (1969), now in *Magnanimitade: Studi su un tema dantesco* (Bologna, 1977) pp. 83-101.

²¹*Ep.*XIII.15-16 (Charity pp. 208, and 210-11); on the necessity for the poem to be persuasive, see *Ep.* XIII.19, and Charity p. 235. Rather than supporting the purely moral interpretation, these words refer to the whole poem as an *exemplum*, not just representing but actually aiming to remove men from the misery of life and lead them to happiness, first on earth and then anagogically in Paradise. This is why the many speculative passages are described as subordinate to the poem's overall ethical and reformist message. On "profetismo" and "tensione escatologica", see G. Padoan, "La mirabile visione di Dante e l'Epistola a Cangrande", *Il pio Enea, l'empio Ulisse* (Ravenna, 1977) pp. 30-63.

²²Besides *Purgatorio* i-ii, see *Purg.*xi.30 and xxx.2 for expressions recalling the phrases "caligine peccatorum" and "qui nescit occasum". *Ad regias Agni dapes*, a hymn for Low Sunday, associates the themes of Christ as the Paschal Lamb, the crossing of the Red Sea, rebirth, and liberty. Raimondi pp.1-13 studies other biblical and liturgical elements in *Purgatorio* i, seeing possible figural references in the images of the sea, the sapphire and the morning-star (see Hollander, *Allegory* p.127).

²³"Gemma animae: 2. De horis canonicis", *Patr. lat.* 172, cols 625-6. Honorius's first reason recalls *Inf.*i.37-40 and his phrase concerning the Church's hymn to her beloved *Par.*x.139-41. See also Raimondi pp.11, 13.

²⁴See *Conv.*IV.v.16; IV.vi.10; IV.xxvii.3; IV.xxviii.13-19; *Mon.*II.v.15,17; see refs in note¹⁵ also.

²⁵Matthew 17:2. Hollander, *Allegory* pp. 124-6. For Moses, Sinai, and other subjects see Kaske, whose identification of Hell as the Old Law is surely wrong when half of Paradise is occupied by adherents to the Old Law.

²⁶Lucan presents Cato as having wished to redeem nations by his death and so bring peace (*Phars.*II.301 ff.); as virtuous and dedicated to justice (II.372 ff.); as devoted to liberty, a true patriot, who urges on his sometimes recalcitrant followers, leads them through the desert, helps them to accept suffering and to die well (see IX, *passim*). Marcia's remarriage to him is in II.326 ff.; during the Civil War, he allowed his grey hair and beard to grow long as a sign of grief for the human race (II.372 ff.). His refusal to consult the oracle of Jupiter Ammon and his belief in the omnipresence of God (IX.550 ff.) are referred to in *Ep.* XIII.22.

²⁷Buti says that Dante chooses Cato as an example of liberty and justice "per far verisimile la sua fizione", that is because in the poem Old Testament figures (formerly in Limbo) and New Testament saints are already in Paradise.

²⁸See Raimondi pp. 34-7; A. Pézard, "Le chant premier du *Purgatoire*", in *Letture del "Purgatorio"* ed. V. Vettori (Milan, 1965) pp. 29 ff.

²⁹Benvenuto calls the angel's boat "navicula Petri", a metaphor for the Church

(*Purg*.xxxii.129). See Chydenius for figures of the Church at various stages of fulfilment.

[30]Hollander makes these points, but by concluding that "Statius comes as the figural messenger of Christ" (*Allegory* p. 69) he reverses the typology completely. Perhaps he is referring to his own theory of "verbal figuralism" (p. 105), thus making his reference to Statius a sort of "internal typology" of the *Commedia* (see note[3]). His tendency to interpret the word "ombra" as "figure" is very confusing, for in the *Commedia* the shades are of course the souls, or, in Auerbach's system, the fulfilments.

[31]On the Jubilee, see A. Frugoni, "Il Giubileo di Bonifacio VIII", *Bullettino dell'Istituto Storico Italiano per il Medio Evo* 62 (1950) 1-121. Benvenuto associates the Exodus and the Jubilee: "This year, which Moses established in the desert, is called *jubilaeus*, and it was the fiftieth, as Josephus relates in book 3 of the *Antiquities*, in which debtors were released by the creditors and slaves were sent away free. During the jubilee, the name of which means liberty, fields were also returned to their previous owners; so Casella says that at this time he was released from Egypt and the power of Pharaoh". Benvenuto also says that Casella went to Rome for the indulgence, thus earning the right to enter the angel's boat despite his late repentance; he also glosses *Purg*.ii.63: "ma noi siam peregrin come voi siete," with the words, "because we are going to the holy mountain for indulgence".

[32]See Chydenius on Jerusalem as the Promised Land and goal of the Exodus (p. 90); a medieval pilgrimage to Jerusalem was a type of the pilgrimage to the heavenly Jerusalem (pp. 76-7); the *Commedia* is a pilgrimage to this Jerusalem made by Dante who could not make one to earthly Jerusalem (pp. 107-8); but Rome, especially the church of Santa Croce in Gerusalemme, was a vicarious Jerusalem (pp. 71-2).

Free Will in Theory and Practice:
Purgatorio XVIII and two characters in the Inferno

Christopher J. Ryan

The first part of *Purgatorio* xviii deals with free will, and it is on that topic that I wish to concentrate. There is good reason for doing so, since free will is central in the *Divine Comedy*, the fact that it is physically central pointing, as material features so often do in the *Comedy*, to something else, namely, to a centrality in the thought of the poem, in the meaning Dante wishes to convey. Dante can be vigorous in his thinking and an appreciation of our canto demands that we attempt to share the poet's desire for clear and precise thought. Still, desire for intellectual vigour in the *Comedy* is not to be equated with love for abstract thought for its own sake: definition and distinction are at the service of Dante's overriding concern, to show men and women how they can find true fulfilment as members of society, a society which, for Dante, embraces eternity and God. I need hardly stress that each moment of discovery in the poem is a stage in a journey, designed to cast light on what has gone before as well as prepare us for further clarification. So I shall attempt to do two things: firstly, to examine in some detail the opening seventy-five lines of *Purgatorio* xviii to give within the short compass available an accurate account of Virgil's description of free will;[1] then, having grasped what the key ideas are, I shall look back to two incidents earlier in the *Comedy* to show how our greater understanding of free will can illuminate what we previously only implicitly understood. When we have analysed *Purgatorio* xviii.1-75, we can better appreciate the forces at work in the characters of Francesca da Rimini and Guido da Montefeltro in the *Inferno*.

Before now going on to treat the philosophical exchange between Virgil and Dante in *Purgatorio* xviii, let us recall the context. The canto opens, so to say, at a midpoint: for, if we consider the first two cantos of the *Inferno* to be a prologue and we leave them aside, then of the ninety-eight strictly other-worldly cantos of the *Comedy*, we are at the half-way mark. Virgil, it turns out, is halfway through his discourse on love which began in the middle of *Purgatorio* xvii; the wayfarers are resting on the top of the steps which lead to the fourth and middle ledge of Mount Purgatory. In Dante's structuring of repentance, you will recall, the lowest three sins are offences against others, the three highest or least serious are offences against oneself; and the middle or fourth ledge contains those who have not loved God with sufficient ardour: "qui si ribatte il mal tardato remo" (*Purg*.xvii.87).

Purgatorio xviii itself divides clearly at line 75. Let us simply note in passing that Dante, with his sensitivity to the role of variety in keeping his readers' interest alive, has three contrast-ing movements in the canto: the refined movement or struggle of the human mind seeking the truth through description and distinction (1-75); a period of rest given over to the quiet contemplation of nature and the slow movement of the moon, with Dante sliding into a gentle sleep (76-87), and notice the round richness of the contrast: "La luna, quasi a mezza notte" (76); and this somnolence in turn being shattered by violent physical movement, by the abrupt appearance and noise of the incessantly running crowd of those guilty of religious sloth on earth. The canto concludes: "e 'l pensamento in sogno tras-mutai" (145). The artistry of the poet is evident in that final line, in the odd transitive "trasmutai": "I changed thought into sleep"; for in *Purgatorio* xix the Siren will appear, she who is the self-created allurement of the intellectually and morally lazy mind.

Let us then, turn back to the beginning of the canto and watch the discourse on love and man's responsibility in love emerge. For emerge it does: like all philosophy worthy of the name it is not a mere game, something done as a relief from "real life". The questions posed and answered here rise naturally, almost inevitably, from the situation of the two men, and speech here is dialogue: between people with distinct characters at a point in their own shifting and growing relationship. The importance of the topic under discussion is signalled in the first few lines, in the stance of Virgil: he looks at Dante intently, anxious to know, as a good teacher, whether what is evident to him is evident to his pupil, whether the pupil is satisfied, or must the implications of what he had said be teased out:

> Posto avea fine al suo ragionamento
> l'alto dottore, e attento guardava
> ne la mia vista s'io parea contento.   1-3

The strength of Dante's desire for knowledge is indicated in that new thirst of: "e io, cui nova sete ancor frugava" (4). But however much Dante's mind may quest for knowledge, his courtesy does not fail him; he hesitates to speak lest he weary Virgil, and it is the latter's readiness to respond which gives Dante the courage to speak:

> Ma quel padre verace, che s'accorse
> del timido voler che non s'apriva,
> parlando, di parlare ardir mi porse.   7-9

I have spoken of the dialogue as taking place within a changing relationship, and two "titles" with which Dante addresses Virgil are indicative both of the central elements in their relationship and the growing shift in emphasis: "Maestro" (10), indicating the leading role of Virgil; the affectionate "dolce padre caro" (13), catching the more purely interpersonal aspect of their friendship. The weight here is, obviously, with the latter in its double adjective "gentle" and "dear", and not accidentally so, for as they near the end of the journey the warmth of Dante's regard for his guide comes more and more to the fore, colouring the intellectual dependence of the Italian on the Latin poet. Whereas Virgil throughout the *Inferno* is addressed or referred to as "master", and that some eighty times, and never there referred to as "father", in the *Purgatorio*, "maestro" is used much less frequently, about thirty times, while "padre" is used a dozen times. Indeed "padre" is used last, and that in the warmest terms. For, when Dante finds, in Eden, that his guide is no longer there, he recalls how he was saved by giving himself to

"Virgilio dolcissimo padre" (*Purg.*xxx.50). I have dwelt for a moment on the warmth of this relationship because it sets the tone for what is to follow: an exchange between men who care for each other in their wider love for the truth. It is this wider love which must now engage our attention.

Having expressed his gratitude for the enlightenment conferred so far, Dante picks up a statement of Virgil which has puzzled him: Virgil has asserted in *Purgatorio* xvii.103-5 that love is the seed of every virtue and every act which deserves punishment. How this is so is not clear to Dante and so he asks Virgil to "dimostrare amore", to make manifest the working, the operation of love:

> Però ti prego, dolce padre caro,
> che mi dimostri amore, a cui reduci
> ogne buono operare e 'l suo contraro.   13-15

Note here the overtones of "reduci". Dante is using the word here with its technical philosophical meaning, as suggested by its etymology. To "reduce" something is to lead it back to its source, to specify the origin, the cause of the thing being discussed. Dante's request then is: make manifest to me the working of love which is the cause of all good and evil action.

Virgil's first reply opens and closes in a surprisingly polemical way:

> "Drizza", disse, "ver' me l'agute luci
> de lo 'ntelletto, e fieti manifesto
> l'error de' ciechi che si fanno duci."   16-18

> "Or ti puote apparer quant' è nascosa
> la veritate a la gente ch'avvera
> ciascun amore in sé laudabil cosa;
> però che forse appar la sua matera
> sempre esser buona, ma non ciascun segno
> è buono, ancor che buona sia la cera".   34-9

His words show how erroneous are those blind leaders who maintain, as lines 34-6 tell us, that every love is good. I will simply note here in passing that it is something of a puzzle whom Virgil has in mind. Most commentators understand Dante here to be referring to the Epicureans,[2] but none, so far as I am aware, has substantiated this claim. Neither as a matter of historical fact nor from what we know of Dante's understanding of their beliefs[3] can the Epicureans be charged with regarding every love as good. Reference is also made frequently to Matthew 15:14 and *Convivio* I.xi.3 ff., but the similarity does not go beyond the verbal. It is implausible to see Virgil's charge as levelled at courtly love poets,[4] since such a sweeping accusation hardly does justice to the view of love common among them – and I should, in any case, find something odd in Virgil's being so incensed by a peculiarly medieval view of love. I hope my rather negative reflections may at least point towards the existence of a not unimportant problem.

The first exposition of the stages through which love develops is, I think, clear enough in itself, as a glance at the text will show:

> Vostra apprensiva da esser verace
>   tragge intenzione, e dentro a voi la spiega,
>   sì che l'animo ad essa volger face;
> e se, rivolto, inver' di lei si piega,
>   quel piegare è amor, quell' è natura
>   che per piacer di novo in voi si lega.
> Poi, come 'l foco movesi in altura
>   per la sua forma ch'è nata a salire
>   là dove più in sua matera dura
> così l'animo preso entra in disire,
>   ch'è moto spiritale, e mai non posa
>   fin che la cosa amata il fa gioire.   22-33

There are two preconditions for love: the existence of a real object; and the cognitive moment of the mind's reflecting that object in idea and image (*intenzione*; 22-4). There are three stages of love proper: love occurs when there is not simply knowledge, recognition, but pleasure, a bending of the mind back towards the object (25-7); this is followed by the second stage, *disio*, when the simple, instinctive, momentary bending in pleasure *within* the mind transforms itself into an active seeking to be united permanently to the object (28-32); and finally the third stage, *gioire* (33), when the first two stages, the momentary pleasure and the lack of fulfilment, the longing, *disio*, give way to union, perfection, joy. I shall wish later to refer back to this passage, but this can best be done after discussion of lines 45-75. But before I move on to Virgil's more substantial account let me draw your attention to one further point. It is commonly thought that desire precedes love. This is true only in a limited sense, for it is also true that love precedes desire. Dante stresses that love is first of all an instinctive reaction of pleasure to a thing, "quel piegare è amor", "that inclination is love, that is nature which by pleasure is bound in you afresh". Only the final stage of love, joy, is preceded by desire: without instinctive love there would be no striving, no calculation, no effort.

When Virgil concludes this speech, there is no hesitation on the part of the pupil. Without waiting to be invited, Dante declares that, while Virgil has revealed love, showed its workings, this has only made him more perplexed. For while Dante was interested in love as the origin of action, it was precisely about love as the origin of *meritorious* action that he enquired, and Virgil's words, says Dante, far from clarifying this aspect seem to preclude it – that is the thrust of his reply:

> ché s'amore è di fuori a noi offerto
> e l'anima non va con altro piede,
> se dritta o torta va, non è suo merto.   43-5

Love as action seems to be entirely shaped from without, from the *esser verace,* from the real object, and if that is the case then the soul's moving to this or that thing is without responsibility. Implicit in this question is the problem: is there something within the soul which guides and shapes love, an *altro piede?*

Virgil begins his reply cautiously, defensively. He can only go as far as reason can penetrate; beyond that is the realm of faith, in which Beatrice is the guide. None the less, reason can go some distance (46-8). The following lines are very dense, and I hope only to pick out some key points. Firstly, Virgil refers to a characteristic specific to the mind of man:

> Ogne forma sustanzial, che setta
> è da matera ed è con lei unita,
> specifica vertute ha in sé colletta,
> la qual sanza operar non è sentita,
> né si dimostra mai che per effetto,
> come per verdi fronde in pianta vita.   49-54

Man (49-50) is described exactly as a substantial form which is not absorbed by, coextensive with, matter, *setta è da matera,* and yet is united to it. Man's essential being, the *forma sustanzial* (49), is not seen in itself as an object; what forms the object of our awareness, our introspection are the actions we perform: I am aware of myself as a subject acting or thinking. A moment's reflection will confirm this: I am never aware of myself as a pure object, a thing: self-awareness is a concomitant of activity, of the *effetti*.

Having noted this essential truth, Virgil goes on to focus on two *effetti* or activities which emerge from the unknown self: the knowledge of the primary truths and the instinctive love of the highest goods:

> Però, là onde vegna lo 'ntelletto
>   de le prime notizie, omo non sape,
>   e de' primi appetibili l'affetto,
> che sono in voi sì come studio in ape
>   di far lo mele; e questa prima voglia
>   merto di lode o di biasmo non cape.   55-60

It is on the latter he concentrates, with some insistence; this *voglia* or love of the highest goods does not of itself merit praise or blame. Let us pause for a few moments to grasp exactly what is being said here. Virgil, and in some sense Dante the poet, is claiming that when love is aroused in the soul by an outside object, there is a double movement of love set up: first and more obviously there is the *piacere*, the bending of the soul as entirely focused on and specified by, absorbed by the particular attracting object; but secondly and alongside that there is a love of the *primi appetibili*, those things or actions which in themselves and prior to all particular, concrete objects are good in themselves.[5] Neither of these is as yet responsible love: one is caused by an outside object, the other arises instinctively within the soul – hence Dante's insistence (59-60) "and this primal will is not itself deserving of praise or blame".

Responsibility enters with the third moment, the application of that primal willing of the highest goods to the particular good naturally loved when presented to man from outside himself. Man has been given the faculty of free choice through which instinct becomes responsible and personalized:

> Or perché a questa ogn' altra si raccoglia,
>   innata v'è la virtù che consiglia,
>   e de l'assenso de' tener la soglia.   61-3

Let us follow that personalization in some detail, "Or perché a questa ogn' altra si raccoglia" (61): free choice has been given to man in order that every willing other than the instinctive willing of the highest goods might gather itself into it. Kenelm Foster has suggested that "si raccoglia" be understood to mean "be gathered into"[6] rather than, as the phrase is usually interpreted, "be in accord with" or in "harmony with", and this I endorse (though I would turn it actively, as the text permits and perhaps requires: "gather itself into"). There is no instance in either the *Divine Comedy* or Dante's minor works in which *raccogliere* means "be in harmony with" and in the majority of cases it means simply "to gather".[7] Free choice then has an aim: to permit the love from outside to gather itself into the already constituted personal desire for the highest goods. How is this aim brought about? Through a double action, or in more scholastic terms, operation. Lines 62-3: "there is in man a faculty which counsels and ought to hold the threshold of assent". Man does not simply have the knowledge of some primary generic goods: he has "la virtù che consiglia", the discursive power, the ability to take a general idea and apply it to a specific case – here the ability to operate on the base of the instinctive desire for the highest goods and measure the particular goods in the light of these. But the operation of this virtue is not exhausted with knowledge, however particular: it *ought* also to hold the threshold of assent. Dante draws this out with another image, that of the sieve: man merits according as he takes the *amori*, the *piaceri*, and passes them through the sieve, retaining the good and dropping, casting away the bad:

> ragion di meritare in voi, secondo
> che buoni e rei amori accoglie e viglia.   65-6

Decision as well as judgment is required. It is these last actions, the double action of the power of free will, which give man his freedom (67-72).[8]

Let me recapitulate: how, Dante has asked, is love the source of good and evil action? The answer is given in two stages: firstly, how love is the source of action; secondly, how love is the source of good (or evil) action. Firstly (19-39), love is the source of action because man has a promptitude to unite with things outside himself (the *piacere*, the *piegare*) and, finding himself only partially united with that thing, he seeks to move from partial, incomplete union to full, permanent union and thus achieve joy, *gioire*. Implicit here is the idea that without that desire for full union and joy there would be no action. Secondly

(50-72), love is the source of *responsible* action, it merits praise or blame, because man can be selective in his love, he can accept or reject the particular love aroused. This he can do because of two other features: his instinctive love for what is truly and most properly good, and the ability he has to apply that instinctive love to the particular love. This application has two moments: the intellectual, the judging of the particular in the light of the instinctive love, and the voluntary, the giving (or withholding) of assent in the light of that further particular judgment. It is implied rather than stated that the action is good if the *assenso* is in accordance with the *consiglio*. Particular love formed from outside; instinctive but general love arising from within; first application of that general love through reasoning or judgment, second application of that general love through the judgment's actually being brought to bear through assent or rejection.

The reward of studying this close-knit passage may be seen if it makes clear how a firm grasp of these ideas enables us to appreciate more deeply the characters we have already met in the *Inferno*. But I feel I ought not to leave *Purgatorio* xviii without taking another quick look at Virgil's first reply to Dante, for it contains, I believe, a richer content than the somewhat uncomprehending reaction of Dante suggests, and, I think it ought to be said, richer than most commentators seem aware. Virgil has in fact already signalled for the attentive listener the change from instinctive to responsible love at the densely packed lines 31-3: he is contrasting *amor* here with *disio*,[9] for the latter is designated a *moto spiritale*, a movement of the spirit, i.e. a conscious move from one stage to the next; and man is responsible for his consciously motivated actions. This same idea is hinted at the emphatic *entra in desire*: desire does not happen, it is entered into, as contrasted with *amor*, by which the soul is taken, *preso*.

There can be few lines in the *Commedia* better known than the generic description of the sensual sinners at *Inf.*v.38-9: "i peccator carnali,/che la ragion sommettono al talento", those who attribute more importance to desire than to reason. Few sinners, too, are given by Dante a more eloquent apparent justification of their sin, a hidden plea that they were not in fact at fault – so eloquent a plea indeed that not a few commentators have argued that Dante is here actually excusing their sin, distancing himself in fact from the condemnation that he is forced to portray in theory.[10] And I suspect that the impetus behind such an interpretation is due in no small measure to the natural sympathy we all have when reason is contrasted with feeling. I disagree with such an interpretation, and wish to show briefly why, in light of *Purgatorio* xviii, I think it is mistaken, and why the putative contrast is misleading.

Francesca's beautiful apologia has *amor* as its subject, and the clear drift of her words is that throughout it is love which is the agent, and that Paolo and herself were sinned against rather than sinning:

> Amor, ch'al cor gentil ratto s'apprende,
>   prese costui de la bella persona
>   che mi fu tolta; e 'l modo ancor m'offende.
> Amor, ch'a nullo amato amar perdona,
>   mi prese del costui piacer sì forte,
>   che, come vedi, ancor non m'abbandona.
> Amor condusse noi ad una morte.
>   Caina attende chi a vita ci spense.   *Inf.*v.100-7

What is not clear from Francesca's speech and what we might have dimly sensed then but are now in a position not simply to sense but to know with lucidity, is that she is speaking of love in a truncated sense, for the love in question is particular love, love as entirely shaped from outside, love as natural love in the narrow sense of *Purgatorio* xviii.25-7 and 31: "that inclination is love, that is nature, which by pleasure is bound in you afresh". A key word here is *preso* which occurs in *Purg*.xviii.31, echoing *Inferno* v.101 and 104; note especially the occurrence of *prendere* and *piacere* in the latter, "mi prese del costui piacer sì forte". There is no mention of that other love, the even more natural love, the *prima voglia* which, according to Dante's psychology, would also be aroused, thus prompting Francesca to measure the narrower, more focused love against broader love. It is a case of special pleading, a disastrous taking of a part for the whole. Note too, that Dante the voyager here seems to accept this truncated view of love, enters into the fiction that the narrow, "un-informed" love is the sole agent: the "disio ch'è moto spiritale" (the desire which is a movement of the spirit) is here surely the *dolci pensieri* of pleasure and it is this which Dante says "led the lovers to the tragic outcome". There is, I think, an element of courtesy in Dante's words here, but more than that there is a partial entry into self-deception. When Dante is finally overwhelmed by the fate of the lovers (142): "e caddi, come corpo morto cade", this is undoubtedly due to the conflict of a whole complex of thoughts and emotions among which, I believe, is his inability to acknowledge fully at this early stage of his journey that the evasion of responsibility for man's most passionate and delicate feelings subhumanizes them. I may conclude this brief look at *Inferno* v by saying that it is only perhaps in the light of *Purgatorio* xviii that we are in a position to appreciate the richness of the generic description "those who subject reason to desire" and not to misinterpret it by too narrow an idea of reason, for we see clearly from the *Purgatorio* passage that *ragione* for Dante is not the mind as *opposed* to the will, reason to love. Rather *reason includes* the deeper love, the *prima voglia* which seeks to encompass, enhance and winnow the particular loves by being articulated through reasoning, judgment and decision. Francesca's failure is not that she is not clever enough. Her sin is first of all a failure to love deeply enough, to love with that primal affection which it is the intellect's role to bring into full awareness. She does not use her reason to bring to bear the one love on the other. Both the attractiveness and the weakness and fallaciousness of Francesca are caught in the gentle elegance of the evasive line which comes near the beginning of her first speech: "se fosse amico il re de l'universo". The enmity of God, she suggests, is his fault: it is he who refuses to be a friend.

A very different, indeed at first sight an entirely different, character from Francesca is Guido da Montefeltro, condemned for fraudulent counselling, whom we meet in lower Hell, in the encounter described in *Inferno* xxvii. I can do no more than touch on him, but I do so because there is, I suggest, an underlying similarity to, as well as a contrast with, Francesca. Guido illustrates how reasoning must not be confused with reason, intellectual agility with mind in its wide Dantean sense. Guido had led a life of political rapacity marked by his ability to use his intellect to gain strategic advantage over his foes. Late in life he repented and entered the Franciscans (in 1296). Two years later, in the story accepted by Dante, he was called upon by Pope Boniface VIII, a Caetani, to help overcome the Colonna family menacing Boniface from their stronghold of Palestrina. How to break the impasse of the siege at Palestrina was the problem. Guido suggested that Boniface promise an amnesty to the Colonnas which he would not observe. It is the conversation recording this which Dante portrays towards the end of *Inferno* xxvii. The lines to which I should like to call your attention are lines 106-7. Boniface recognizes that Guido hesitates because he fears eternal punishment for his sin and Boniface declares that he forgives him antecedently. Guido recalls his reaction to this promise:

> Allor mi pinser li argomenti gravi
> là 've 'l tacer mi fu avviso 'l peggio   *Inf.*xxvii.106-7

As with Francesca, responsibility is shuffled off: "mi pinser"; his weighty arguments *drove* me. Unlike the case of Francesca, we feel immediately that this is nonsense. How could such a facile proposition to offer forgiveness for an as yet uncommitted (and by that very fact unrepented) sin, be forgiven? Yet Guido, even in Hell, regards Boniface's word as *argomenti gravi.* Where in the case of Francesca the underlying deeper love, the *prima voglia*, is obscured by concentration on narrow, purely instinctive carnal love, here this underlying love is obscured by concentration on *consiglio*, discursive reasoning, calculation. This reasoning fails because it is cut off from the underlying love, it is mental agility cut off from feeling, feeling for his own *voler* to sin, feeling for the victims of his fraudulent counsel. Where Francesca fails to reflect, Guido fails to reflect on the proper basis, on his own deeper feeling or love. It is when both are in harmony, the reasoning sharpening and focusing the love, that both morality and freedom in its highest sense are found.

Notes

[1]A bibliography of modern readings of this canto is found in the Casini-Barbi-Mazzoni *Purgatorio* (Florence, 1973), p. 413. Translations in this paper are from Sinclair (London, 1948).

[2]So for example among major modern commentators: Casini-Barbi-Mazzoni (Florence, 1973) p. 399; Sapegno II (Florence, 1968) p. 196; H. Gmelin, *Die Göttliche Komödie* II (Stuttgart, 1968) p. 287; Singleton, *Purgatorio* (Princeton, 1973) p. 420. More tentative is M. Porena (Bologna, 1955) II, p. 176. Significantly A. Pézard makes no reference to this passage in "Un Dante épicurien", *Mélanges offerts à Étienne Gilson*

112   Christopher Ryan

(Toronto, 1959) pp. 499-536.
³See *Conv.*III.xiv.15; IV.vi.11-12; IV.xxii.4 and 15; *Inf.*x.14-15.

⁴This is the view of Porena (note² above), who comments rather wildly: "E col discorso di Virgilio Dante ha voluto, senza troppo parere, condannare tutti coloro che son propensi a farsi una scusa dell'amore irresistibile … rappresentati nell'Inferno da Francesca e nel mondo da poco meno che tutta l'umanità e niente meno che da tutti i poeti d'amore" (p. 176).

⁵What precisely Virgil means by *primi appetibili* is not explained and I have followed the text, translating vaguely: "highest goods". A discussion of these words would have to consider not simply possible parallels in scholastic usage but also whether Dante is not deliberately portraying Virgil as unable to focus clearly on the supreme good.

⁶K. Foster, "Dante and Eros", *Downside Review* 84 (1966) p. 267, now in his *The Two Dantes* (London, 1977) p. 42.

⁷"Raccogliere" is used nineteen times in the *Commedia*. It means "to gather physically", "to collect" in *Inf.*iii.110; xiii.142; xiv.23; xvii.105; xviii.18; xxiv.104; xxvii.81; *Purg.*v.109; viii.62; xxviii.19; *Par.*xxii.96. Of the remaining eight more figurative uses, see especially *Purg.*iv.3 and 68, and above all *Purg.*xiv.72 (where the word is used with respect to understanding in a similar fashion to its application to willing in *Purg.*xviii.61): "poi ch' ebbe la parola a sé raccolta."

⁸In "Il libero arbitrio e la storiella dell'asino di Buridano" *Nel mondo di Dante* (Rome, 1944) pp. 285-303, B. Nardi discusses Dante's ideas on free will. Stimulating, but here imprecise, Nardi is incorrect in what appear to be his two main conclusions namely (*i*) that Dante believed that the exclusive agent in man of free choice is the intellect, such that the will cannot refuse to follow what the intellect judges to be good; (*ii*) in upholding this belief Dante was following a school of thought (the "Latin Averroists") led by Siger of Brabant and condemned in 1277 at Paris by Bishop Tempier. While Nardi bases his view of Dante mainly on *Mon.*I.xii and *Par.*iv.1-9 he sees the same doctrine in *Purg.*xviii (pp. 294-5). Confining ourselves to the latter, we may note that lines 62-3 distinguish the moments of judgment and assent and the *de'* of line 63 indicates that the assent is not always in accord with the judgment. More broadly the doctrine of rational determinism which Nardi ascribes to Dante is incompatible — as philosophers and theologians of the time were not slow to point out; see A. San Cristobal-Sebastian, *Controversias acerca de la voluntad desde 1270-1300* (Madrid, 1958) — with belief in what Dante is here at pains to uphold, man's capacity to merit praise or blame. The faults in Nardi's analysis are the more regrettable in that even distinguished Dante scholars when commenting on *Purgatorio* xviii refer their readers to his article without a cautionary word.

⁹I therefore disagree with J. A. Mazzeo when he interprets lines 25-7 as referring to the moment of free choice, *Structure and Thought in the "Paradiso"* (Ithaca, 1958) p.61. Critics are divided on whether *di novo* in line 27 should be understood as "firstly" or "again". I think the former is determined by the run of the argument.

¹⁰Any attempt such as mine to summarize succinctly the debates which have surrounded the interpretations of this canto cannot do justice to the nuances in positions adopted. For a sensitive reading of the canto, with much valuable bibliographical information, in which the author attempts to steer a middle course between what he somewhat infelicitously terms the doves and hawks, see P. Dronke: "Francesca and Héloise", *Comparative Literature* 27 (1975) 113-35. Evidently I must be numbered among the milder hawks.

Dante and Statius: Purgatorio XXI-XXII

J.H. Whitfield

Perhaps we should set to preside over these cantos the line that Dante used in the beginning:

O de li altri poeti onore e lume   *Inf*.i.82

and by which he expressed at once his affection and his allegiance to Virgil. Here, those sentiments will find their climax for the simple reason that the geometry of the *Comedy* will not allow Dante to place the accent upon Virgil at the moment of his eclipse, because there the actors of the scene are himself and Beatrice. But if we do adopt that line from the *Inferno* as our guide in Purgatory we had better couple with it two lines from the present text as cautionary riders to the theme of Virgil's excellence. The first is from *Purgatorio* xxii: "la fede, sanza qual ben far non basta" (*Purg*.xxii.60). And the second, at the outset of this episode of Dante and Virgil meeting Statius, is Virgil's full confession that this line — which was his own addressed to Statius — is a condemnation of himself: "che me rilega ne l'etterno essilio" (*Purg*.xxi.18). This is the divide between Virgil and Statius, that the one can answer *Yes*, and go forward with Dante towards beatitude, while the other: "O de li altri poeti onore e lume", has to answer *No*, and go back into Limbo.

It has been said that we have in this episode the solidarity of culture, Dante's belief in the supremacy of poetry.[1] You will see at once the limitations of that judgment. For if it is faith which decides the fate of Virgil and of Statius, while poetry gives an opposite, but inoperative, assessment, then poetry is outweighed by faith: "la fede, sanza qual ben far non basta." (*Purg.*xxii.60). It is here that we run into our main difficulty. For, if we do concede (and Dante as it will be clear does so reluctantly) that Virgil had to answer *No*, by what right or even by what stretch of the imagination could Statius answer *Yes*? And who is Statius to measure himself either in faith or poetry with Virgil? Did he not write when the glories of the Augustan age had gone, did he not live in the unchristian Roman world of the first century A.D., two centuries and more before Constantine embraced the faith?

For us Statius is the flattest and the tamest of the Latin epic poets. But it will be plain for you from the start that if Dante singled him out for this high honour, he, and the Middle Ages with him, had for Statius a very different estimate. We need not look further than Dante; and if we take the first place where he marks up the ratings we shall find in *De vulgari eloquentia* II.vi that the four regular poets are for him, and in this order: Virgil, Ovid (the Ovid of the *Metamorphoses*), Statius, Lucan. If we move on to *Convivio* IV.xxv, we shall find amongst the lessons to be learnt from Statius's characters, the overall judgment: "E però dice Stazio, lo dolce poeta". Now Dante's debt to Ovid, the second-ranking of the Latin poets, is wide, is vast; but for various and obvious reasons he cannot play the card of Ovid at this point; and that of Lucan he has already played with Cato. That leaves only Statius, "lo dolce poeta", a recommendation culled from Juvenal,[2] which Statius repeats here about himself: "Tanto fu dolce mio vocale spirito" (*Purg.*xxi.88). And Dante also drops the name of Juvenal, who had revealed to him the cult of Statius for the *Aeneid*:

> Onde da l'ora che tra noi discese
> nel limbo de lo 'nferno Giovenale,
> che la tua affezion mi fe' palese.   *Purg.*xxii.13-15

Statius, for the Dante of the *Comedy*, is what he seemed to be in the days of the *Convivio* and the *De vulgari eloquentia*.

We may still be surprised at his appearance and feel that it is not prepared for within the *Comedy*. When we look briefly back, we see that Dante called on Statius at some prominent points and that it may be our own unfamiliarity with the *Thebaid* and the *Achilleid* (the two works which Dante and the Middle Ages knew of Statius) which prevents them registering with us. The first, perhaps the most significant, is with Capaneus in *Inferno* xiv, that strong, or seeming-strong, blasphemer of the gods for whose unfaith Statius wrote the most memorable of his lines: "Virtus mihi numen et ensis/quem teneo" (*Theb*.III.615; My God is my own strength. That and the sword I bear), with that other contemptuous dismissal of the gods: "Primus in orbe deos fecit timor" (*Theb*.III.661; fear first created gods within the world). No wonder that Capaneus is for Statius the *contrepied* of Virgil's Ripheus: "Superum contemptor et aequi impatiens" (*Theb*.III.602; despiser of the gods, and heedless of the right). Then in the famous encounter with Ulysses in *Inferno* xxvi, Statius lurks in the background when Ulysses is condemned for the trickery which made Achilles abandon Deidamia and her isle of Scyros. And in another celebrated place, the setting of the scene for the Conte Ugolino and his prostrate enemy, the Archbishop Ruggieri, it is the hatreds of Thebes (which Dante thought he saw in the divided flame of those evil counsellors, Ulysses and Diomedes) which provide the precedent, with Tydeus gnawing out the skull of Menalippus. One may almost disregard the echoes of Statius earlier in *Purgatorio*: Dante's own awakening, after being transported up the mountain, compared to that of Achilles on Scyros and in feminine attire (*Purgatorio* ix); or the necklace of Harmony, remembered within the catalogue of pride (*Purgatorio* xii). For it will be evident that as a poetic contributor to the matter, and the style, of the *Comedy*, Statius is as lightweight in comparison to Virgil as we are like to find him deficient as a poet.

He has, however, this second distinction: as well as being third in that quadrumvirate of poets, he is one of the four only pagans whom Dante, by some special alchemy, rescues from damnation and promotes either to Purgatory or else to Paradise. They make for us an odd assembly: in *Purgatorio*, Cato and Statius; in *Paradiso*, Trajan and Ripheus. Of these the easiest to understand is Cato, especially in view of Dante's homage to him throughout the *Convivio*. From *Pharsalia* II.383, Cato was: "Nec sibi, sed toti se credere genitum mundo" (born, he thought, not for himself but for mankind). There is a long Christian interpretation of Cato, the one who is sacrificed for the many. Next Trajan, subject of a pious legend in which a Roman province, asking the favour of his presence and portrayed as a female suppliant on a bas-relief, became a widow seeking justice (*Purgatorio* x and *Paradiso* xx), and Trajan's pursuit of justice won him the prayers of Pope Gregory and the reversal of his fate. With him in *Paradiso* xx and in the very eye of the imperial eagle, which symbolizes Justice, Dante put Ripheus, who has no substance other than one line, one epithet, in Virgil's *Aeneid*: "iustissimus unus/Qui fuit in Teucris et servantissimus aequi" (*Aen.* II.426-7; the justest man within the Trojan ranks, the most observant of the right). The opposite, as I said, of Capaneus, nor did Statius write of him *aequi impatiens* without remembering Ripheus: *servantissimus aequi*. For Ripheus there is no medieval legend and those who say that Dante takes his faith so seriously as never to invent forget usually to discuss Ripheus. It is true also that they may add that for both Dante and the medieval mind it needed but the slightest hint to find the allegory that Christianized the inventions of the pagan world.[3] This is to admit what the first statement denied, that the invention of a meaning not meant originally is of the essence of the medieval approach to the heritage of Rome. Let us leave Ripheus, as Dante's own trophy for Christianity; our concern is with Statius.

Dante in these two cantos offers us unequivocally a Christian Statius: one who will go on with Dante and is ready to discourse to Dante, as Virgil had been, on points of doctrine, then to step with him into the sacred wood and launch himself among the blessed. Cato and Trajan, similarly chosen, had their legends thick about them: does Statius stand with them, or with Ripheus? Round this important point the battle of criticism has swayed to and fro. If it has proved anything, it is that others than Dante, by Dante's time or in Dante's time, had conceived of Statius as a Christian. But it should also be apparent that if Dante finds moral allegories in classical authors, as they do, and Christianizes Statius, as they do, he is moving with them and with the spirit of his (medieval) times, consciously or unconsciously. And if we cannot put our finger on his reasons for baptizing Statius, theirs have some relevance for us.

You may think these prolegomena are too long; and, if we are to look even cursorily at an episode which spills over two cantos, it is time we turned to the text. Actually it begins before the end of *Purgatorio* xx with the quaking of the mountain and the *Gloria in excelsis Deo*, where Dante, to make his setting clear, finds for the quake the parallel of Delos, shaking at the birth to Latona of the two eyes of the world: "li due occhi del cielo" (*Purg.*xx.132), Apollo and Diana, the *mundi lumina* which symbolize for Dante the two equally providential institutions, Empire and Papacy, which should, which for Dante *shall*, preside over the world. And to make sure we do not miss the burden of the *Gloria in excelsis Deo*, Dante and Virgil stand chilled with fear, as did the shepherds who first heard that song: "come i pastor che prima udir quel canto" (140). Nor will it surprise you, with such an omen, that the rhyming word, for Dante's and Virgil's going, is "santo": "poi ripigliammo nostro cammin santo" (142).

We had to look at the end of *Purgatorio* xx to make sure that we are not mistaken when we find the background to *Purgatorio* xxi purely and resolutely christological. We start with Dante thirsting for the answer to the mystery and his thirst is that of the Samaritan woman at the well:

> La sete natural che mai non sazia
> se non con l'acqua onde la femminetta
> samaritana domandò la grazia   *Purg.*xxi.1-3

Who can doubt that Dante means to find the same living water? Then even more directly, the setting of the scene switches from the moment of the birth to that of the resurrection; Dante and Virgil assume the role of the disciples on the road to Emmaus:

> Ed ecco, sì come ne scrive Luca
> che Cristo apparve a' due ch'erano in via,
> già surto fuor de la sepulcral buca   7-9

Make no doubt, if Dante and Virgil assume the guise of the apostles on their way to Emmaus the shade who appears to them, and who in fact is Statius, assumes the role of Christ himself. Like the disciples, Dante and Virgil do not observe his coming until he gives what is for an ancient poet a curious form of greeting: "O frati miei, Dio vi dea pace" (13), to which Virgil gives the appropriate reply. Now the notes to the Barbi-Casini edition of Dante put forward the idea that Virgil answered as he did to Cato, suitably. But Dante did not write that Virgil gave *a* suitable reply, but that he gave *the* suitable reply. When Statius said *Pax vobiscum* and Virgil "rendéli 'l cenno ch'a ciò si conface" (15), what could he be answering but *Et cum spiritu tuo?* And what point would there be in depriving Virgil of this, while leaving Statius with its counterpart?

Now Statius is a liberated soul and the whole purpose of the earthquake and the *Gloria* was his acquisition of the grace sought by Dante and the woman of Samaria. Dante will not retract the Christlike setting he has given Statius. But Virgil is another matter and Virgil's candour will not let him leave a false impression for a moment. So he revises his form of greeting (16-18); peace for Statius but not for himself: "che me rilega ne l'etterno essilio" (18). You see the gap, the chasm, which Dante has opened up between Statius and Virgil: the first as Christ on his way to Emmaus, the second an inhabitant of Hell. It will be the task of the rest of the episode, not to reverse the roles, but to afford to Virgil the most flattering of compensatory poetic homage. On the surface, this comes from Statius; but it would not sound so real, or so triumphant, if it did not come from Dante too. And this is why, when Statius asks some explanation of the pair, and Virgil tells him of that circumstance which arouses curiosity in all the souls of Purgatory, of Dante being still alive, Statius does not respond with any flicker of interest on that score. We are not going to be concerned here with Dante, only with Virgil. For this concentration of the focus Dante quickly sweeps aside the question also of the earthquake: natural phenomena have no place within Purgatory proper, and the mountain-top can quake, but only within superior order, for the liberation of a soul, without its base. Or the base, for natural reasons (by dry and hot vapours), without the top. How can that be? "Non so come" (*Purg*.xxi.57; I do not know).

Naturally, that ignorance is relative, and we see the limit between the natural and the supernatural world; just as we learn the long terms of Statius's path to liberation and beatitude (and you will realise that he has some twelve centuries of expiation to account for). Of all these preliminaries let me give attention to one detail, where Statius explains "la religione de la montagna" (41-2). It has, as we have seen, a new significance, conveys a supernatural order. But it is verbally a reminiscence of Virgil, an act of homage by allusion from one poet to another, from this poet and his creator Dante to the greatest of the poets, Virgil. What Statius has in mind is the *religio loci* of the *Aeneid*

VIII.349-50. I mention this as a hint, because when we come to the climax of *Purgatorio* xxi, from line 82 on, where Statius answers Virgil directly with an account of himself, his words are thick with reminiscences of Virgil or, more especially, of Virgil seen through Dante's eyes. Look how Statius echoes what our Virgil in the *Comedy* said to Dante: "Nel tempo che'l buon Tito" (82), as against: "e vissi a Roma sotto 'l buono Augusto" (*Inf*.i.71). The *goodness* of Augustus consisted in the establishment of the Empire and of peace; the *goodness* of Titus comes also as Emperor, and in the punishment of the sacrilege of the Jews by the destruction of Jerusalem. And if you hesitated, where Dante paused over the "giusta vendetta" (*Purg*.xxi.6), which on the surface was the punishment of the "avari", you were right to take it more widely, as the premonition of this tercet for Titus:

> Nel tempo che 'l buon Tito, con l'aiuto
> del sommo rege, vendicò le fóra
> ond' uscì 'l sangue per Giuda venduto   82-4

(The time when Titus, by the help of God, avenged the wounds whence flowed the blood that Judas sold). Just as this tercet itself looks forward to *Paradiso* vi, where Justinian records again the vengeance of the same Titus, with the same sanction, that of Rome:

> poscia con Tito a far vendetta corse
> de la vendetta del peccato antico.   *Par*.vi.92-3

In the meantime Statius puts forward his claim to stand with Virgil: "col nome che più dura e più onora / era io di là" (*Purg*.xxi. 85-6). And what name, pray, was that? I only ask rhetorically, since I gave the answer as the leitmotiv of the episode: "O de li altri poeti onore e lume" (*Inf*.i.82). It is what Dante said of Virgil; just as what Statius says of his material: "cantai di Tebe, e poi del grande Achille" (*Purg*.xxi.92), echoes what Virgil said to Dante:

> Poeta fui, e cantai di quel giusto
> figliuol d'Anchise che venne da Troia.   *Inf*.i.73-4

There is no need to dwell upon Dante's error (*Purg*.xxi.89) in making Statius from Toulouse, when he was really born in Naples. It is an error of Dante's time, born out of ignorance of Statius's *Sylvae*. Alongside it there is the one bit of literary criticism Dante knew for Statius, that one adjective (whose motivation I find hard to guess) which Dante drew from Juvenal's *tanta dulcedine captos* (with so much sweetness) (VII.84) in the *Convivio* (IV.25): "Tanto fu dolce mio vocale spirto" (*Purg*.xxi.88). It is the close of Statius's speech which interests us, for here the theme of Virgil, which so far has been circulating underground, comes out into the open. It is based directly on what Statius said himself at the end of the *Thebaid* (XII.816):

> Vive, precor, nec tu divinam Aeneida tempta,
> Sed lunge sequere, et vestigia semper adora.

This is Statius addressing his own work, and hoping (like Horace, *non omnis moriar*) that it will survive. Yet modestly he distances it from the "divine" *Aeneid*, which the *Thebaid* follows, but far behind, with reverent adoration. Boccaccio will echo Statius correctly, at the end of the *Filocolo*,[4] but for Dante, Statius's modesty is only modesty, and his achievement is achievement:

> Al mio ardor fur seme le faville,
> che mi scaldar, de la divina fiamma
> onde sono allumati più di mille;
> de l'Eneida dico, la qual mamma
> fummi, e fummi nutrice, poetando.   *Purg*.xxi.94-8

The *Aeneid* as the poetic nurse, the breast from which both Dante and Statius suck, is a metaphor beloved of Dante, and though the line in the next canto: "che le Muse lattar più ch'altri mai" (*Purg*. xxii.102), was written for Homer, it is a tribute which Dante gives more naturally to Virgil. Then look how Virgil springs into prominence with his own name and with an accompanying cloud of alliterative *v*'s:

> E per esser vivuto di là quando
> *v*isse *V*irgilio, assentirei un sole
> più che non deggio al mio uscir di bando.
> *V*olser *V*irgilio a me queste parole
> con *v*iso che, tacendo, disse "Taci";
> ma non può tutto la *v*irtù che *v*uole.   *Purg*.xxi.100-5

So we come to that human comedy of Virgil's modesty and Dante's knowing until, with Virgil's sanction, Dante can tell Statius what his eyes have already flashed:

Questi che guida in alto li occhi miei,
è quel Virgilio dal qual tu togliesti
forte a cantar de li uomini e d'i dèi.   124-6

It is the verb that you should look to there for your clue, for it is once again the word which Dante used in the beginning and it takes us back to that theme, which is to be dominant in *Purgatorio* xxii, of honour — honour naturally for Virgil:

tu se' solo colui da cu' io tolsi
lo bello stilo che m'ha fatto onore.   *Inf.*i.86-7

The canto ends rather differently from the way in which it began. There Statius was as Christ on the way to Emmaus, here he forgets beatitude, which you will see (101-2) he is ready to postpone for Virgil's sake, and his own status as a shade, and in his eagerness to embrace the author of his inspiration risks clasping, instead of Virgil's feet, the empty air. So to close the canto, Statius finds for us, on Virgil's account, a line which can epitomize the range of Dante's art, his giving substance to what else had none: "trattando l'ombre come cosa salda" (*Purg.* xxi.136; treating the shadows as a solid thing). By now we should have Statius, who has everything, and Virgil, who has nothing: Statius, I mean, who goes on to Paradise, and Virgil, who goes back to Hell. It is this balance which the new canto will redress. It begins with a reminiscence in a different and this time a legitimate key, of Francesca's compulsive love for Paolo in *Inferno* v: "Amore, acceso di virtù, sempre altro accese" (*Purg.* xxii.10-11), as against "Amor, ch' a nullo amato amar perdona" (*Inf.*v.103). Since Virgil learnt from Juvenal (*tanta dulcedine*) of Statius's cult for himself, he has returned affection with affection. But how, he asks with infinite delicacy, how could *you* have yielded to the sin of greed. And here apart from the surface language, which is, as we shall see, significant, we must remember *radix malorum est cupiditas* (avarice is the root of evil) fits especially Dante's view of the world and what is wrong with it. It is greed from which Christ came to free the world. It is the circle of greed which Dante and Statius are leaving behind them. The earthquake which ushered in the two eyes of the world reminds us of the principle of the *Monarchia* (I.xi.11): "Remota cupiditate omnino, nichil iustitie restat adversum" (when greed has wholly gone, justice has no enemy). So how could Statius himself be tainted by greed?

> Come poté trovar dentro al tuo seno
> loco avarizia, tra cotanto senno
> di quanto per tua cura fosti pieno?   *Purg*.xxii.22-4

I said that Virgil asks with infinite delicacy: and you will see, first, how Virgil disclaims the credit which Statius gave to him and to the *Aeneid*: "sanz' essa non fermai peso di dramma" (*Purg*.xxi.99), when he answers: "per tua cura" (*Purg*.xxii.24). And even more, look what Virgil admits him to: "tra cotanto senno" (23). Nominally it is the great wisdom of Statius which surely left no room for avarice. But we have met the phrase before and it carries still the implications and the associations of Dante's other use for it, when he was himself admitted into the company of the great poets: "sì ch'io fui sesto tra cotanto senno" (*Inf*.iv.102).

So Statius takes his place for Dante, if not for us, with the immortal names of poetry. It follows of course that the taint of greed does not cling to him, a wrong assumption because we did not know (how could we, since Dante had not hinted at it?) that avarice and prodigality are punished together in the circle so far labelled as of the "Avari" only. In parenthesis, I would say that Dante did not invent the prodigality of his Statius. It was an attribute of the rhetorician from Toulouse whom he mistook for the poet. Now repeatedly we find Dante taking from Juvenal the notion of the sweetness of Statius's poetry and speaking of the news which Juvenal brought to him in Limbo of Statius's reverence for the *Aeneid*. But the point of Juvenal's concern with Statius was the poverty of poets in spite of their genius. There is no hint in Juvenal that Statius was poor because he had been profligate; he was poor as all good poets are, because the world cares for other things than poetry. But Statius picks up the word which Virgil used when he transferred the merit from himself to Statius. "Per tua cura", said Virgil, you cultivated your mind. If it was my care, says Statius, you gave the impetus,

> E se non fosse ch'io drizzai mia cura,
> quand'io intesi là dove tu chiame.   *Purg*.xxii.37-8

In *Purgatorio* xxi we had the general confession of Statius of his dependence on Virgil. In *Purgatorio* xxii each modest enquiry of Virgil brings from Statius the particular rejoinder: It was you who put me on the path. We had better not say that this canto is the apotheosis of Virgil, because to use such language would deny the accompanying reality. But it is the highest tribute that can come from one poet to another; and of course it comes all the more warmly in that Statius speaks, but Dante dictates the terms. There is a difficulty, a crux not easily resolved, in that the first text to which Statius appeals as prompter of his reformation from prodigality is twisted by Dante to a sense which conspicuously it did not have.

> Quid non mortalia pectora cogis,
> Auri sacra fames? *Aen.*III.56-7

(To what will you not drive men's hearts, o cursed thirst for gold?) It is Virgil's comment on Polydorus killed by Polymnestor so that he could seize the treasures of Priam. Here *sacra* is a euphemism and what is hard to know is whether there are limits beyond which the thirst for gold will not drive men. I shall leave unanswered the question whether Dante mistook the sense, or whether this is an *aemulatio* which allows him the liberty to extend his author's meaning. (I should add that nowhere else does Dante show an inclination to warp his Virgil consciously; nor is the interpretation which in a moment he will place on the Fourth Eclogue in this same category).

So Statius, by his confession, would be in Hell, had it not been for Virgil's timely warning. But when you wrote of Thebes, of the mutual hatred of Eteocles and Polynices, "disse 'l cantor de' buccolici carmi" (*Purg.*xxii.57), you do not seem to be a Christian?

> non par che ti facesse ancor fedele
> la fede, sanza qual ben far non basta. 59-60

Usually, when Dante wishes to name Virgil he does so directly without the need for periphrasis. But this periphrasis, "disse il cantor de' buccolici carmi" (57), takes us straight to the second quotation from Virgil which pointed the way for Statius and, once again, what seemed merely a request for enlightenment can be turned back as a triumphant compliment. *It was you*: you made me a poet and you made me a Christian. "Tu prima m'inviasti" (64); "Per te poeta fui, per te cristiano" (73). Whatever innocent enquiry Virgil makes of Statius, Statius returns it to him as the sole author of his destiny. We are at the heart of the second canto and we had better pause to look more closely at Statius's second quotation out of Virgil.

> Ed elli a lui: "Tu prima m'inviasti
> verso Parnaso a ber ne le sue grotte,
> e prima appresso Dio m'alluminasti.
> Facesti come quei che va di notte,
>   che porta il lume dietro e sé non giova,
>   ma dopo sé fa le persone dotte,
> quando dicesti: 'Secol si rinova;
>   torna giustizia e primo tempo umano,
>   e progenie scende da ciel nova.'
> Per te poeta fui, per te cristiano."   64-73

For Dante's purposes it was usually enough that Virgil was the prophet of the Empire, but here for Statius he becomes the prophet of the Redemption also.

> Ultima Cumaei venit iam carminis aetas;
> magnus ab integro saeculorum nascitur ordo.
> Iam redit et Virgo, redeunt Saturnia regna:
> Iam nova progenies caelo demittitur alto.
>   *Ecloga* IV.4-7

Everybody since the fourth century had seen this prophetic text of Virgil and most had given it a Christian context (even if some, as St Jerome, had been more sceptical). Dante not only adopts it for Statius, thereby pushing back its history as a Christian announcement by a full three centuries, but makes of it the hinge between their destinies. The light which Virgil gave to Statius projected behind Virgil's back and, to the triumph of Virgil as the poet's double inspiration, we have the shadow: of Virgil unable to save himself.

> Facesti come quei che va di notte,
>   che porta il lume dietro e sé non giova.   67-8

In the matter of thirst for gold (*auri sacra fames*) it is Dante alone who puts a meaning, but an impossible one, on to Virgil's text. Of the Fourth Eclogue Dante was speaking in harmony with his time; and you will see how subtly its translation has been doctored to give it a Christian connotation. Not the beginning of a new span of centuries, but in the singular the *saeculum* — this world as opposed in Christian terminology to the next world — renewed by the Redemption. No wonder, so translated, that Statius saw its consonance with Christian preachers. But the merit of his conversion is more Virgil's than it is theirs: "Per te poeta fui, per te cristiano" (73). The telltale second-person pronoun (It was you) comes back: "e la parola tua" (79), "Tu dunque, che levato hai il coperchio" (94). Yet Statius, so persuaded, so convinced and converted, was tepid in his new belief. He dared not show what he really thought and, when Domitian persecuted the Christians, Statius bewailed their fate but was not ready to share in it. In secret he was baptized, in public he was a pagan still.

> E pria ch'io conducessi i Greci a' fiumi
>   di Tebe poetando, ebb' io battesmo;
>   ma per paura chiuso cristian fu'mi,
>   lungamente mostrando paganesmo.   88-91

So we end the episode, which began with Statius in the guise of Christ upon the pathway to Emmaus, with the same Statius afraid to show his faith. I say we end the episode, but that is not quite true. What we have left is the conversation between Virgil and Statius in which the former satisfies Statius's curiosity about the poet companions of Virgil in Limbo, whereby Dante supplies some names that were no more than names to him, something that is true both of the Greek and of some Latin poets. And with them there is naturally that Homer "che le Muse lattar più ch'altri mai" (102): the line which Dante uses for Homer and thinks for Virgil. And with the poets amongst that honourable company of Limbo, there are the heroes whom they wrote about, to whom Dante ascribes a reality he did not know they lacked. For how could Ripheus take his place in Paradise if he was not for Dante a historic fact? In *Inferno* iv we glimpsed this for Virgil's characters and it is fitting here we learn it now for Statius: not Eteocles and Polynices, not Jocasta, but all the gentle heroines of the *Thebaid* and the *Achilleid*, from Antigone to Deidamia, are here. And they include strangely enough one who has little right to be named as in Limbo, because Dante has forgotten that he had already condemned her to the circle of the soothsayers. This is Manto, the "figlia di Tiresia, e Teti" (113).

I have dutifully pointed out that sometimes Dante nods, having good precedent in Homer. But I hope I will be excused if I do not reproach him with his lapse, or seek excuses for it, or if I do not follow on, spying, as Dante did, on the poetic arguments of Virgil and Statius. All we are permitted is a peep:

> Elli givan dinanzi, e io soletto
> di retro, e ascoltava i lor sermoni,
> ch'a poetar mi davano intelletto.
> Ma tosto ruppe le dolci ragioni . . .   127-30

It would be nice of course if we could listen in. But I cannot supply the details and I have also left the main substance of our argument untouched. The two cantos were written, it has been said *ad majorem Virgilii gloriam*;[5] yet in effect Dante has rejected Virgil and chosen Statius. For the first problem we must ask, why? For the second we must ask both, why? and, how?

We may start again with that declaration of Statius about Virgil's role as prophet:

> Facesti come quei che va di notte,
> che porta il lume dietro e sé non giova,
> ma dopo sé fa le persone dotte.   67-9

According to the Barbi-Casini commentary the germ of this simile can be found in lines of Ennius quoted by Cicero. It may be that Ennius supplied the germ; but what he said was very different, more akin to what Dante says on the multiplication sum of charity:[6]

> Homo qui erranti comiter monstrat viam,
> Quasi lumen de suo lumine accendat, facit.
> Nihilominus ipsi lucet, cum illi accenderit.[7]

(Who kindly shows a wanderer his way lights as it were a lamp from his own light. He does not light himself the less when he has lit another). In this matter of similes, Dante's is more famous, but Ennius's surely is more sensible; for who can carry a light which is of use only to others after him and by no means to himself? Yet I suspect that Dante felt he had no choice. Virgil at his date can be a prophet, especially of Empire, but there were no preachers of Christianity for him to listen to; and if Dante had "saved" Virgil, against tradition, he would have lost Virgil as his guide, as the symbol of that *scola* (*Purg.*xxi.33) which is human reason this side faith. We should have lost the magnification of Virgil in these two cantos; and if Virgil were still here he would have lost the authority he had, to become an also-ran with Dante. Which is after all, what happens now to Statius, who began his career with us as a shadow reminding us of Christ and goes on to a dwindling part by Dante's side. Look for him in the index to *Paradiso*, you will realise by his non-appearance there that Dante cast him for a temporary role, had no real use for him but as a foil to Virgil's excellence. And as a footnote to Virgil's, necessary, relegation I would surmise that Dante "saved" Ripheus in Virgil's stead and as a token of his will to "save" his author.

Dante then needs Virgil as his prophet. But prophecy must be of use, or what use is it? That is the *why* of Statius, who fits the twin needs, by his dates, and by the medieval rating of his poetry. But what, you will say, about the *how*? Well, Dante gives us a hint:

> E pria ch'io conducessi i Greci a' fiumi
> di Tebe poetando, ebb' io battesmo.   88-9

When he wrote the last three books of the *Thebaid* (X-XII) Statius was a Christian, though he hid this from the world. One may ask, did Dante learn this interesting fact from some tradition, or from his spying out the symptoms in Statius's poetry? Now it transpires, since the effort of medieval exegesis of classical texts was to make them look forward as the Old Testament to the New, that there were those who found a Christian Statius, especially in his account of the Altar of Clemency (*Theb*.XII.481), which has seemed to many to be assimilable to the Altar of the Unknown God. More recently, Giorgio Padoan has made a brave effort to shift attention to Theseus, the slayer of the Minotaur, who like that other slayer of monsters, Hercules, was capable of taking on the guise of the Redeemer in the medieval gaze.[8] Unfortunately, Padoan makes this case for Theseus as "Redentore" more convincingly as a general proposition than he does for Theseus as depicted by Statius. And certainly, since Statius was a "chiuso cristian", Dante may have meant that he left a pagan surface to his poetry, as to his life, for those reasons of timidity towards Domitian. In which case it is no good our looking for what he left out and Dante could not hope to find, and all we have is Dante's word for it. I think that we can see the "Why" much better than the "How". Dante needed Statius as the touchstone and the product of Virgil: whether he found him Christianized in the tradition of his time, or wrote his baptismal certificate himself, is hard for us to say. So let us leave them, while they are still together as a trio on the slopes of Purgatory, where Dante twice bestows on

Statius and on Virgil an epithet which equates them for us, in spite of their different destiny. In *Purgatorio* xxvii they are "i gran maestri" and even more picturesquely in *Purgatorio* xxiv they receive one of those Dantesque feudal appellations which puts them equal with the great nobles who stand around the throne. For where God himself is "lo imperador che sempre regna" it is feudal dignitaries who stand closest to Him. For proof of this we have only to look ahead to *Paradiso* xxv, where Dante is examined on Hope by the apostle James. St James addresses Dante thus:

> Poi che per grazia vuol che tu t'affronti
> lo nostro Imperadore, anzi la morte,
> ne l'aula più secreta co' suoi conti,
> sì che, veduto il ver di questa corte.   *Par*.xxv.40-3

In Paradise God in his innermost chamber is surrounded by his counts, in Purgatory Virgil and Statius are also of that company,

> e io rimasi in via con esso i due
> che fuor del mondo sì gran marescalchi.
> *Purg*.xxiv.98-9

Not, you will notice, just Statius, who is saved, but Statius and Virgil equally. The analogy in nomenclature, for Virgil and Statius on the one hand and for the apostles on the other, is a reminder that for Dante, Rome, as personified in Virgil, is a full part of the providential scheme of history.

Notes

[1]M. Santoro, "Virgilio personaggio della *Divina Commedia*", *Cultura e scuola*, 14 (1965), 343-55 (p. 353), speaks of "la solidarietà della cultura", "l'eccellenza della poesia", of meetings with "poeti e dotti di ogni età" in the poem. Santoro (p.352) quotes Flora: "L'incontro di Stazio con Virgilio è la prima poesia dell'umanesimo", which is an odd assessment. Compare with this the judgment of E. Paratore, "Dante e il mondo classico", *Tradizione e struttura in Dante* (Florence, 1968) pp. 25-54; previously in *Dante*, ed. U. Parricchi (Rome, 1965), 109-29 (p. 127) when he speaks of "l'irriducibilità della personalità e dell'opera di Dante negli schemi dell'Umanesimo rinascimentale. Egli è un perfetto figlio del Medioevo." See also p.129 in the same article.

[2]Juvenal VII.82-6: "Curritur ad uocem iucundam et carmen amicae Thebaidos, laetam cum fecit Statius urbem promisitque diem: tanta dulcedine captos adficit ille animos tantaque libidine uolgi auditor . . ."

[3]See the interesting passage in G. Padoan, "Il mito di Teseo e il cristianesimo di Stazio", *Lettere italiane*, 11 (1959) 432-57, where Padoan first rebukes Sapegno, who had suggested that the Christianity of Statius might be an invention, based maybe on some legend. We must understand, says Padoan, that the concept of *"finzione"* is alien in Dante, and to underline this he stresses the "serietà morale e religiosa rigorosissima" (pp. 434-5) of Dante. But in the next paragraph he concedes that Dante needed little to set his imagination to work, and quotes Parodi on this little: "un qualsiasi frusto e grossolano canovaccio" (p.435). I find it hard to reconcile such opposing judgments, so closely juxtaposed.

[4]G. Boccaccio, *Il filocolo* (Bari, 1938) p.564.

[5]A. Ronconi, "L'incontro di Stazio e Virgilio", *Cultura e scuola*, 14 (1965), 566-71 (p. 567).

[6]*Purg*.xv.49-57:

> Perché s'appuntano i vostri disiri
> dove per compagnia parte si scema,
> invidia move il mantaco a' sospiri.
> Ma se l'amor de la spera supprema
> torcesse in suso il disiderio vostro,
> non vi sarebbe al petto quella tema:
> ché, per quanti si dice più lì "nostro",
> tanto posside più di ben ciascuno,
> e più di caritate arde in quel chiostro.

[7]Quoted by Cicero in *De officiis* I.xvi. Ennius's simile might more readily become the basis for *Purg*.xv.49-57 than for *Purg*.xxii.67-9.

[8]G. Padoan, "Il mito di Teseo e il cristianesimo di Stazio", *Lettere italiane* 11 (1959), 432-57.

Dante's Virgil: Purgatorio XXX

Jennifer Petrie

Purgatorio xxx describes one of the great moments of transition in the *Commedia*, when Virgil disappears and Beatrice takes his place. This makes it a suitable canto in which to treat of Dante's two guides. And, although in many respects this is the canto of Beatrice, I take primarily as my subject Dante's Virgil, first and foremost his character and significance in the poem, and only secondarily, Virgil, the Roman poet who influenced Dante,[1] before I finally come to Beatrice. As Dante moves from one guide to another, so he moves from one way of thinking to another and also from one way of writing poetry to another. In Roberto Mercuri's phrase, there is "un salto qualitativo".[2]

Indeed, by making use of two guides, Dante makes the main division in his other world fall here at the end of the *Purgatorio* rather than where there is an obvious division, at the end of the *Inferno*: between the realm of the damned in Hell, and the realm of the saved in Purgatory and Heaven. In doing this there are clear artistic advantages in that Dante, by isolating in some sense the *Paradiso*, can present Hell and Purgatory as a balanced, antithetical pair, both places of torment and yet so different. Nevertheless, the use of two guides, one of whom is a pagan, unfit to enter Heaven, yet fit to lead Dante through a

Christian Hell and Purgatory, is a strange procedure.

As is well known, Dante's Virgil has been understood from the fourteenth-century commentators onward to represent Reason. Beatrice by contrast is understood as Theology, or Reason perfected by Revelation. In recent years, however, this interpretation has often been criticized as over-schematic or as a misreading of Dante's allegorical method.[3] This method, it is argued, is not "personification allegory" (like that of the *Roman de la Rose* or of medieval morality plays), but rather it follows the patterns of medieval Biblical exegesis as set out by Dante in the *Letter to Cangrande*[4] and in particular that of "typology" – the "fulfilment" of one event by another in a scheme of historical correspondences centring on the life, death and resurrection of Christ. In this view Virgil's role in the *Commedia* in some way "fulfils" his life on earth.[5]

Clearly, it is reasonable to assume that there should be some correspondence between Dante's fictional Virgil and the historical Virgil, even without having recourse to biblical typology. However it would, I believe, be wrong to be over-dismissive of the traditional view of Virgil representing Reason. This may at times have been applied too thoroughly and too schematically in such a way as to reduce the remarkably lifelike action of the poem to scenes from a sort of morality play. But in the wider structure of the poem as well as in the many didactic passages, the traditional view makes sense. The "story" of the *Commedia* in its barest outline is that of the journey of a man from a state of utter moral disorientation (the "selva oscura", the moral significance of which is made explicit at the end of *Purgatorio* xxx) to the knowledge of God. This journey takes him through the discovery of moral evil (*Inferno*) and of ways of overcoming moral evil (*Purgatorio*) to a vision of a spiritual order of truth and love (*Paradiso*). "Reason" is an appropriate guide in the moral lessons of the first two realms, but for the spiritual, supernatural lessons of the *Paradiso*, the guidance of Revelation is needed. The initiative is taken by the three "donne benedette" (*Inf.*ii.124), the Virgin Mary, St Lucy and Beatrice herself. Virgil is the *instrument* of Beatrice: in the salvation of Dante's soul, Reason is the instrument of Grace.

Virgil's *didactic* role in the *Commedia* certainly corresponds to the idea of "Reason". When answering Dante's question on how love can be reconciled with moral responsibility, Virgil begins (*Purg.*xviii.46-8):

> Quanto ragion qui vede,
> dir ti poss' io; da indi in là t'aspetta
> pur a Beatrice, ch'è opra di fede.

Beatrice's role as Theology is most transparently set out a little later in the same canto: "La nobile virtù Beatrice intende/per lo libero arbitrio" (73-4). A similar instance occurs in *Purgatorio* vi.44-5 where Virgil, replying to a question about prayer, refers Dante to Beatrice, whom he describes as "quella", "che lume fia tra 'l vero e lo 'ntelletto."

Schematic and uninspiring as these allegorizations may sound, they are, I think, essential structural props in the making up of the poem; and the two figures of Virgil and Beatrice cannot be fully understood without them.

But there is more to Virgil than the bare abstraction "Reason". If Dante's poetry involves the world of abstractions, it also involves the concrete world of historical reality. (Hence the relevance of "typology" to an understanding of Dante's allegory). So perhaps more helpful for an understanding of Dante's Virgil (outside the didactic episodes) than the abstraction "Reason" is the idea of the pagan classical world which Virgil exemplifies as the poet of Rome. This world, for Dante, can in fact be seen as a concrete embodiment of the abstract notion of "natural reason" or reason as seen apart from Christian Revelation. For Dante the achievements, virtues, political and moral insights of the pagan world are the achievements of natural reason historically realized under the guidance of Divine Providence, but outside Christian Revelation. Dante's "humanistic" admiration for this culture is enormous, to the extent of seeking in it the divinely appointed guide for man in all temporal affairs.

In the *Monarchia* Dante argues that the pagan Roman Empire grew, under the guidance of providence, to be the principle of world government. Roman law was the embodiment of universal law. And within this order man was best able to achieve his earthly, temporal happiness "operatione proprie virtutis", through the activity of man's own natural virtues, unaided by grace, but guided by "phylosophica documenta", the teachings of the pagan philosophers. This goal of temporal happiness, achieved by man's own human efforts is represented by the Earthly Paradise, the Garden of Eden. The other goal, that of eternal happiness, cannot be achieved without grace and the guidance of "documenta spiritualia" which transcend the limited human reason.[6] This may serve as a commentary on Dante's two guides, Virgil, who leads his pupil as far as the Earthly Paradise, and Beatrice, the guide through the celestial Paradise. In the *Monarchia* Dante insists on the autonomy of man's secular "humanistic" activities, which in political terms means the strict separation of Church and State. Here, I think, is an important key to the figure of Virgil and to the fact that he is not saved. Virgil must remain a pagan to the end because the world of pagan culture, of reason and nature, must preserve its autonomy. A Christian guide or a Christianized pagan would not have provided the necessary contrast with Beatrice and might have blurred Dante's insistence on the positive achievements of man apart from the Christian faith, within the limits of reason and nature. Paradoxically it is Dante's humanism which "damns" Virgil.

The tragic element which accompanies the treatment of the fate of the character Virgil reflects, I think, a tension between Virgil seen as a representative or allegorical figure and Virgil seen as an individual person, the object of Dante's growing affection as the poem progresses. On the one hand there is a statement of the achievements and limits of unaided human reason and virtue, and on the other the problem of the justice of the personal condemnation of this good man Virgil.[7] Such tensions are perhaps inherent in Dante's method of writing which at once involves a Christian view of individual salvation necessarily treating each character as a person in his or her own right, and invests the characters with a moral, intellectual or theological significance which itself can affect their placing in the next world. It is certainly true that Dante sees the question of the justice of the condemnation of the individual "good pagan" as a problem and raises it explicitly in *Paradiso* xix. But he leaves it unresolved as something humanly insoluble, comprehensible only in terms of a divine justice which transcends man's limited understanding, but from which, nevertheless, all human notions of justice derive. Dante also allows for the salvation of a few individual pagans, all "special cases".[8] No doubt he could have made a special case for Virgil but he refrains from doing so.

But why, it may be asked, did Dante choose Virgil as his representative of pagan culture? If his structural and didactic role corresponds to the idea of "reason", would not Aristotle be more appropriate? Virgil guides Dante through a world of moral self-discovery, where he learns about sin, justice, penance and self-discipline; would it not be more appropriate to have a pagan moralist such as Aristotle again, or Cicero, whose influence can be found in the moral structure of Dante's *Inferno*?[9] Many answers can be given to this and the most significant have all to do with the fact that Virgil is a poet, indeed the poet, "nostra maggior musa" (*Par*.xv.26); "de li altri poeti onore e lume" (*Inf*.i.82).[10] Throughout the *Commedia* Dante's own self-consciousness is apparent as a poet and as a poet who is setting himself an extraordinary task. In one sense Dante's journey is his poem and on several occasions he compares his tremendous literary enterprise to a sea-voyage.[11] Significantly, both his other-worldly guides are associated in some way with poetry and moreover with Dante's own poetry. Beatrice was the inspiration of his youthful lyrics, of his self-discovery and "coming-of-age" as a poet. This self-consciously "poetic" angle on Beatrice is already apparent in the *Vita nuova*.[12] Virgil is welcomed as a literary inspiration (*Inf*.i.85-7):

> Tu se' lo mio maestro e 'l mio autore,
> tu se' solo colui da cu' io tolsi
> lo bello stilo che m'ha fatto onore.

These well-known lines raise problems in connection with the precise nature of Virgil's influence on Dante. However I am at present concerned less with these than with the fact that Virgil is from the beginning acclaimed as Dante's greatest literary inspiration. Dante is like his Statius for whom the *Aeneid* was "mamma" and "nutrice, poetando" (*Purg*.xxi.97-8). One could perhaps say that the *Inferno* and the *Purgatorio* are "Virgilian" in inspiration in the very broad sense that they set out, if not to imitate Virgil at least to emulate him, to write poetry on a similar scale; but that the inspiration of the *Paradiso* is akin to that of the *Vita nuova* — associated with Beatrice.

Of course the differences between the *Divina Commedia* and Virgil's *Aeneid* are considerable. Dante himself seems to be drawing attention to a major formal difference in *Inferno* xx-

xxi, when Virgil's description of the *Aeneid* as "l'alta mia tragedia" (*Inf.*xx.113) is followed shortly afterwards by Dante's reference to his own poem as "la mia comedía" (*Inf.*xxi.2). The distinction for Dante is as much one of style as one of content. "Tragic" is the term used by Dante in the *De vulgari eloquentia* II.iv.5-6 for the most elevated type of style; "comic" for an intermediate style. And indeed while Dante may have learnt much from Virgil the styles of the two poets are certainly dissimilar.[13] Moreover the narrative forms are quite different and also the approach to historical events and characters.

There are, however, many echoes of Virgil's poetry[14] and Dante makes considerable use of Virgilian themes. Most important among these are the central theme of the journey of Aeneas for the sake of the founding of Rome and that of Aeneas's visit to the Underworld in *Aeneid* VI. These play a significant part in the structure and conception of the *Commedia*. Aeneas's journey is for the purpose of founding Rome, the city destined to have an eternal empire, to give justice to the world.[15] Dante is led by Virgil to the Earthly Paradise of natural human perfection which, as we have seen, in the *Monarchia* represents the temporal good of man to be aimed at within a world-order presided over by the Roman Empire. It may be noted that in *Monarchia* II, when Dante is trying to prove that Rome was divinely destined to rule the world, his main authority — whom he constantly quotes — is Virgil: "Poeta noster".

Aeneas's journey and discovery of his destiny requires a visit to the Underworld to see the shade of his father Anchises. Dante's journey echoes this, from his hesitations in *Inferno* ii.32, "Io non Enea, io non Paulo sono", to his meeting in Heaven with his ancestor Cacciaguida (compared at *Par.*xv.25 to Anchises), who tells Dante of his destiny and his mission as a poet (*Par.*xvii).

For Dante therefore, as for Dante's Statius, the *Aeneid* was mother and nurse. Statius may indeed provide a model in his debt to Virgil for Dante himself. For Statius Virgil was first of all a literary inspiration (*Purg.*xxi.94-9); secondly, the poet who through one line of the *Aeneid* led him to repent of his extravagant living (*Purg.*xxii.37-42); and thirdly, the poet who attracted him to Christianity (*Purg.*xxii.64-93). In the *Commedia* Virgil the character is for Dante what the poet was for Statius, a moral guide and a guide towards Christianity (represented in the *Commedia* by Beatrice). Clearly this corresponds to something seen by Dante in Virgil's poetry. In *Inferno* ii.67-9, Beatrice appeals to Virgil to help Dante through his "parola ornata". The concept of "ornatus" is most important in medieval rhetoric and poetics[16] and corresponds in a literary work to the formal beauty which is understood as something distinct from content but which can serve to make the content attractive to the hearer or reader. The beauty of Virgil's language, Beatrice seems to imply, will ensure that Dante, the poet who has seen in Virgil his master in "bello stilo" (*Inf.*i.87), will listen to Virgil when he will listen to nobody else.

As for the content of Virgil's poetry, Dante probably saw it, in part at least, through the moralizing, allegorizing spectacles of his cultural tradition. The late Latin writer Macrobius in his *Saturnalia* saw the *Aeneid* as a compendium of all human wisdom and knowledge.[17] Fulgentius, the sixth-century commentator on Virgil, read into the *Aeneid* an allegory of the various stages of man's life. Dante certainly knew this interpretation of the *Aeneid* as he himself uses it in *Convivio* IV.[18] The view of Virgil as a moral or philosophical poet continued through the Middle Ages beyond Dante. A generation later Petrarch was to see the *Aeneid* as a philosphical work "de perfectione humana".[19] Meanwhile as we have seen, Dante recognized that Virgil was the poet of Rome and Rome for Dante meant above all justice: it was the city intended as centre and capital of a world-order designed for the good and fulfilment of man.

Virgil's poetry then, offers a vision of human perfection and of the attainment of a just human society and, through the poet's "parola ornata", makes this vision attractive. The idea is reminiscent of Lucretius's image of honey on the edge of the medicine-cup but Dante possibly takes it further. In *Convivio* II.xi Dante says that every poem has two clearly distinct aspects: "bellezza" and "bontade".[20] The "bellezza" lies in the formal aspects, "l'ornamento de le parole", and is achieved through the poet's skill in handling grammatical, rhetorical and metrical techniques.[21] The "bontade", on the other hand, resides in the "sentenza", the meaning or content. The two aspects are quite separable: one may enjoy the beauty of a poem even if one has no idea of what it is about. A literary work may have "bellezza" without "bontade" (and vice versa); in other words it could have a meaning which would be untrue or immoral while having a beautiful form. The implications of this may be seen at times in the *Commedia*. Francesca in *Inferno* v presents herself in a beautiful way, using beautiful language, but is a sinner in Hell. Ulysses leads his men on their "folle volo" (*Inf.*xxvi.125) with an eloquent speech (112-20). In *Purgatorio* xxvi the poets Guido Guinizelli and Arnaut Daniel are both praised in the highest terms for their *style*: the "dolci detti" (112) of Guido, the "father" of writers of sweet and elegant "dolci e leggiadre" love-poetry (97-9); the craftsmanship of Arnaut, the "miglior fabbro del parlar materno" (117). Both poets are burning in the circle of the lustful. This of course need not be taken as an indictment of their poetry, merely of their lives; but the very choice of these two poets as examples of lust surely must reflect in some way on their works. It was the example of the courtly romance of Lancelot which led to the adultery of Paolo and Francesca (*Inf.*v.127-38) and in speaking of her own love she echoes, in line 100, "Amor, ch'al cor gentil ratto s'apprende", a famous poem of Guinizelli himself.[22] It seems likely Dante is accusing his two masters in love poetry and, by implication himself in some of his poems, of a morally irresponsible "bellezza" without a corresponding "bontade". Virgil on the other hand in the *Aeneid* IV, presents love as a destructive passion, a moral "culpa",[23] an impediment to Aeneas's journey which the hero has to leave behind and which destroys Dido. Dante's view of love is, in the case of Beatrice at least, a much more positive one, but the moral dimension of Virgil's treatment of Dido is a significant background to *Inferno* v. Dido, it will be remembered, is one of the sinners punished with Francesca. In Virgil the beauty of form is balanced by the moral seriousness of the content.

This is in part at least, I believe, the significance of Dante's dream of the Siren (*Purg.*xix) and Virgil's role in it. In this dream Dante sees a hideously ugly, deformed, stammering woman. He looks at her and beneath his gaze, she becomes beautiful, loses her stammer and begins to sing. She is the fascinating Siren who lures sailors away by her song. At this point there appears "una donna" "santa e presta" (26); she summons Virgil and he, with his eyes fixed on the lady, rips open the Siren's dress revealing her foul-smelling belly; and

Dante awakes.

The interpretation of the figures has been much discussed.[24] It is clear from later in the canto that the Siren represents the three sins of avarice, gluttony and lust (*Purg.*xix.58-9). These have been defined (*Purg.*xvii.133-9) as an excessive love for goods which are not the ultimate good. The meaning of the lady is less clear, but the general associations of virtue, truth or justice are evident. Virgil is usually understood as Reason, revealing sin for what it is. His action may be seen as corresponding to his role in the *Inferno*. The fact that the Siren becomes beautiful under Dante's gaze is a little more difficult to explain: the general idea seems to be that evil is tempting only in so far as man allows it to be. Dante's gaze is sometimes associated with sloth as it is in the circle of the slothful that the dream occurs.[25] However the implication that Dante is too lazy to notice how ugly the woman is seems a little strange: she is so self-evidently hideous. Another interpretation stresses the idea of subjectivity or self-projection in the sins represented by the Siren.[26] It is an interesting interpretation, but somewhat difficult to relate to Dante's ideas on love and moral responsibility as they are set out in the *Commedia*.

In my opinion Dante's view of poetry may be relevant here. The Siren's charm resides above all in her song and in it she uses all the techniques of language as seductively as she can:

> "Io son", cantava, "io son dolce serena,
> che ' marinari in mezzo mar dismago;
> tanto son di piacere a sentir piena!"   *Purg.*xix.19-21

Repetition, alliteration and assonance all serve to produce a sense of alluring sweetness. It is all "bellezza"; there is no "bontade" as the "meaning" of the Siren is the sin she represents. Perhaps then Dante's gaze which makes the Siren beautiful is connected with his power as a poet to embellish whatever he wishes. Dante may here be accusing himself of having at times embellished sin through poetry. Virgil, the poet of justice with his eyes on the lady (whether she represents truth or justice or virtue), reveals sin as it is.[27]

Later in the same canto Virgil exhorts Dante to turn his eyes away from earth to the "logoro" or "lure" (the image is from falconry) whirled by God in the heavens. This is one instance of a frequently recurring idea in the *Purgatorio*: that of the beauty of the heavens calling man and drawing him upwards towards God:

> Chiamavi 'l cielo e 'ntorno vi si gira,
> mostrandovi le sue bellezze etterne.   *Purg.*xiv.148-9

The principle of "bellezza" and "bontade" applies to Creation: the visual beauty of the universe is its outward attraction, drawing men towards its inner meaning. Virgil's poetry reflects God's Creation, in that the formal beauty serves to draw the reader to goodness and truth. This is the example which Dante as a poet is to follow.

Finally, for Dante, Virgil's poetry points towards Christianity, even though it never gets there. As a poet Virgil signifies more than "Reason"; he has certain insights foreshadowing the Christian faith. Hence Statius is attracted to Christianity because he sees a certain harmony between its teaching and Virgil's Fourth Eclogue (*Purg.*xxii.70-81), the strange poem foretelling the birth of a child who is to restore the Golden Age of primeval happiness. In *Purgatorio* xxviii when Dante, Virgil and Statius have reached the Earthly Paradise, the lost Garden of Eden, situated at the summit of Dante's mountain of Purgatory, Matelda, its beautiful guardian, explains that the poets of ancient times who wrote of the happiness of the Golden Age perhaps had "dreamt" of the lost Eden:

> Quelli ch'anticamente poetaro
> l' età de l'oro e suo stato felice,
> forse in Parnaso esto loco sognaro. *Purg.*xxviii.139-41

This idea of a myth hinting at a Christian truth might be taken as applicable to other pagan myths — certainly much of Dante's use of mythology in the *Commedia* suggests this.[28] Virgil as a poet, as *the* poet, through myth is able somehow to point beyond the limits of natural reason. Poetry can therefore be seen as the culmination of human achievements; hence Statius speaks of himself as a poet: "col nome che più dura e più onora / era io di là" (*Purg.*xxi.85-6).

Dante rejects any notion of *conscious* prophecy in the case of the Fourth Eclogue or elsewhere; he does not, as some medievals may have done, see Virgil as a "Gentile prophet".[29] Virgil's light is of benefit to those coming after him, but not to himself (*Purg.*xxii.67-9). Virgil remains a pagan poet, his work is the culmination of natural human achievement. Here again one may observe the paradox of Dante's "Christian humanism": his elevated claims for pagan poetry (and poetry in general as an autonomous human activity) mean that his Virgil is not saved by his own insights.

Purgatorio xxx provides an epilogue to the entire present-ation of Virgil in the two first *cantiche*. It describes, as I said, the transition between the world of Virgil and that of Beatrice. There has been a pause: Virgil has formally taken his leave of Dante at the end of *Purgatorio* xxvii, declaring his own work completed and proclaiming his pupil free and able to follow his own "piacere" (131). However, although Virgil can see no further "of himself" (*Purg*.xxvii.129), he continues to be present in the background. He smiles at Matelda's words on the ancient poets (*Purg*.xxviii.145-7) and in *Purgatorio*xxix.57 he is as astonished as Dante is at the sight of the mysterious allegorical procession, representing Revelation of which he knew nothing, and his face appears "carca di stupor" to Dante's scrutiny. Virgil is passive, out of his depth, and yet admitted to this lost Eden which he had hinted at in his own poetry of the Golden Age.

Through the middle of the forest of the Earthly Paradise there runs a stream which seems to serve as a barrier. Virgil pass beyond it. Dante has not crossed it, although he has longed to do so to reach the beautiful Matelda on the other side (*Purg*.xxviii.70-5). It is on the other side of this stream that the mysterious procession appears and finally, Beatrice herself. Dante cannot cross the stream and come over to Beatrice until he has broken down and repented of his infidelity to her.

Between the world of Virgil then and that of Beatrice, there is a gap and a barrier. And this corresponds to a certain discontinuity on the level of understanding. Virgil has led Dante to believe that Beatrice will be welcoming: laughing and happy (*Purg*.vi.48), her eyes smiling (*Purg*.xxvii.136), but he is wrong. He has proclaimed Dante free and morally purified, "libero, dritto e sano è tuo arbitrio" (*Purg*.xxvii.140), and he is right from his own point of view. But when Dante encounters Beatrice he has to repent — radically — of something which is perhaps not conceivable in Virgil's terms. And it is here in *Purgatorio* xxx at the moment of Beatrice's appearance and Dante's realization that he is alone, without the support of

Virgil, that this "gap" is expressed most powerfully.
The beginning of the canto strikes a note of expectancy and strangeness, a sense of the unpredictable. The allegorical procession has stopped, with the triumphal chariot (the centre of the procession) immediately opposite Dante. The participants give three mysterious calls or chants in Latin (11, 19, 21) which give a sort of liturgical solemnity to the expectation which they express. The first two are biblical (or liturgical); [30] the third, by a remarkable juxtaposition is from Virgil himself (*Aen*.VI.883), from the passage in which Anchises predicts the untimely death of the young Marcellus. Out of context, however, the phrase: "manibus o date lilia plenis", need not contain any explicit reference to this episode.[31] The precise reference of the lines is hard to determine, and their enigmatic nature is probably deliberate. Clearly, however, there is a tribute to Virgil. Here at least his poetry and the language of the bible are, prior to Beatrice's coming, allowed to touch.

The suspense is further prolonged by the simile of the rising sun (22-7) and the description of the "cloud" of flowers thrown by the angels (28-30). At last Beatrice appears:

> sovra candido vel cinta d'uliva
> donna m'apparve, sotto verde manto
> vestita di color di fiamma viva.   31-3

The emblematic tone of the language, the colours of faith, hope and charity, the olive wreath of wisdom, fit Beatrice's role as a figure in the pageant, as "Lady Theology". But in the characteristic verb "apparve" and indeed in the use of symbolic colours for Beatrice's dress, the language echoes strikingly certain passages in the *Vita nuova*: "Apparve vestita di nobilissimo colore, umile e onesto, sanguigno, cinta e ornata a la guisa che a sua giovanissima etade si convenia" (*VN* II.3) and "ne l'ultimo di questi die avvenne che questa mirabile donna apparve a me vestita di colore bianchissimo" (*VN* III.1). If her role in the *Commedia* is Theology, she is also the Beatrice of the *Vita nuova*.

Dante experiences a recovery of his childhood love and the fear that marked it. Like a frightened child he turns to Virgil:

> Tosto che ne la vista mi percosse
> l'alta virtù che già m'avea trafitto
> prima ch'io fuor di puerizia fosse,

> volsimi a la sinistra col respitto
> col quale il fantolin corre a la mamma
> quando ha paura o quando elli è afflitto,
> per dicere a Virgilio: "Men che dramma
> di sangue m'è rimaso che non tremi:
> conosco i segni de l'antica fiamma".   40-8

Dante's childlike and affectionate dependence on Virgil, often apparent in the course of the poem, is expressed to its fullest degree in the word "mamma". Line 48, Dante's last words to Virgil, is a quotation from *Aen*.IV.23: "agnosco veteris vestigia flammae". They are the words of Dido as she realizes that she is falling in love with Aeneas. There is perhaps an inappropriateness in the reference to Dido: her passion is condemned in *Inferno* v. It does, however, serve to heighten the sense of dread which accompanies Dante's feeling: the line of Virgil has now acquired a personal meaning for him. At the same time the reference to Dido possibly hints at the gulf between Virgil and Beatrice.

It is at this point that Dante realizes that Virgil has gone. Here we see the remarkable boldness of Dante's art. Instead of attempting in any way to attenuate the sadness of losing Virgil, he heightens the painful element. He could have let Virgil depart after his solemn leave-taking at the end of *Purgatorio* xxvii; but Dante prefers to give full expression to a sense of desolation, of being abandoned when he wanted Virgil's support and companionship:

> Ma Virgilio n'avea lasciati scemi
> di sé, Virgilio dolcissimo patre,
> Virgilio a cui per mia salute die'mi;
> né quantunque perdeo l'antica matre,
> valse a le guance nette di rugiada
> che, lagrimando, non tornasser atre.   49-54

Beatrice seems momentarily almost forgotten in this eloquent lament for Virgil, as if she like the Earthly Paradise were no compensation for his loss. It might be better to say that she is too intimidating for her presence to be a compensation at this stage. Her first words cut sharply into the lament without any introduction:

> Dante, perché Virgilio se ne vada,
> non pianger anco, non piangere ancora;

ché pianger ti conven per altra spada.   55-7

The first word Beatrice speaks is Dante's name. This is the only occasion in which it occurs in the *Commedia* and Dante (63) virtually apologizes for its use here. The uniqueness – and rhetorical impropriety – of this use of Dante's name gives it all the more force. Beatrice is striking at the core of Dante's personality at this moment when, for the first time since the beginning of the poem, Dante is alone without the guidance and support of Virgil.

The remainder of the canto consists of Beatrice's accusation against Dante which is addressed to the angelic bystanders. It can be summarized briefly as follows. Dante in his youth was a person of exceptional promise such as could lead to remarkable achievements, but which could also, if wasted, do correspondingly great harm (109-20). During her lifetime Beatrice had turned Dante's inclinations to the good (121-3), but after her death he had turned away from her, led astray by specious images of good (124-32). Dreams and memories of her were of no avail: he fell so low that finally only the sight of Hell could save him. For this purpose Beatrice had begged Virgil's help (133-41).

Here Beatrice's significance in the poem is hinted at and in the next canto it is made more explicit. His love for her had led him to desire God, the ultimate good (*Purg*.xxxi.22-4). Her beauty was the summit of natural beauty to him (49-51); her death brought home to him the transitoriness of all earthly goods and the need to look beyond this world for permanence (52-7). But Dante had not learnt his lesson and so had dissipated his life.

Beatrice, like Virgil, is both a poetic and a moral inspiration. In her, in a different way, beauty leads on to goodness. Dante's literary and poetic "humanism" takes another form in her case. In a way that is not true of Virgil's poetry or of classical culture in general, her beauty made the world of faith attractive to him. Her death especially, is associated with his sense of another world. The figure of Beatrice allows for a continuity in Dante's thought between human love and the love of God. In the case of Virgil there is a discontinuity: as a poet of truth and justice he can lead Dante towards the love of God and towards Beatrice, but no further. And so Dante must give up Virgil and leave his world behind in order to enter that of Beatrice. It is a tribute both to Virgil and to the seriousness with which Dante approaches the *Paradiso*, the spiritual world of Beatrice, that the transition is not an easy one.

Notes

[1]For a full bibliography on Virgil in the *Commedia,* see "Virgilio", *Enc.d.* V, 1030-49.
[2]R. Mercuri, "Conosco i segni de l'antica fiamma", *Cultura neolatina* 31 (1971) 237-93. (I am grateful to Dr R. Kirkpatrick for recommending this article).
[3]See for example, R. Hollander, *Allegory in Dante's Commedia"* (Princeton, 1969).
[4]*Dantis Alagherii Epistolae*: *The Letters of Dante* ed. Paget Toynbee, second edition (Oxford, 1966), *Epistola* X.7 (p.173) or *Epistola* XIII elsewhere.
[5]For a discussion of this form of allegory see P. Armour's essay above.
[6]*Mon.*III.xv.7-8: "Duos igitur fines providentia illa inenarrabilis homini proposuit intendendos: beatitudinem scilicet huius vite, que in operatione proprie virtutis consistit et per terrestrem paradisum figuratur; et beatitudinem vite ecterne, que consistit in fruitione divini aspectus ad quam propria virtus ascendere non potest, nisi lumine divino adiuta, que per paradisum celestem intelligi datur. Ad has quidem beatitudines, velut ad diversas conclusiones, per diversa media venire oportet. Nam ad primam per phylosophica documenta venimus, dummodo illa sequamur secundum virtutes morales et intellectuales operando; ad secundam vero per documenta spiritualia que humanam rationem transcendunt, dummodo illa sequamur secundum virtutes theologicas operando, fidem spem scilicet et karitatem."
[7]For a very thorough discussion of the theological problems raised by Dante's "good pagans" and of the condemnation of Virgil in particular see K. Foster, "The Two Dantes" in *The Two Dantes and Other Studies* (London, 1977) pp. 156-253.
[8]These are Cato (*Purg.*i.75: assuming that this line does refer to Cato's ultimate salvation); Trajan (*Par.*xx.44-8; 106-117); the Trojan Ripheus (*Par.*xx.67-72; 118-129). For these characters see J.H. Whitfield's discussion of *Purgatorio* xxi-xxii above.
[9]See Sapegno's note on *Inf.*xi.22-4.
[10]See *Inf.*iv. for "l'altissimo poeta" (80), "fannomi onore" (93) and "quel segnor de l'altissimo canto" (95-6).
[11]Two conspicuous instances are *Purg.*i.1-3 and *Par.*ii.1-18.
[12]I am thinking especially of the build-up to the first *canzone,* "Donne ch'avete intelletto d'amore, *VN* XVII-XIX, in which Dante describes his search for "matera nuova e più nobile che la passata" (*VN* XVII). His literary self-consciousness is also apparent in his analyses of his poems, and his justification of his use of the personified "Amor" in *VN* XXV.
[13]See J. H. Whitfield, *Dante and Virgil* (Oxford, 1949) pp. 61-106 for a discussion of the differences between the two poets. Whitfield stresses Virgil's refined and ennobling use of style and character in his presentation of history, as opposed to Dante's use of the familiar, material and homely in character and style, in his presentation of a spiritual world.
[14]For Virgilian echoes in the *Commedia,* see *Enc. d.* V, 1044-9.
[15]*Aen. I.278-9:*

> his ego nec metas rerum nec tempora pono:
> imperium sine fine dedi.

and *Aen.* VI.851-3 (quoted *Mon.*II.vi.9):
  tu regere imperio populos, Romane, memento
  (hae tibi erunt artes), pacique imponere morem,
  parcere subiectis et debellare superbos.
[16]See C.S. Baldwin, *Mediaeval Rhetoric and Poetic* (New York, 1927).
[17]For Virgil's "fortune" in the Middle Ages, see D. Comparetti, *Virgilio nel Medio Evo* 2 vols (Florence, 1937).
[18]*Conv.*IV.xxvi, in which Aeneas is used to illustrate the virtues of "gioventute". See *Conv.*IV.xxiv.9: "lasciando lo figurato che di questo diverso processo de l'etadi tiene Virgilio ne lo Eneida".
[19]*Invective contra medicum*, ed. P.G. Ricci (Rome, 1950), III, p.66.
[20]*Conv.*II.xi.4: "E però dico al presente che la bontade e la bellezza di ciascuno sermone sono intra loro partite e diverse; ché la bontade è ne la sentenza, e la bellezza è ne l'ornamento de le parole; e l'una e l'altra è con diletto, avvegna che la bontade sia massimamente dilettosa."
[21]*Conv.*II.xi.9: "ma ponete mente la sua bellezza, ch'è grande sì per construzione, la quale si pertiene a li gramatici, sì per l'ordine del sermone, che si pertiene a li rettorici sì per lo numero de le sue parti, che si pertiene a li musici."
[22]*Inf.*v.100; the *canzone* is "Al cor gentil rimpaira sempre amore", ed. M. Marti, *Poeti del Dolce stil novo* (Florence, 1969) pp. 57-62. Dante himself echoes this poem in *VN* XX.
[23]*Aen.*IV.172: "coniugium vocat, hoc praetexit nomine culpam." See also *Aen.*IV.221: ". . . oblitos famae melioris amantes" and 267: "heu, regni rerumque oblite tuarum".
[24]See G. Paparelli, "La 'femmina balba' e la 'donna santa e presta' nel XIX del *Purgatorio*" in *Ideologia e poesia di Dante* (Florence, 1957) pp. 203-221; also G. Padoan, "Sirene", *Enc. d.* V, 268-9.
[25]See the discussion of this episode by Hollander, *Allegory* pp. 139-43.
[26]K. Foster, "Dante and Eros", *The Two Dantes* p.52: "The whole stress then of this wonderful episode is on the *subjectivity* of carnal sin".
[27]It may be worth noting that each of the three circles of avarice, gluttony and lust has its poet or poets: Statius for avarice, Forese and Bonagiunta for gluttony and Guido Guinizelli and Arnaut Daniel for lust. For an interesting discussion of associations between the discipline of Purgatory and the poet's discipline see R. Kirkpatrick, *Dante's "Paradiso" and the Limitations of Modern Criticism* (Cambridge, 1978) pp. 57-60. The association of the sirens and poetry can be found in Boethius, *De Consolatione Philosophiae* I.i.35. Philosophy drives away the Muses, whom she calls "sirens" and "harlots", "scaenicae meretriculae": her own muses will replace them. Dante himself uses the image of the sirens for "worldly" poetry, as compared with the songs of the blessed in Heaven in *Par.*xii.7-9:
  canto che tanto vince nostre muse,
    nostre serene in quelle dolci tube,
  quanto primo splendor quel ch'e' refuse.
[28]For example the parallelism of the rebellion of the Giants and that of Lucifer (*Inf.*xxxi and xxxiv; *Purg.*xii.25-33); Proserpina and Eve (*Purg.*xxviii.49-51); Glaucus's metamorphosis into a sea-god and Dante's "transhumanization" in Heaven (*Par.*i.67-72); as well as Dante's adaptation of the pagan underworld of his *Inferno* (and the bold placing of the Lethe in his Earthly Paradise) and the parallel pagan and Christian examples of vice and virtue in the *Purgatorio*.
[29]See Comparetti, *Virgilio* II pp. 86-96.
[30]The first is from Canticles 4:8; the second echoes Matthew 21:9; Mark 11:9; Luke 19:38 (and also the *Sanctus* in the Mass). The first could be applied to Beatrice; in the second, although Dante alters the verb from third to second person, he preserves the masculine form "Benedictus" and the phrase would seem to be addressed to Christ.
[31]There could, however, be a link between the death of the young Marcellus and that of Beatrice.

Paradiso X: Siger of Brabant

M. B. Crowe

Who is the philosopher in the *Paradiso*? Is it, perhaps, Dante himself? To say so would demand an investigation far beyond the scope of this paper; for it would mean a study of Dante's philosophical opinions and all their far-reaching applications in the *Divine Comedy*. The scope of this study is the more modest, but still difficult one of identifying "the philosopher" among the great variety of personalities that people Dante's *Paradiso*. Is it Thomas Aquinas, for whom he had such a regard? Or Bonaventure? Or Albert the Great? Boethius or Dionysius? Or Siger of Brabant, whose appearance in the *Paradiso* reflects so exactly the enigmas of his career at Paris?[1]

But is philosophy not out of place in the *Paradiso*? Practically all the great names in philosophy, from the ancient Greeks down to Dante's own day, are in the *Divine Comedy*. The greatest of them, however, are in the *Inferno*; Socrates, Plato, Anaxagoras, Thales, Empedocles, Heraclitus, Cicero, Seneca, Avicenna, Averroes and many others together with the one who was, in Dante's eyes, the greatest of them all, Aristotle:

> Poi ch'innalzai in poco più le ciglia,
>   vidi 'l maestro di color che sanno
>   seder tra filosofica famiglia.
> Tutti lo miran, tutti onor li fanno   *Inf*.iv.130-3

Surely the *Paradiso* is the place for the theologian, not the philosopher. When theology, the queen of the sciences, appears on the scene what function remains for the handmaiden, the *ancilla*, philosophy? Is not the exclusion of philosophy suggested by the fact that Virgil, who has guided Dante for most of his journey in the other world, gives way to Beatrice in the *Paradiso*? And Beatrice, in her turn, gives way to Bernard, the doctor of mystical theology. The medievals, including Dante, took Virgil for a philosopher in the broad sense, a man possessed of wisdom. This wisdom, however, pales by comparison with faith and, above all, vision. It is not by chance that Dante's epitaph by Giovanni del Virgilio begins: *Theologus Dantes nullius dogmatis expers.* For his contemporaries he was not Dante the philosopher.

Yet one has the feeling that the question is more complex. For Dante was a philosopher and thought of himself as such. In the exordium to his *Quaestio de aqua et terra* he described himself, in a phrase reminiscent of St Paul's self-identification as the "least of all the saints", as "inter vere philosophantes minimus". No consideration of Dante can omit his constant preoccupation with philosophy. He is after all not merely the poet of the *Divine Comedy*, although it is to that masterpiece he owes his immortality. The *Convivio* and the *De Monarchia*, to go no further, are works remarkable for their philosophical content and they are literally stuffed with authorities cited in support by Dante the scholar. It is not too much to say that Dante was obsessed with philosophy. No part of the *Divine Comedy*, certainly not the *Paradiso*, can be really intelligible without some knowledge of the background to Dante's philosophical view of the universe. The medieval imprint of his thought was fundamentally philosophical. The image of man and the world with which he worked was laced with philosophical conceptions, astronomical, cosmological, anthropological. We cannot easily today enter into these conceptions (the image is now properly described by C. S. Lewis as "the discarded image"),[2] but they are nonetheless philosophical. Nor were they simply picked up by Dante in a sort of osmosis from his environment. They were the result of deep study by one who must be counted one of the most learned men of his age. Between the *Vita nuova*, which is already packed with philosophical allusions, and the *Convivio*, Dante went through some sort of intellectual crisis. What precisely it was cannot be certainly known. But it may not be altogether fanciful to see it as his feeling the need, in some personal and dramatic way, for a principle of unity, an intellectual point of vantage from which to survey and order his experiences, his knowledge, his observations. It is the traditional role of philosophy to offer an answer to such a need. And the fact is that Dante, when he comes to write the *Convivio*, eulogizes the Lady Philosophy, in a way that reminds the reader of the vision of philosophy in the golden book that so influenced Dante and the entire Middle Ages, Boethius's *Consolation of Philosophy*: "veramente è donna piena di dolcezza, ornata d'onestade, mirabile di savere, gloriosa di libertade" (*Conv.* II.xv.3).

We can, then, scarcely hope to discover the philosopher in the *Paradiso*, if there be one, without knowing something of Dante's philosophy and of the manner of his acquiring it. As to his formal initiation in philosophy, one's thoughts turn naturally to the Dominican *studium* at Santa Maria Novella. This Florentine *studium* became a *studium generale* in 1295; but even before the separation of Florence from the Roman province of the Dominicans in 1288, it was a well-known school. Beatrice died in 1290; and it is perfectly plausible to think of Dante, in great need of consolation, betaking himself to the school of the friars, shortly to receive the accolade of recognition as a fully-formed school of philosophy and theology. Here he could have heard the lectures of Fra Remigio de' Girolami, a pupil of Thomas Aquinas. Fra Remigio was the son of a Florentine merchant, Chiaro Girolami, and may even have been a friend of Dante as a layman before he set off for Paris to study law. It was in Paris that Remigio turned to the study of philosophy and took the Dominican habit — in both matters acting, quite probably, under the spell of Thomas Aquinas, then (1269-1272) in his second period as master-regent in the University. This was the period when the Averroistic crisis was threatening to tear the University apart, so that Fra Remigio, returning to his native Florence, could bring the most vivid recollections of the philosophy of St Thomas locked in ferocious combat with the speculations of the Aristotelians in the Arts Faculty led by Siger of Brabant. Made *lector* at Santa Maria Novella even before his ordination as a priest, Fra Remigio taught at Florence for forty-two years until his death in 1319, two years before Dante. From his writings Fra Remigio appears not merely as a fine speculative mind, at home in the most difficult questions of philosophy and theology, but also as a thinker with a practical cast of mind, one capable, in a phrase of Martin Grabmann's, of connecting the Thomistic world of thought with the storms of life.[3]

Another friar whom Dante may possibly have heard at Santa Maria Novella was Fra Nicola Brunacci. Fra Nicola seems to have become *lector* only in 1299, by which time Dante was well launched in public life. There must be some doubt whether he can be counted among Dante's teachers. But the two must certainly have met in the Florence of the turn of the century. If so, Fra Nicola provides another connection with Aquinas; for he seems to have travelled to Paris with Aquinas in 1268-69.

Whatever of these historical relationships, what is undoubted is Dante's high appreciation of the thought-synthesis of St Thomas, a synthesis that included not merely the Fathers and Christian theologians but, and more particularly, the philosophy of Aristotle. The major controversies in the intellectual life of the thirteenth century centred precisely upon the reception of Aristotle, whose works had become progressively available to the Latin West since the late twelfth century. Up to then Western Europe knew Aristotle only for his logic and that due to the happy circumstance of his logical works having been translated and commented upon by Boethius in the sixth century. When the rest of Aristotle became known, at first in corrupt Latin versions of Arabic versions of Syriac versions of the original Greek, the impact was enormous. Here was a thinker who, without the benefit of Christianity, had evolved a powerful system of thought in which there were answered the great questions of man and the world, of life and destiny. Some of the answers were, on their face, inconsistent with Christianity — the assertion of the eternity of the world, for instance, or the denial of a personal immortality of the soul. For some this may simply have added spice to the enterprise of interpreting Aristotle; to some it suggested the idea that a proposition might be provable in philosophy and yet false by comparison with theological certainties; to still others, the inconsistency simply confirmed their view that Aristotle was a pagan burning in Hell, whose opinions need not be taken into account.

Nowadays we may tend to take the Aristotelianism of

Aquinas for granted. His contemporaries did not take it for granted and the series of condemnations of Aristotle at Paris and at Oxford in the thirteenth century, in which Aquinas was not untouched, shows it. When Dante described Aristotle as the "maestro di color che sanno", this was more than an academic judgment; it was the brandishing of a banner.

What was it to be an Aristotelian? That, for Dante as for his predecessors in the thirteenth century, was the question. What Paris said, as the uncontested intellectual centre of Europe, should be decisive. But what did Paris say? Paris, unfortunately, spoke with many voices. It took the white heat of controversy, notably that between Siger of Brabant and Thomas of Aquin, to refine and purify the notion of a Christian Aristotelianism of the kind that Dante could embrace half a century after the drama of Aristotle had been fought out at Paris. These are matters to which we must return.

But first it is time to put the question more insistently: Who is the philosopher in the *Paradiso*? Let us, so to speak, interrogate Dante himself. In the *Paradiso* alone — neglecting the "filosofica famiglia" of the *Inferno* and thinkers like Cato of Utica in the *Purgatorio* — there are about thirty personalities who might in some sense be called philosophers. It is clear that nearly all the shapers of the medieval mind are here; and it is equally clear that few, if any of them are in Paradise for their philosophy. They include Albert the Great, Anselm, Aquinas, Augustine, Bernard, Boethius, Bonaventure, Dionysius, Hugh of St Victor, Isidore, Peter Lombard, Peter of Spain (the logician, later Pope John XXI), Richard of St Victor and Siger of Brabant. Does this short list, in alphabetical order, contain "the philosopher"? The question may, for the moment, be turned by asking another. Is there any claimant to the title who has escaped Dante's net? Is there any notable omission in the list?

If one were to ask a contemporary to name the philosopher *par excellence* of the Middle Ages the answer might very well come: Peter Abelard. The extraordinary influence of Abelard in the first half of the twelfth century, when students flocked from all parts of Europe to sit at his feet, is a factor in explaining the intellectual hegemony of Paris in the latter half of that century and thereafter. It was as a dialectician — a logician — that Abelard made his reputation and his moderate realist solution to the "universals" problem became a commonplace

of thirteenth-century dialectics. He turned later, less success-
fully, to theology where his suspect opinions and his provocative
exposition of them, led to his eventual condemnation at the
Council of Sens in 1141. This condemnation was largely the
work of St Bernard, whose place in Dante's *Paradiso* could
scarcely be higher. Why, one may ask, does Abelard not appear
at all, not even in the *Inferno?* If not as a heterodox theologian,
then surely as a superb dialectician, he had claims. Indeed one
would not have been surprised to find the story of Heloise and
Abelard immortalized in the manner of the story of Paolo and
Francesca in the *Inferno.* [4] It is true that the story of Heloise and
Abelard is better known to us than that of Paolo and Francesca;
and this is not entirely due to the romantic embellishments of
the nineteenth century. Abelard's *Historia calamitatum
mearum* and the *Correspondence* with Heloise constitute a
document as moving and personal as, say, the *Confessions* of
St Augustine. But there is no echo of this in the *Divine Comedy.*
The reason cannot be just the ecclesiastical condemnation; for
that reason, as we shall see, should also exclude Siger of
Brabant who, on the contrary, enjoys a position of considerable
distinction in the *Paradiso.* This, too, is a matter to which we
must return.

In the interim may we continue to circle about our main
question by looking again at the philosophy of Dante. Rather it
will be useful to look at two broad themes within that
philosophy. First let us take the *cosmogonia dantesca* which
has been the object of so many studies.

It is evident that the understanding of the *Divine Comedy* is
much impaired unless the reader has an adequate conception of
the geography of the *Inferno, Purgatorio* and *Paradiso.* But the
phrase *cosmogonia dantesca* means much more than the three-
dimensional image of the after-world. It includes the mental
structure, imagery and speculation, through which medieval
man understood his world and his own place in it. The
discarding of this image, under pressure from the advances of
science more than philosophy, presents the greatest obstacle to
our understanding of the medieval world. The abandonment of
geocentrism for heliocentrism is only one, although important,
detail in which our universe differs from that of Dante's
contemporaries. Space and time are problems for the post-
Einsteinian culture of our day; but space and time have always

been philosophical problems and, despite all our advances, what Plato and Aristotle said about time and place cannot be dismissed as simply irrelevant. When the medievals thought about God or angels, or separated souls or the after-life — and how much of the *Divine Comedy* is taken up with such themes — they inevitably speculated about time, eternity and *aevum*. Dante is no exception. On such matters he turned, like many of his contemporaries, to Aristotle and even to the Arabic commentators on Aristotle. So too, for the complicated astronomical system in which the heavenly bodies are carried around the earth on crystalline spheres and where their relative positions are explained by a system of cycles and epicycles; Aristotelian suggestions, one might say, but greatly overlaid by the explanations and refinements of Ptolemy and the Hellenistic and Arab calculators. Our space-conscious age has to make a deliberate effort to recapture such details and their implications.

The more directly philosophical matters, like creation, or the pure being of God, or the status of separated souls, do not present the same opaqueness to modern minds, because they are still philosophical problems. In these areas, too, Dante's debt to Aristotle and to Aristotle's Arab interpreters, Avicenna and Averroes, is well-documented. The point is that Dante looked to the science of his day to inform him on such matters. Already in the thirteenth century that science was bursting the bonds of the liberal arts. The arts of the trivium (grammar, rhetoric and dialectic) could scarcely contain philosophy; and those of the quadrivium (arithmetic, geometry, astronomy and music) were quite inadequate to contain all that was beginning to be known about the universe. The autonomy of the positive sciences, claimed against philosophy, was still a thing of the future and no distinction can be made between Dante the philosopher and Dante the scientist. Questions about prime matter, the totally indeterminate substrate of all being outside of God, creation, the soul, its parts and functions, the freedom of the will, these and many other topics, many of them exceedingly complex and technical, are despite their abstractness given a local habitation and a name in the *Divine Comedy*. They all point to the Aristotelian Unmoved Mover which, as final cause, is the source of all movement in the universe and becomes the Christian God of love:

l'amor che move il sole e l'altre stelle. *Par.*xxxiii.145
These highly abstract notions can be expressed in the superb
imagery of a consummate artist only because he has taken the
trouble to understand what he is talking about. He has gone to
the sources, to the Aristotelians of his time and notably to St
Thomas Aquinas. For these were matters upon which Aristotelian philosophy, particularly in the interpretation of the
Arabs, had much to say and much of it controversial.

A similar situation obtains in a second area of Dante's
thought, that concerned with the relationship between philosophy and theology or, we may say, between reason and faith.
Once again it is a broad theme which one cannot do much more
than outline. It is, no less than the *cosmogonia dantesca*, part of
the framework of the *Divine Comedy*, providing not the material
images of the poem but an important part of the intellectual
context in which it was written. The distinction between
theology and philosophy is one that we may be tempted to take
for granted. We may be more cautious when we reflect that one
of the first to expound it clearly and unambiguously was St
Thomas Aquinas who tells us that theology relies upon data of
divine revelation whereas philosophy has to do with the objects
of human rational investigation.[5] The distinction was to be a
critical one in the Averroistic controversies that involved St
Thomas with Siger of Brabant at Paris 1269-1272. For the
moment we may be content to note that Dante's inclinations
were strongly on the side of an independent philosophy. There
seems to be no evidence that he would accept the description of
philosophy as the *ancilla theologiae*; he saw the function of
philosophy as that of "a collaborator far prouder and far more
independent. It is through its splendour and magnificence as a
daughter of God, *by virtue of the miracle of its own existence
and of the effects which it produces on man through its special
quality*, that philosophy, a miracle to be seen every day, helps us
to deem possible the miracles of Christ which we did not see".[6]

The experience of truth described early in the *Paradiso*
connects truth with the vision of God:

Io veggio ben che già mai non si sazia
    nostro intelletto, se 'l ver non lo illustra
    di fuor dal qual nessun vero si spazia.   *Par.*iv.124-6

The presence of Beatrice, recalling here the Lady Philosophy of

Boethius's *Consolation of Philosophy*, encourages Dante:

> Questo m'invita, questo m'assicura
> con reverenza, donna, dimandarvi
> d'un'altra verità che m'è oscura.   *Par*.iv.133-5

There are, of course, matters beyond the grasp of philosophy; but even here philosophy helps greatly towards the ultimate understanding.

Not unconnected with the distinction of faith and reason is Dante's view of the relation of Church and State. He made no secret of his conviction of the necessity of a separation of Church and State or, in the concrete terms of his time, Papacy and Empire. His *De Monarchia* is sufficient testimony of his views, views by no means shared by most of his contemporaries and stayed by arguments which many found less than cogent, but views, nevertheless, that were in the long run of history to gain acceptance. These were views for which Dante suffered much, including exile. It is little wonder that the papalist side of the argument fared badly in the *Divine Comedy* and it is no accident that Popes like Boniface VIII and Nicholas III appear in the *Inferno*. The independence claimed by Dante for State against Church may parallel the autonomy claimed for philosophy vis-à-vis theology. How could Dante not sympathize with one — is it Siger of Brabant? — who suffered for that autonomy?

It is time to begin to draw together the seemingly disparate threads of the argument of this paper. The process may be introduced by a brief chronicle of events at Paris half a century before the writing of the *Divine Comedy*. These cast long shadows, reaching right into Dante's *Paradiso*. The events in question took place in the early 1270's and to situate them we may conveniently contrast the earlier (1255-1259) and the later (1269-1272) sojourn of St Thomas Aquinas as master-regent in the Faculty of Theology at Paris. First time around, the laurels of the *magister in sacra pagina* fresh on his brow, Aquinas launched into his incomparable teaching career. He had published, as the regulations demanded, his *Commentary on the Sentences of Peter Lombard* and was about to embark upon his *Summa contra gentiles*. Aristotelianism was already causing ripples on the surface of academic calm. The condemnations of Aristotle's "natural philosophy" (in practice, his metaphysics and his psychology) of 1210, 1215, and 1231 had fallen into desuetude and the cultivation of Aristotle in the Faculty of Arts was being viewed with increasing suspicion by the Faculty of Theology. The texts of Aristotle were unsatisfactory by reason of the tortuous nature of their transmission, in a centuries-long process, through Syria and the Arab world to Spain, where they were finally translated into Latin. The help of the great Arab commentators, Avicenna and Averroes, was welcomed, and the danger posed by Aristotelianism to orthodox theology was compounded.

In all this affair the position of Aquinas was delicate. That he was a sound theologian goes, today, without saying. But not all of his fellows in the Faculty of Theology were sure. Some thought he went too far in the direction of Aristotle. As a young man he had, after all, early learnt of Aristotle and Averroes when, before becoming a Dominican, he studied under Master Peter of Ireland at Naples. He later studied at Cologne under Albert the Great, in the period of Albert's Aristotelian paraphrases. Could he be relied upon against the Aristotelians in the Arts Faculty? It seems that he could; here again the long perspective of history allows us to see more clearly than his contemporaries. Indeed, there is good reason to think that the "gentiles", against whom the *Summa contra gentiles* was written, were the arabizing Aristotelians in the University.

Be that as it may, the situation had radically changed for the worse by the time of Aquinas's second Paris sojourn. It was unusual for a master to be invited to a chair of theology for a second time; and the reason for this invitation lay precisely in the crisis that faced the University of Paris. The enthusiasm of the young masters of arts for Aristotle had gone beyond all bounds and left little room for deference to theological orthodoxy. The crux was in Aristotle's views about the eternity of the world and the difficulties about personal immortality. The difficulties were exacerbated by the interpretations of the "Arabs", i.e. Avicenna and Averroes, leaning towards the denial of creation, the extinction of personal responsibility, the abandonment of the notion of Divine Providence and the unicity of the intellectual soul. The leader of these Aristotelian masters of arts was Siger of Brabant; and it was to meet the danger presented by Siger and his followers that Aquinas returned to Paris. His strength was that, as he himself was an Aristotelian but an orthodox one, he could meet the masters of arts, and indeed Avicenna and Averroes, on their own ground. His work *De unitate intellectus*, usually called *contra Averroistas*, was the academic *coup-de-grâce* for the Paris Aristotelians. But, needless to say, the matter did not end there, nor for long afterwards. We shall see more presently of the riots and the disturbances, and the condemnations in which Thomas himself did not escape unscathed. For the moment we may simply note that, during his stay in Italy between the Paris periods, St Thomas had met, at the court of Urban IV in Orvieto, a Dominican *confrère*, William of Moerbeke, whose help was invaluable. Moerbeke was a missionary in the East, an excellent Greek scholar, and he provided the West, and Aquinas in particular, with a series of accurate translations of the Greek texts of Aristotle to replace the faulty and defective versions current until then.

The question must finally be put: Who is the philosopher in the *Paradiso*? Virgil, representing human reason at its best, who has guided Dante through the *Inferno* and the *Purgatorio* as far as the Earthly Paradise, has disappeared. Beatrice enters this terrestrial Paradise in the chariot of the church and represents revelation, faith. When, later, Dante penetrates the empyrean it is Bernard, the doctor of contemplation, who undertakes his guidance. But what of the theologian-philosophers in *Paradiso* x and xii? Surely amongst these we may hope to find the philosopher of the *Paradiso*? And here we meet the enigma of Siger, which has exercised generations of Dante scholars.

Entering the fourth Heaven, that of the sun or light, Dante and Beatrice meet a group of twelve spirits who, by their brightness, stand out against the sun. They form a crown or garland and circle about Dante and Beatrice in a kind of ballet. When Dante wishes to know who they are, St Thomas does the honours:

> Io fui de li agni de la santa greggia
>   che Domenico mena per cammino
>   u' ben s'impingua se non si vaneggia.   *Par*.x.94-6

He introduces his neighbour on the right, his old teacher, Albert the Great:

> Questi che m'è a destra più vicino,
>   frate e maestro fummi, ed esso Alberto
>   è di Cologna, e io Thomas d'Aquino.   *Par*.x.97-9

St Thomas then points out in turn the lawyer, Gratian, who helped in both civil and canon law: "che l'uno e l'altro foro aiutò"; then Peter Lombard, the author of the *Book of Sentences* upon which every medieval master of theology had to write his commentary; then the wise king Solomon, followed by Dionysius the Areopagite or rather the author of the neo-Platonic treatises that went under the name of that distinguished man converted by St Paul. Then comes Orosius, who wrote a complement to St Augustine's *City of God*. He is followed by Boethius, Isidore of Seville, the Venerable Bede and Richard of St Victor. Last of all, completing the circle and consequently flanking St Thomas on the left as Albert does on the right, comes Siger of Brabant. The puzzle is not merely the presence of Siger in such company, given that he was the defeated opponent of Aquinas, but the quite unusual deference shown to him. He is introduced in two tercets; of the others only Solomon and Boethius get such full treatment:

> Questi onde a me ritorna il tuo riguardo,
>   è 'l lume d'uno spirto che 'n pensieri
>   gravi a morir li parve venir tardo:
> essa è la luce etterna di Sigieri,
>   che, leggendo nel Vico de li Strami,
>   silogizzò invidiosi veri.   *Par.*x.133-8

Who was this Siger who, thinking grave thoughts, longed for death and had formerly taught "invidiosi veri" in the Street of Straw? Little enough was known about him in the centuries between Dante and the nineteenth century. And when modern scholarship began to lift the veil the riddle of his appearance in such distinguished company in the *Paradiso* was only increased. He was known to have been condemned for his part in the Averroistic controversies in Paris in 1270 and it was clear that he was the person mainly aimed at in the Great Condemnation of 219 Propositions by the Bishop of Paris, Stephen Tempier, on 7 March 1277. He was thought to have fled the University and for long Dante's reference was the only indication of his manner of death. Then there came to light a letter of John Peckham, Archbishop of Canterbury, addressed to the University of Oxford and dated 10 November 1284. In it Peckham, speaking of the unicity of the substantial form in every corporeal individual (a view defended by St Thomas among others), said that the two principal defenders of this opinion perished miserably beyond the Alps although they did not belong to that region.[7] It is now clear beyond reasonable doubt that the reference is to Siger of Brabant and his companion Gosvin of La Chapelle.

What was this miserable death? In 1881 Ferdinand Castets published the text of a thirteenth-century Italian poem entitled *Il Fiore*, attributing it to Dante. It is possible that the author was another Florentine, a doctor of medicine, called Durante, who died in 1305.[8] The poem is modelled on Jean de Meung's *Roman de la Rose* and consists of 232 sonnets. In sonnet 92 Falsembiante (the Faux-semblant or personification of hypocrisy of the *Roman de la Rose*) speaks:

> Mastro Sighier non andò guari lieto.
> A ghiado il fe' morire a gran dolore,
> nella corte di Roma, ad Orbivieto.

Was Siger executed, put to the sword? At the Papal Court at Orvieto? The question was, as might have been expected, keenly debated, amongst others by Pierre Mandonnet, whose epoch-making *Siger de Brabant et l'averroisme latin au XIIIe siècle* first appeared in 1899. Just at this time came another dramatic discovery, in this case a passing reference in the *Monumenta Germaniae Historica.* Here the writer, apropos of the Emperor Rudolph in whose reign Albert the Great engaged in controversy with Siger of Brabant, describes how Siger, having to leave Paris, went to the Roman Curia where shortly afterwards he was stabbed by his cleric in a fit of madness.[9]

"Curiouser and curiouser!" It is difficult to see in the subject of this story the honoured colleague of St Thomas Aquinas in the fourth Heaven of Dante. Nevertheless it does now appear, in the light of three quarters of a century of research since Mandonnet first turned his attention to the Avveroist controversies at Paris, that Siger has far and away the best title to be called "the philosopher of the *Paradiso*". A simple rehearsal of the conclusions of that research should convince all but the most sceptical.[10]

There can be no doubt that Siger was the leader of the "Averroist party" among the masters of arts in the University of Paris. Nothing is known of the origins of Siger, except that he came from the Duchy of Brabant. He first appears in a document drawn up by the Papal Legate, Simon de Brion, who had been called in to settle disturbances in the University of Paris in 1266 and it appears that he was a canon of the Church of St Paul at Liège. Brabant belonged to the diocese of Liège; and the canonry was certainly a sort of scholarship enabling Siger, who must have shown promise, to go to Paris to study. At Paris he lived up to that promise intellectually in becoming a master of arts and an influential teacher. But he was also a strong character with more than a touch of flamboyance and in fact, a faction leader. The Arts Faculty was divided into four nations, French, Normans, Picards and English, the French at this time outnumbering the other three nations. Once a month the nations elected a Rector of the University — an office that was to grow in importance and finally eclipse that of Chancellor, which belonged to the Faculty of Theology. The quarrel that Cardinal Simon de Brion was called in to settle was the result of a series of rather discreditable episodes in the relations between the nations. The French, in a majority, elected a Rector whom the other nations refused to acknowledge; Siger, who was named as a leader of the anti-French party, may even have been elected Rector by his supporters. There followed riotous behaviour, the kidnapping of rivals and even the assault on the Church of Saint-Jacques and the attempt to prevent the Dead Office being sung in the memory of William of Auxerre, a former professor in the Faculty of Theology. Simon de Brion took the affair firmly in hand, named the culprits, including Siger, decreed that the Rector should be elected only four times a year and laid down a system of resolving disputed elections. Siger's first appearance was not a happy one.

Much more significant, however, than the faction-fighting of the nations was the polarization of the University between the Aristotelians in the Faculty of Arts, led by Siger, and the conservatives in the Faculty of Theology. The intensity of the quarrel and the enormity of its implications brought about, as we have seen, the recall of Thomas Aquinas to Paris in 1269. The battle lines are drawn. St Thomas's opuscule on the *Unity of the Intellect* was clearly directed against Siger and against the authority of Averroes which he claimed. This indeed, of all the suspect teachings of Siger and his followers, was the most destructive; for to assert that there is only one intellect (however qualified) for the entire human race is to make nonsense of individuality, responsibility and immortality. Siger replied. It was not in his character to remain silent and he throve on controversy. But the inevitable ecclesiastical intervention took place; Stephen Tempier, Bishop of Paris, a former master in the Faculty of Theology and former Chancellor of the University, issued a condemnation of 13 propositions in 1270. This condemnation, clearly directed against Siger and his followers, was a dress rehearsal for the Great Condemnation of 1277.

Between the first and the second of these condemnations there was a lull followed by more riots and tumults that need not be detailed here. What was not appreciated until comparatively recently, and a result of the better knowledge of Siger's works, is that Siger seems to have changed his mind. It would be too much to say that he became a Thomist, even if one could pin an exact meaning on that term in the thirteenth century. But his later writings do manifest an Aristotelianism that is no longer irreconcilable with Christian thought. He still appeals to exclusively philosophical sources; he is not a theologian; and Aristotle is still the authority *par excellence*; but the synthesis now resembles that of St Thomas. There is no need to postulate a dramatic conversion; that would surely not have gone un-recorded in the case of so outstanding a figure on the University scene. But a gradual development in the direction of orthodoxy, stimulated it may be by the powerful argument of Aquinas's *De unitate intellectus*, can plausibly be read into Siger's later writings. He is beginning to look a much more presentable candidate for the task of representing philosophy in the *Paradiso*.

Have we proved too much? How explain Dante's curious and cautious references to Siger in the *Paradiso*, his grave thoughts, the death slow in coming and, above all, those "invidiosi veri" which he taught in the Street of Straw? The answer lies in the reconstruction now possible of the last years of Siger's life.

Even before the condemnation of 1277 Siger, with two of his associates, Bernier of Nivelles and Gosvin of La Chapelle (all three with Liège connections), was summoned before Simon de Val, Inquisitor of France, charged with heresy. Despite his apparent change of heart and the fact that, over the previous six or so years, he had not taught truths contrary to the faith, Siger was vulnerable because of his past and his writings. He could hardly expect a sympathetic hearing in France — Bishop, Chancellor, Legate and Inquisitor, not to speak of the Faculty of Theology, all seemed ranged against him and all had good reasons for distrusting him. Siger may well have despaired of getting a fair trial in the court of the Inquisitor. On the other hand, if he had a clear conscience in the matter of heresy, he would easily appeal to the Papal Curia, the more so as the reigning Pope was John XXI who, as Peter of Spain, had taught logic (and was consequently in the Faculty of Arts) at the University of Paris. What happened in the event is mainly conjecture, for no evidence has come to light concerning any process at the Curia. John XXI died on May 20, 1277, killed accidentally in the collapse of a ceiling in the Papal Palace at Viterbo. The Curia was subsequently transferred to Rome and later to Orvieto, under Martin IV elected in 1281. Here, some time before 1284 (the date of Peckham's letter already mentioned) Siger died, assassinated by a demented cleric. Peckham's letter is likely to be well-informed on the matter, for he was at Paris 1269-1271 when the controversies about Siger raged; and he was lector at the Papal Curia 1276-1279 when the trial of Siger may very well have taken place.

Was Siger found guilty of heresy? Hardly; for contumacious heretics were burnt. If he was guilty and recanted the penalty would have been perpetual imprisonment. It seems more likely that he was absolved of the formal charge of heresy but possibly detained in a kind of house-arrest and, because of his former career and influence, refused permission by the Curia to take up his teaching career again. The fact that he could have had the services of a *clericus*, a scribe or secretary presumably, is an indication that whatever the imprisonment it was not of the stricter kind. But such a detention, with close censorship of what he might write and close surveillance of all his activities, would have severely restricted a fiery and impetuous spirit like Siger's to a miserable existence in which death was welcomed as a release. Siger was not much over forty years of age when he met his tragic end.

We have in this question as much certainty as we are likely to get. It is always possible that future research will throw up further revelations about Siger of Brabant; but they are unlikely to alter the present picture in any substantial way. Dante was probably aware of the drama of Siger's career and he cannot but have been impressed by Siger's suffering for his philosophical opinions. As himself a rather eclectic and easy-going, although devoted, follower of St Thomas, Dante would not have worried unduly about differences between Thomas and Siger, above all if he knew that those differences had been mended before Siger's death. He would have been more impressed by the common fidelity to Aristotle in Siger and Thomas. It must not be forgotten that St Thomas was suspected, and even condemned, by those whose views about the hegemony of theology Dante could not accept.

Finally, a significant and important detail, Siger was and always remained a philosopher, a master of arts. He never proceeded to theology or taught in a Faculty of Theology. What better or more appropriate representative of philosophy in the *Paradiso*?

Notes

[1]C. Vasoli, "Sigieri (Sighieri) di Brabante", *Enc. d.* V, 238-42.

[2]C.S. Lewis, *The Discarded Image* (Cambridge, 1964).

[3]M. Grabmann, "Die Wege van Thomas von Aquin zu Dante: Fra Remigio de' Girolami O.Pr.", *Deutsches Dante-Jahrbuch* 9 (1925), 1-35, reprinted in *Dante Alighieri: Aufsätze zur Divina Commedia* ed. H. Friedrich (Darmstadt, 1968) pp. 201-35; Charles T. Davis, "An Early Florentine Political Theorist: Fra Remigio De' Girolami", *Proceedings of the American Philosophical Society* 104 (1960) 662-76. For him and for his contemporary Fra Nicola Brunacci, who follows in the text, see also: P. Mandonnet, *Dante le théologien* (Paris, 1935); and C.T. Davis, "Education in Dante's Florence," *Speculum* 40 (1965) 415-35.

[4]See note[10] in the essay by C. Ryan above.

[5]*Summa theologiae,* Ia,q.1,a.1. The distinction elaborated by St Thomas and ever since accepted was foreshadowed in the Jewish translators from the Arabic working at the courts of Frederick II and Manfred in Sicily. See J. Sermoneta, "Pour une histoire du thomisme juif", *Aquinas and the Problems of his Time* (Louvain, 1967) pp.130-1.

[6]E. Gilson, *Dante the Philosopher* (London, 1948) p. 119.

[7]Charles T. Martin, *Registrum Epistolarum Fratris Joannis Peckham*, Volume III (London, 1885) p.842, "dicuntur conclusisse dies suos in partibus transalpinis, cum tamen non essent di illis partibus oriundi".

[8]For the text I have used F. Castets ed., *Il fiore: poème italien du XIII siècle en CCXXXII sonnets, limité du Roman de la Rose par Durante* (Paris, 1881). For a survey of opinions see G. F. Contini on the *Fiore* in *Enc. d.* II, 895-901.

[9]Martin of Troppau's Chronicle "Continuatio Brabantina", *Monumenta Germaniae*

Historica 27, *Scriptorum* Tomus XXIV (Hanover, 1879) p. 263: "Qui Sygerus, natione Brabantinus, eo quod quasdam opiniones contra fidem tenuerat, Parisius subsistere non valens, Romanam Curiam adiit ibique post parvum tempus a clerico suo quasi dementi perfossus periit". See C. C. J. Webb, "Some Notes on the Problem of Siger", *Medieval and Renaissance Studies* 2 (1950) 121-7.

[10]The fullest and most recent account is F. Van Steenberghen, *Maitre Siger de Brabant* (Louvain, 1977). See also R. Hissette, *Enquète sur les 219 Articles condamnès à Paris le 7 mars 1277* (Louvain, 1977).

Dante the Philosopher – Historian in the Monarchia

Michael Richter

> Cumque, inter alias veritates occultas et utiles, temporalis Monarchie notitia ultilissima sit et maxime latens et, propter non se habere immediate ad lucrum, ab omnibus intemptata, in proposito est hanc de suis enucleare latibulis, tum ut utiliter mundo pervigilem, tum etiam ut palmam tanti bravii primus in meam gloriam adipiscar. (*Mon*.I.i.5).

(Now since the truth about temporal monarchy is the most beneficial and most hidden of all these other beneficial and concealed truths, and yet has been neglected by all because it leads to no immediate reward, I intend to draw it out of the shadows into the light. There I shall be able to examine it for the benefit of the world, and to my own glory gain the palm of so great an enterprise.)[1] It would not be surprising if these lines which conclude the first chapter of the *Monarchia* had been written after the completion of the remainder of the work. What was Dante's immediate concern? He claims it to be the unrewarding philosophical pursuit of truth but he is more specific than that. The second chapter sheds more light on the matter:

> Est ergo temporalis Monarchia, quam dicunt 'Imperium', unicus principatus et super omnes in tempore vel in hiis et

super hiis que tempore mensurantur. (*Mon.*I.ii.2)
(The temporal monarchy that is called the Empire is a single command exercised over all persons in time, or at least in those matters which are subject to time.) The medieval European scene was dominated by the struggle between the empire and the papacy from the late eleventh century, first over investitures and then in the opposition of various popes to the Staufer dynasty, a struggle which found its clearest expression in political and philosophical works on the nature of the empire and its relationship with the papacy. Scholars may find it difficult therefore to accept Dante's words that "the truth about the temporal monarchy . . . has been neglected by all". What palm did Dante think he had earned by dealing with this subject? What was original in what he had to say and to what extent does it "gain the palm"? These questions cannot, of course, be fully answered in a paper of this length; I shall restrict myself to only a few topics of the *Monarchia*. However, due to the length of the *Monarchia*, it is necessary to be somewhat selective in the topics covered. I am concerned mainly with evaluating the significance of monarchy in this work of Dante's comparing it with other statements of his on the same subject, although I will have to exclude the *Commedia* because this would go far beyond the limits of this paper.

Dante's fame rests mainly on his poetical works written in the Tuscan vernacular. The *Monarchia*, in contrast, is written in Latin prose, a fact too rarely commented upon by scholars. I believe, however, that the choice of language in this work is as significant for a full understanding of it as in the case of Dante's poetry, where language and content are rightly considered together. I shall return to the topic of the Latin language in the *Monarchia.*

What were Dante's motives for writing the work other than those already mentioned? This question, together with that of the date of composition, is part of the difficulty of commenting on the *Monarchia*. Yet we are not completely left in the dark. There are some hints in the work itself which throw light on these issues. Let us take first his intention in writing the work:

> Verum quia naturalis amor diuturnam esse derisionem non patitur, sed, ut sol estivus qui disiectis nebulis matutinis oriens luculenter irradiat, derisione omissa,

lucem correctionis effundere mavult, ad dirumpendum vincula ignorantie regum atque principum talium, ad ostendendum genus humanum liberum a iugo ipsorum . . . Nam per hoc quod romanum Imperium de iure fuisse monstrabitur, non solum ab oculis regum et principum, qui gubernacula publica sibi usurpant, hoc ipsum de romano populo mendaciter extimantes, ignorantie nebula eluetur, sed mortales omnes esse se liberos a iugo sic usurpantium recognoscent. (*Mon*.II.i.5-6)

(Since natural love cannot bear to maintain derision, so, just as the summer sun breaks through the morning mists and shines forth in splendour, natural love disperses derision, and prefers to shed the light of correction, to break the chains of ignorance binding kings and princes . . . For by showing that the Roman empire was founded upon right not only shall I disperse the clouds of ignorance veiling the eyes of kings and princes, who usurp the control of public affairs and falsely imagine that the Roman people did likewise, but I shall also enable all men to acknowledge themselves as free from their yoke.) Again:

Maxime enim fremuerunt et inania meditati sunt in romanum Principatum qui zelatores fidei cristiane se dicunt. (*Mon*.II.x.1)

(It is those who boast of being defenders of the Christian faith who have most agitated and meditated foolishness against the Roman primacy.) Also:

Desinant igitur Imperium exprobrare romanum qui se filios Ecclesie fingunt. (*Mon*.II.xi.7)

(And so let those who make themselves out to be sons of the church stop their attack upon the Roman empire.) These passages identify those against whom the work was directed: they were the kings and princes as well as those Christians (presumably ecclesiastics) who worked or spoke against the empire in Dante's time. These references show that the work was written in response to the political realities of the time. But of what time? Evidence for the dating of the *Monarchia* is even more scant:

cum insuper doleam reges et principes in hoc unico concordantes: ut adversentur Domino suo et Uncto suo, romano principi. (*Mon*.II.i.3)

(I saw the sorry spectacle of kings and princes agreeing upon only one thing — resistance to their Lord, to the anointed One, the Roman Prince.) In this Dante refers clearly to his own experience. The only emperor anointed in Dante's lifetime was Henry VII of Luxemburg who received the papal blessing in 1312 but who died in shame and misery in 1313, after Pope Clement V had opposed the imperial claim to universal overlordship. This reference to Henry VII offers a firm *terminus post quem* for the writing of the *Monarchia*. More problematical, on the other hand, is an alleged cross-reference to the *Paradiso* in Ricci's edition of the *Monarchia*.[2] Accepting this at its face value, we would have to regard the *Monarchia* as completed very late in Dante's lifetime. I find it impossible to reconcile this with the nature of its content.

Scant as these references are, they enable us to place the *Monarchia* firmly later than two other pieces of writing which (apart from the *Commedia*) throw light on Dante's attitude to the empire. These other writings are the *Convivio*, written in vernacular prose, a work broken off unfinished about 1306-7, and three letters, known as "the political letters", written in Latin prose, which can be firmly assigned to the years 1310 and 1311.

Let us now turn to the contents of the *Monarchia*. The task which Dante set himself is outlined with admirable clarity (*Mon*.I.ii.3):

> primo nanque dubitatur et queritur an ad bene esse mundi [monarchia] necessaria sit.

(The first is the question whether it — the temporal monarchy — is necessary for the well-being of the world.) This topic Dante deals with in *Mon*.I.v-xv:

> secundo an romanus populus de iure Monarche offitium sibi asciverit

(the second is whether it was by right that the Roman people took upon itself the office of the Monarch.) This discussion fills *Mon*.II.ii-xi:

> et tertio an auctoritas Monarche dependeat a Deo inmediate vel ab alio, Dei ministro seu vicario.[3]

(And thirdly there is the question whether the monarch's authority is derived directly from God or from somebody else, some minister or vicar of God.) Dante treats this topic in *Mon.*III.i-xiv. This leaves altogether six chapters dealing either with preliminaries or with additional matter (*Mon.*I.i-iv; II.i; III.xv). We shall come back to them later. It is evident from this that the topic of the *Monarchia* is developed further in each book. The first book deals with the concept of the empire as such and may be labelled philosophical. The second book deals with a specific empire, that of classical Rome, and we may call this historical. The third book refers to Dante's own time. Since the universal authority of Henry VII was being seriously challenged at this time, Dante's advocacy of the supremacy of the medieval Christian empire was highly controversial. Considering the Roman Empire of antiquity and the medieval Christian empire together could well constitute the novelty which Dante claims for his work. It certainly constitutes a novelty when compared with Dante's other statements on the empire. Assuming that the philosophical dimension is present in all of Dante's remarks on the empire, the relevant chapters in the *Convivio* (IV.iv and v) deal in addition only with the historical aspect. In contrast, the "political letters" emphasize the controversial contemporary aspect. We will examine these passages both individually and in conjunction with the *Monarchia* so that we may be able to appreciate the full significance of the *Monarchia* in the development of Dante's views of the empire.[4]

Monarchia I: Is the monarchy necessary for the well-being of the world? Dante takes Aristotle's statement that any community should be ruled by a single person to its logical conclusion by claiming that what applies to the family, the village, the city and the kingdom also applies to mankind as a whole: that it is to be ruled by one man. This ruler of the world is called *monarcha*: emperor (*Mon.*I.v.1; *Conv.*IV.iv.1-4).

Similarly, affairs are best managed when they are managed according to the intentions of the first mover, God. In a typically radical statement, Dante follows on from that "Ergo humanum genus uni principi subiacens maxime Deo assimilatur" (*Mon.*I.viii.4; when mankind is subject to one prince it is most like to God.) Again based on Aristotle, Dante further argues that the world is best ordered when justice is strong, justice being the opposite of greed ("cupiditas"; *Mon.*I.xi.11; *Conv.*IV.iv.4). The emperor is free from greed because he has nothing left to desire as his commands find their limits only at the ocean's edge (*Mon*.I.xi.12). This is another argument that the universal empire would be to the benefit of mankind.The emperor, by definition just, can have no enemies (*Mon.*I.xi.19). With this we have indicated the main arguments for the necessity, as Dante says (or, as we would perhaps prefer, the desirability) of a universal monarchy for the well-being of the world. Dante, however, does not stop here. He acknowledges the existence of lower forms of political organization, and of these the *regna* are the most important. The following remarks seem to be necessitated by the fact that there existed *regna* in Dante's Europe. No doubt he recognizes their legitimate existence (*Mon.*I.v.8). He readily acknowledges that peoples, kingdoms and cities differ from each other in many essential ways so that they have to be ruled by different laws, but he adds that the rulers of these smaller political units should act under the monarch since they bear the same relationship to him as does the practical intellect to the speculative intellect (*Mon.*I.iv.7). The princes of the smaller units should not negotiate among themselves without reference to the universal monarch because "eo quod cura ipsorum a cura illa suprema descendit" (*Mon.*I.xi.16; their tutelage is derived from his.)

We encounter in *Monarchia* I a mixture of philosophical and historical-political arguments, but this is brought to a new height at the very end of this book: Dante states in the concluding chapter that since the Fall of Man the perfect monarchy has existed once, and once only, and that when the world was at peace at the time of Caesar Augustus (*Mon.* I.xvi.1). This remarkable statement which leads on to *Monarchia* II is not found in the *Convivio*, a work that otherwise, though in much less detail, shows many parallels to the *Monarchia* without any remarkable differences.

Monarchia II: This book deals with a specific empire, the one and only world power that ever existed, that of ancient Rome. The arguments adduced — surely the most remarkable part of the treatise as a whole — find many parallels as well as some differences in emphasis in Dante's description of the role of Rome in the *Convivio*. In the *Monarchia* he adds some further thoughts, but it is best to start with a brief summary of the arguments in the *Convivio*. He proceeds in the following manner: Some people would argue that Rome acquired the empire by force. This is a mistaken view, for the election of a supreme ruler must proceed from God. The Romans were the sweetest people: "E però che più dolce natura . . . che quella de la gente latina" (*Conv.*IV.iv.10). The control of the empire was won by the most deserving people; this statement is supported by a quotation from Virgil. Force was not the moving cause but the instrumental cause of the empire (*Conv.*IV.iv.12). Rome's origin and special progress came from God, a topic that Dante further elaborates in the following chapter.

Convivio IV.v deals essentially with Christ's birth and life and their relevance to Rome. Obviously Heaven and Earth would be best disposed when Christ came. Thus Rome was ordained by Divine Providence (*Conv.*IV.v.4, and similarly again 10-11). This providence is best seen in the parallel origin of Rome and Christ. Christ's family originated from David just at the time when Rome had its origin with the arrival of Aeneas from Troy. This showed the divine election of the city (*Conv.*IV.v.5-6). Luke the Evangelist testified that at the time of Christ's birth the whole world was at peace. Dante then considers Rome before the birth of Christ. The city was uplifted and brought to its height, as he believed, by the divine citizens who were infused with divine rather than human love. The author adduces many examples, of which perhaps the most remarkable is the epithet, "sacratissimo", used of Cato (*Conv.*IV.v.16). These people were instruments through which Divine Providence worked in the Roman Empire. A number of miracles were performed for the preservation of the Empire from her external enemies. Dante concludes with the statement that he has shown that the "spezial nascimento e spezial processo da Dio pensato e ordinato, fosse quello de la santa cittade" (*Conv.*IV.v.20). With this Dante ends his digression on the Roman Empire and turns to other subjects.

This material in the *Convivio* provided him with a basis when taking up the subject again in *Monarchia* II. As will be seen the treatment there is remarkably different. There are, besides parallels, changes of emphasis as well as additions and a whole new line of argument.

In *Monarchia* II we find the same opening statement. Close inspection reveals that the Romans made their acquisitions not only by force but also by divine authority. Dante starts from the following premise: "divina voluntas ius est" (*Mon.*II.ii.4;

right is willed by God). He discusses the implications of this statement in two separate ways and deals in fact with two separate issues. First he argues at length that the conquest of the world by the Romans happened lawfully. What he calls in one place "predestinatio divina" (*Mon*.II.iii.17) is treated in *Monarchia* II.iii-vi more specifically as the work of "natura" rather than the work of God. We may confine ourselves here to two summary statements:

> non dubium est quin natura locum et gentem disposuerit in mundo ad universaliter principandum;

and: Propterea satis persuasum est quod romanus populus a natura ordinatus fuit ad imperandum: ergo romanus populus subiciendo sibi orbem de iure ad Imperium venit. (*Mon*.II.vi.8,11)

(There can be no doubt that nature has ordained a place and a people designed to rule over the whole world; and: We have now shown convincingly that the Roman people were intended by nature to rule the world; therefore the Roman people in subjugating the world attained the Empire by right.) Turning to the second point he makes in *Monarchia* II, he deals more briefly with the divine will, significantly opening chapter xi with a discussion of "divinum iudicium" (the counterpart to "natura" of chapters iii-vi). The main argument, however, comes in the last two chapters where he shows that the existence of the Roman Empire at the time of Caesar Augustus was eschatologically necessary (*Mon*.II.x,xi).

We are confronted thus in *Monarchia* II with a historical-secular as well as a theological argument. We should look at both more closely. The statement that the Romans were the most noble people (*Mon*.II.iii.2) we have already encountered in the *Convivio*. In both works Virgil is adduced as the authority for this statement. But while in the *Convivio* Virgil is mentioned only once in this context and without any special epithet, in the *Monarchia* he is introduced as "divinus poeta noster" (our divine poet), a unique epithet even in the *Monarchia*, while in the whole of *Monarchia* II Virgil is referred to as an authority on no less than fourteen other occasions, generally as "poeta noster" (our poet), "vates noster" (our prophet).[5] For this part of Dante's thesis, Virgil is easily the most important single authority.[6]

Dante continues: Whoever wills the good of the community, thereby wills the advancement of right. By subjecting the world to their rule, the Romans acted for the benefit of the community (*Mon*.II.v.1-3). Their deeds clearly showed that this "populus ille sanctus pius et gloriosus" (*Mon*.II.v.5; holy, pious and glorious people) neglected their personal comfort for the benefit of mankind. "Unde recte illud scriptum est: Romanum imperium de fonte nascitur pietatis" (*Mon*.II.v.5; Thus it has justly been written: "The Roman Empire was begotten in the womb of piety".)[7] According to Aristotle, some people are born to rule, others to obey, and there can be no doubt that nature ordained the Romans to rule, as had been shown so adequately ("subtiliter") by Virgil (*Mon*.II.vi.7-11).

We can detect here in the author a more enthusiastic attitude towards the classical Roman past than appeared in the *Convivio*. It is more than that. One may say that the Roman past is seen with different eyes. This can best be brought out by a brief textual comparison of the way in which the noble behaviour of famous Roman citizens is presented in the *Convivio* and the *Monarchia*.

Convivio IV.v.12: . . . noi troveremo lei essaltata non con umani cittadini, ma con divini, ne li quali non amore umano, ma divino era inspirato in amare lei. E ciò non poeta né dovea essere se non per ispeziale fine, da Dio inteso in tanta celestiale infusione. (13:) E chi dirà che fosse sanza divina inspirazione Fabrizio infinita quasi moltitudine d'oro rifiutare, per non volere abbandonare sua patria? . . . (15:) Chi dirà di Quinzio Cincinnato, fatto dittatore e tolto da lo aratro, e dopo lo tempo de l'officio, spontaneamente quello rifiutando, a lo arare essere ritornato? Chi dirà di Cammillo, bandeggiato e cacciato in essilio, essere venuto a liberare Roma contr'a li suoi nimici, e, dopo la sua liberazione, spontaneamente essere ritornato in essilio per non offendere la senatoria autoritade, sanza divina istigazione?

Monarchia II.v.6: Sed quia de intentione omnium ex electione agentium nichil manifestum est extra intendentem nisi per signa exteriora . . . (8:) . . . Nunquid non bonum comune intendisse dicendi sunt qui sudore, qui paupertate, qui exilio, qui filiorum orbatione qui amissione membrorum, qui denique animarum oblatione bonum publicum exaugere conati sunt? (9:) Nonne Cincinnatus ille sanctum nobis reliquit exemplum libere deponendi dignitatem in termino cum, assumptus ab arato, dictator factus est . . . et post victoriam, post triumphum, sceptro imperatorio restituto consulibus, sudaturus post boves ad stivam libere reversus est? (11:) Nonne Fabritius altum nobis dedit exemplum avaritie resistendi cum, pauper existens, pro fide qua rei publice tenebatur auri grande pondus oblatum derisit, ac derisum, verba sibi convenientia fundens, despexit et refutavit? . . . (12:) Nunquid non preferendi leges propriis commodis memorabile nobis exemplar Camillus fuit qui, secundum Livium, dampnatus exilio, postquam patriam liberavit obsessam, spolia etiam romana Rome restituit, universo populo reclamante, ab urbe sancta discessit . . .?

(But since external signs are the only means by which a free agent's intentions can be detected by any other person . . . For how could it be denied that they were inspired by desire for the common good who through poverty, through exile, through loss of their children and mutilation of their limbs, and finally by the sacrifice of their very lives, strove to promote the public welfare? Has not the great Cincinnatus provided us with a blessed example of how titles should be utterly laid aside at the proper time? He who . . . was called from the plough to be dictator, yet after his triumph and victory handed back the sceptre of command to the consuls, and returned of his own free will to sweat away at the plough behind his oxen. And did not Fabricius afford us a noble example of how to resist avarice? For, poor though he was, his loyalty to the republic led him to scoff at the great weight of gold offered to him; and having scoffed at it he then rejected the offer in terms worthy of the man he was. And have we not been given a memorable example of how to put the law before personal advantage by Camillus, who, according to Livy, was under sentence of exile yet delivered his fatherland from siege, restored the spoils to Rome, even the spoil taken from Rome, and then took his leave of the holy city . . .?)

According to the *Convivio*, the deeds of the Romans were divinely inspired. However, mention of this inspiration is conspicuously absent in the *Monarchia* which refers instead to work for the benefit of the "bonum comune". There is another difference. In the *Convivio*, approval is given to the good deeds of the past; in the *Monarchia*, the same deeds are presented, in pseudo-Christian terms, as incentives for future action. When in the *Monarchia*, the work of Cincinnatus for example is described as "sanctum nobis . . . exemplum", from the context, "sanctum" must be classified as a non-Christian term, and even more so when we hear of the "divina istigazione" in a corresponding passage in the *Convivio*.

We can detect a similar de-Christianization of the past in other sections of the *Monarchia*; those religious epithets that remain have to be seen as primarily non-Christian. Thus once Virgil is even graced with the term "divinus poeta". Correspondingly, those blessings which in the *Monarchia* are ascribed to "natura" in the *Convivio* are attributed to God.

This change of emphasis has a remarkable counterpart in the second sequence of arguments in *Monarchia* II, where Dante discusses the relationship between the Roman Empire and the coming of Christ. We find, as in the *Convivio*, the chronological coincidence of the Roman Empire and Christ's birth when, according to Luke, the world was at peace, but here, in contrast to the *Convivio*, Christ's choosing to be born under the authority of Rome proves the legitimacy of the empire. The legitimacy of Rome thus becomes an eschatological necessity. If the Roman Empire had not existed as of right at the time of Christ, the validity of the act of salvation would have been undermined, as otherwise Adam's sin would not have been legitimately atoned for by Christ. Pontius Pilate as the "iudex ordinarius" (*Mon*.II.xi.5) and vicar of Tiberius Caesar must be considered as having passed judgment legitimately if this action were to be a contribution towards a valid act of salvation.

Only these considerations make clear the complex meaning of Dante's statement that "right is willed by God".

When we compare the argument in the *Monarchia* with that in the *Convivio*, a significant shift of emphasis emerges. In the *Convivio*, the Romans are hallowed, as it were, by being born chronologically at the same time as the House of David; this point is not taken up in the *Monarchia*; on the contrary, Dante virtually says that the Roman Empire, existing legitimately at the time of Christ, gave respectability and an aura of credibility to Christ's death. Whereas in the *Convivio*, the Romans were under divine influence even at the time of the foundation of the city, in the *Monarchia* they appear to be uninfluenced in this way even at the time of Christ's work on earth. In other words, while in the *Convivio* the pre-Christian Romans had in some way participated in God's work, in the *Monarchia*, if Dante's argument is to stand, the empire has to remain unaffected by Christ's being condemned by the Romans. Thus while the Romans of classical times are presented in the *Convivio* as quasi-Christians, in *Monarchia* II the Roman Empire was emphatically a non-Christian empire.

This conclusion, perhaps not so dramatic in itself, assumes however, a new importance when we see that his argument about the nature of the empire at the time of Caesar Augustus and of Christ's birth relates to the work as a whole only if the empire which he is describing in *Monarchia* III is of a similar kind to that of Caesar Augustus. To this we must now turn.

Monarchia III: From what source does the monarch derive his authority?

It should be stressed that in this part of his treatise Dante is dealing with the empire of the Christian era; what he is discussing is the relationship between the emperor and the pope. He touches on many familiar aspects of this controversy. He treats the relationship as analogous with that of the sun and moon, that of the two swords, of Levi and Judas, of Saul and Samuel. He also discusses the Petrine mission described in Matthew 16:19 (*Mon.*III.iv-ix). He does not devote the same amount of attention to these *minutiae* as many of his predecessors had done, but what he does say makes it very clear that he is aware of these discussions. He brushes aside rather neatly the question of the Donation of Constantine as well as that of the apparent precedent for the emperor's dependence on the pope implied by Charlemagne's accession to that office (*Mon.*III.x and xi). Most important in Dante's argument is the statement that the empire was in existence prior to the Church and therefore the Church could not be regarded as having given the empire a new dimension "causa illius virtutis" (*Mon.* III.xii.3). Here we have clearly the link between *Monarchia* II and III. Dante has proved ostensibly that the monarch derives his authority directly from God.

Since *Monarchia* III deals with the Christian empire, the view of the empire put forward in Dante's three "political letters" offers valuable comparative material. They give the previous argument its contemporary political relevance although it has been said that "it is difficult to read any definitive political programme, still less a political philosophy, into the three political epistles",[8] it would be irresponsible to dismiss these scraps of information on Dante's view of the empire even though the letters in isolation do not constitute a complete political philosophy. They have to be compared with the Christian empire as portrayed in *Monarchia* III.

In *Epistola* V.3, written about September-October 1310, we read: "maiestas [Caesaris] de fonte defluat pietatis" (It is from the Fount of Piety that [Caesar's] sovereign greatness flows). This was a commonplace statement in the medieval imperial chancery though it ultimately goes back to classical Roman times.[9] This statement does not occur in the *Convivio* but it does appear in *Monarchia* II.v. It is not quite clear whether "pietas" as mentioned in *Monarchia* II with reference to classical Rome has the same meaning when applied to Henry VII of Luxemburg. What is clear, however, is that in *Epistola* V "pietas" means Christian piety. That this letter was written firmly within the tradition of the medieval Christian empire is shown by the way in which Dante continues: "Hic est [Caesar] . . . quem Clemens nunc Petri successor luce Apostolicae benedictionis illuminat" (*Epistola* V.10; This is the emperor . . . whom Clement, the present successor of Peter, irradiates with the light of the Apostolic blessing).There is a slight similarity to this in *Monarchia* III when Dante writes that "lucem gratie . . . benedictio summi Pontificis infundit illi" (*Mon*.III.iv.20;[10] the light of grace . . . which is dispensed by the supreme Pontiff). Oddly enough in the *Monarchia* Dante does not regard this as a sign that the emperor derives his authority from the pope. *Epistola* V was written before Henry VII of Luxemburg, German king and future emperor, had received the papal blessing which would make him emperor. The advocates of papal supremacy at that time argued that this act of blessing demonstrated the superiority of the papacy over the empire and frequently quoted Hebrews 7.7 in support of this: "sine ulla autem contradictione, quod minus est a meliore benedictur" (and beyond all dispute the lesser is always blessed by the greater). In my view it is of the utmost importance that in the *Monarchia* Dante does not discuss, though he mentions briefly, *how* the Christian emperor *is made* but merely his position *when he is* emperor. In the context of the contemporary historical situation and the contemporary controversies this was a most serious omission.

It is true that Dante deals with the relationship of emperor and pope from *Monarchia* III.vi onwards, and this is where we would expect to get an evaluation of the act of papal blessing. Instead, he refutes the argument that the authority of the empire depends upon the authority of the Church, just as the lowly craftsman depends upon the architect, ". . . auctoritatem Imperii ab auctoritate Ecclesie dependere velut artifex inferior dependet ab architecto" (*Mon*.III.iv.1). We may consider here one of Dante's many arguments on this point, namely the allegory of the sun and the moon, a favourite theme of medieval papalists. Dante comes to the conclusion: "dico ergo quod licet luna non habeat lucem habundanter nisi ut a sole recipit, non propter hoc sequitur quod ipsa luna sit a sole" (*Mon*.III.iv.17; So I say that although the moon receives the fullness of light from the sun alone, it does not follow that the moon is derived from the sun.) The Pope's blessing, which is central to the message of Dante to Henry of Luxemburg, is mentioned in this passage of the *Monarchia* and is given the following meaning:

> regnum temporale non recipit esse a spirituali, nec virtutem que est eius auctoritas, nec etiam operationem simpliciter; sed bene ab eo recipit ut virtuosius operetur. (*Mon*.III.iv.20)

(The temporal monarchy does not owe its existence to the spiritual government, nor its power, which constitutes its authority, nor even its operation as such — though it certainly receives from the spiritual government the energy to operate more powerfully.) This interpretation would not be shared by contemporary thinkers, for if the pope could not confer "auctoritas" then the papal blessing could be dispensed with.

While the relationship between the two powers is mentioned here only in passing, Dante devotes more attention to historical precedent when he says that Charlemagne's apparent dependence on the papacy was counterbalanced by the popes' dependence on the Ottonians. Dante was mistaken about Charlemagne, who, contrary to popular belief, was not consecrated (that is, crowned and anointed) emperor by the pope, but in 800 was merely acclaimed in a manner which consciously imitated classical Roman practice. The first historically attested imperial anointing by a pope took place in

816 when Charlemagne's successor Louis the Pious was so blessed. Yet, although Dante could not have known this, he would have been delighted to learn that even in the opinion of such a conservative ninth-century churchman as Rabanus Maurus this anointing of the emperor depended on the pope. It was the *papal* interpretation which put such great emphasis on the act of anointing, and from the time of Louis the Pious onwards, certainly into Dante's time, the king who became emperor (normally the king of the Germans, who since the twelfth century was also known as king of the Romans) had to be anointed by the pope. Not long after Dante's death however, though for reasons which differed from his, in 1338 the German electors argued, as was subsequently laid down in the act *Licet Iuris*, that "the emperor becomes true emperor merely by the election of those to whom belongs the election, and he does not need anybody's confirmation or approbation."[11]

After this lengthy digression we conclude that in *Epistola* V Dante refers to the emperor clearly as the Christian emperor who receives illumination from the greater of the two lights. Unlike the account in the *Monarchia*, Henry VII's empire according to this letter "did not begin with Troy but with Christ's birth"[12] at the earliest. In other words, the emperor discussed in *Monarchia* III was not Henry VII. The difference can be pinpointed quite clearly: "imperium Romanum" had two irreconcilable meanings: it could mean (and was so understood by Dante in *Monarchia* II as well as in *Convivio* IV.iv-v) "classical and pagan", but it could also mean "medieval and Christian" since by the sixth century "Roman" had become virtually a synonym for "Latin Christian". It is in the latter sense that the term "imperium Romanum" is used in *Epistola* V and appears to be used in *Monarchia* III.

We see the same awareness of the contemporary situation in Dante's other two political letters, those of 1311. In *Epistola* VI, Dante refers to the "sacrosanctum Romanorum imperium" while in *Epistola* VII, written to the emperor himself, he addresses him: "Dei ministrum et ecclesiae filium, et Romanae gloriae promotorem" (minister of God, son of the Church and promoter of Roman glory). Finally in the same *Epistola* VII, Dante reminds Henry VII of the greatness of the Empire: "You took no account, we must suspect, of the fact that the glorious power of the Romans is not cramped within the limits of Italy...

for it hardly consents to be encircled by the ineffectual stream of the ocean". This, of course, is one of the philosophical definitions of the emperor's power in *Monarchia* I.xi.12.

We may sum up the result of the comparisons which have been made so far. It appears that Dante's views as expressed in the *Convivio*, in the political letters and in the *Monarchia* are not consistent; but the differences between these works have been generally neglected.[13] As a consequence, the *Monarchia* is not given that special position within Dante's works which it surely deserves. I maintain, and have already given some evidence to support the view, that Dante's main argument in the *Monarchia* is emphatically different from that in the *Convivio* and in the political letters, and that in the *Monarchia* this argument is not free from ambiguity. We should be fully aware of this ambiguity and on this basis assign the work its proper place in Dante's writings. We may also find an answer to our initial question of what Dante means when he says that the truth about the temporal monarchy is most neglected.

The answer is already partly provided by the foregoing analysis. What makes the *Monarchia* rather different from similar writings of Dante's time and earlier is, briefly, his selection of the Roman Empire of the time of Christ, and thus the pagan Empire, as a model. This model could only be relevant if it possessed all the main features which Dante regarded as essential to the empire of his time. We have seen that he found support for his admiration of the classical Roman Empire in the writings of some of the classical authors, prominent among whom was Virgil. As a native of Italy, Dante found it easier to accept accounts of Rome's former glories for the future than would have been possible for a writer from outside Italy for whom the Roman Empire would not necessarily have been so closely linked with the geographical realities of Rome and Italy. In this context it is surely important that Dante refers to Virgil as "our poet", a phrase in which this little possessive pronoun bridges the gap between the classical Roman past and Dante's time. If I seem to be labouring this point I do no more than Dante does when he makes this original statement.

For this apparently effortless bridging of the gap between the classical Roman past and the time of the Italian Trecento is surely the most remarkable feature of Dante's treatise, and it has important implications. When Dante states towards the end of *Monarchia* III that the Roman Empire had existed before the Church and therefore does not owe its existence to the Church, he thereby bridges the gap between the classical past and the Trecento. But at what a cost! His argument carries weight only if it is accepted that the empire about which he writes in the *Monarchia* fits the model Empire of classical Rome. This would imply that the coming of Christianity had left the nature of the empire basically unaffected, a conclusion which Dante had explicitly stated elsewhere. That he was not consistently of this opinion is shown by the reference to the Christian empire of the Carolingians and the Ottonians where the fact of a close relationship between empire and Church was acknowledged though not further elaborated. Here Dante is ambiguous in his use of the term "empire". The ambiguity is rooted in the fact that he examines the classical past more closely than any of his predecessors.

How could Dante hold such an opinion, how could the gulf between classical pagan Rome and the Christian empire be bridged? There are two possible answers to this question. One is that the gulf was apparently bridged by linguistic means, and the second is that Dante saw that ultimately the gulf could not be bridged and so abandoned the attempt.

For the first answer I come back to the point raised towards the beginning of our discussion: why was the *Monarchia* written in Latin? Throughout western Christendom in the age of Dante philosophers still used the Latin language as the universally accepted language of learning for their writings. Latin had also been, as we already mentioned, the language of classical Rome, and thirdly, Latin was the language of the western Church during most of its history. For in the West the Church was grafted on to the Roman Empire. Although the Church derived originally from the Judaeo-Hellenic world in the East, and although Greek and Hebrew were recognized, together with Latin, as the sacred languages of the Church, in practice Latin ousted Greek and Hebrew more and more from daily usage until it was eventually the main and exclusive language of the Christian Church in Western Europe. This historical process has important linguistic implications. For the Romans already had a religion in their empire when Christianity arrived there, a religion which then had an elaborate vocabulary of ritual and hierarchy. Much of that vocabulary was adopted by the Roman Christians who believed that the contents of the terms of worship were changed even though much of the terminology remained the same.

In the light of this we can see how the pagan Romans could be described in Latin terms which, at face value, were perfectly acceptable to Christians. Thus in the important fifth chapter of *Monarchia* II[14] where Dante extols the qualities of the Romans in the time of the Empire, he describes them as "populus ille sanctus pius et gloriosus", and two of these adjectives are religious terms which occur both in pagan Rome and the Christian religion. Thus *apparently* the Roman people of antiquity showed those qualities which were later to be considered so essential to the good Christians. Indeed, just after this phrase, another even more surprising statement occurs: "Romanum imperium de Fonte nascitur pietatis". Dante introduces this phrase by the words "recte illud scriptum est" and the phrase can indeed be traced back to the classical Roman Empire (see note[7] above). Yet the medieval imperial chanceries which used this phrase surely held that this was intended to apply to the Christian empire only. However, when Dante uses the phrase and the term "pietas", he consciously refers back to pre-Christian Rome and implicitly denies that there was a qualitative difference between the Roman and Christian empires.

We can be quite sure that the author did not make this transition from the Christian present to the pagan past unintentionally or, as it were, by default. Generations of scholars have performed an immensely valuable task in tracing the sources of Dante's writings. We have already mentioned the instructive case of Dante's quoting the exemplary behaviour of pagan Romans. It has been shown, conclusively, in my view, that Dante took these examples not from his own reading of the classical authors but that he used St Augustine's *De civitate Dei* as his source while giving his argument a twist very different from that of Augustine. This case, along with many others in which he quotes both Scripture and accepted ecclesiastical authorities, particularly St Thomas Aquinas, shows that Dante's raising of the pagan past to the level of acceptability in the *Monarchia* was not unintentional. We may be surprised by this, but we can draw no other conclusion.

There are other indications in the *Monarchia* which point in the same direction. On several occasions, he refers to God in terms which are somewhat removed from those of basic Christian teaching. In the *Monarchia*, God and nature, "deus et natura" are often used interchangeably as synonyms[15] to the extent that Walter Ullmann called this view one of theistic cosmology not specifically Christian.[16] The cumulative effect is a debasement of the term "Deus" which to a Christian ear loses specifically Christian connotations. This is one more way in which Dante tries to establish a continuity between the Roman past and his own time, a continuity which is not materially affected by the advent of Christianity. In the light of these impressions, the empire which Dante is discussing appears to be a basically secular monarchy.

This interpretation receives support from other sections of his work. It has been said rightly, I believe, that every political philosophy has underlying it a basic view of man. For to the philosopher man and society are inextricably linked. We must therefore ask what view of man Dante put forward in the *Monarchia*, and this approach is justified by the fact that the treatise is indeed preceded by a few remarks about the nature and the aim of man. The relevant passages occur in *Monarchia* I.iii. and iv.

Dante asks: ". . . quid sit finis totius humane civilitatis" (*Mon.*I.iii.1; what is the ultimate end of human society as a whole?) He argues that each individual as well as each group of human beings has specific aims but that the highest aim is that which God has established for the whole of the human race by his art, which is nature: "Deus ecternus arte sua, que natura est" (*Mon.*I.iii.2). Man's unique distinction is to perceive things by use of the intellect. He then continues:

> . . . patet quod humanum in quiete sive tranquillitate pacis ad proprium suum opus, quod fere divinum est . . . liberrime atque facillime se habet. Unde manifestum est quod pax universalis est optimum eorum que ad nostram beatitudinem ordinatur. (*Mon.*I.iv.2)

(It is in the tranquillity of peace that mankind finds the best conditions for fulfilling its proper task which is almost divine. Hence it is clear that universal peace is the most excellent means of securing our happiness.) The goal to which all man's actions should be directed is thus identified as the establishment of universal peace. The aims outlined for humanity are essentially secular aims. E. H. Kantorowicz calls these aims a "moral-ethical goal which is a goal in itself and is para-ecclesiastical".[17] Indeed, the aims of the community are set above the aspirations of the individual who is expected to bow to this higher purpose. We may now find it easier to accept that in the *Monarchia* Dante could argue in favour of an empire of the classical Roman type which preceded Christ and was unaffected by his life. This argument is conclusive as long as its premises are accepted. Kantorowicz adds that Dante took the "human out of the Christian compound and isolated it as a value in its own right — perhaps Dante's most original accomplishment in the field of political theology".[18]

But of course the premises upon which the *Monarchia* is built have not been universally accepted, least of all in Dante's time. Having outlined man's "beatitudo" in *Monarchia* I.v as the striving towards peace, Dante takes up the theme of man's "beatitudo" in the very last chapter of his treatise:

> Duos igitur fines providentia illa inenarrabilis homini proposuit intendendos: beatitudinem scilicet huius vite, que in operatione proprie virtutis consistit et per terrestrem paradisum figuratur; et beatitudinem vite ecterne, que consistit in fruitione divini aspectus . . . que per paradisum celestem intelligi datur. Ad has quidem beatitudines . . . per diversa media venire oportet.
> (*Mon.*III.xv.7)

(Unerring Providence has set man to attain two goals; the first is happiness in this life which consists in the exercise of his own powers and is typified by the Earthly Paradise; the second is the happiness of eternal life which consists in the enjoyment of the divine countenance and is typified by the heavenly Paradise. These two sorts of happiness are attained by divers means.) Thus at the end of the treatise Dante openly admits that he only discussed one facet of the human personality, namely the secular aspect. He is aware that man has a religious side, and he also knows that this requires a different kind of provision. Dante's Earthly Paradise as portrayed in the *Monarchia* is therefore no preparation for the heavenly Paradise. This admission of course also applies to his discussion of the imperial office, and we should add that in the very last section of the *Monarchia* Dante has something remarkable to say on the relationship between the emperor and the pope: "Illa igitur reverentia Cesar utatur ad Petrum qua primogenitus filius debet uti ad patrem." (*Mon*.III.xv.18; Caesar is obliged to observe that reverence towards Peter which a first-born son owes to his father.) Étienne Gilson went out of his way to show that this undoubted attitude of compromise runs through the whole of the *Monarchia*.[19] I cannot agree with him in this. I see the treatise as being, for the most part, a description of a world government having mainly secular aims both for society and for the individual.

This brings me to the second possible answer to Dante's attempt to bridge the gulf between classical and Christian Rome. From the way in which I described the outline and treatment of the *Monarchia* the treatise appears incomplete in itself. For Dante describes only one side of human nature while acknowledging the existence of another important aspect. Already in *Convivio* IV.xxii.18 Dante argued that there is a supreme happiness ("somma beatitudine") towards which man strives but which he cannot attain on earth. At the end of the *Monarchia*, he takes another step forward and, as we saw above, describes the second side of man as "beatitudo vite ecterne que consistit in fruitione divini aspectus". Here he puts into one sentence the task which was still before him, the description of man's other "beatitudo", which the *Commedia* was to contain. In contrast to his position in the *Convivio*, Dante in the *Monarchia* is no longer satisfied with the treatment of man's earthly happiness alone.

So the *Monarchia* appears as an important signpost towards the *Commedia*. Other indications support this, and they must be mentioned briefly. Virgil who was to lead Dante through the *Inferno* into the Earthly Paradise in *Purgatorio* xxix is Dante's guide in the *Monarchia* in precisely the same area. Admittedly the *Monarchia* describes only "terrestrem paradisum" and thus Virgil deserves the place of honour which he is given. The *Monarchia* is the first work in which Virgil appears in this prominent position throughout. We may say likewise that in the *Monarchia* Dante goes only as far as Virgil is able to guide him. But it was a considerable step forward from the *Convivio*.

Dante had exhausted the subject as far as possible within those limits which he had initially set himself. For the further treatment of the subject he abandoned Latin, that cosmopolitan language of scholarship, and instead used the highly individualistic vernacular.

Looking back over our analysis, we may recapitulate as follows. The views put forward by Dante in the *Monarchia* are not all new, neither as regards his own works nor those of his contemporaries. What make the *Monarchia* a work of value in its own right however, are, on the one hand, changes in detail from what he had expressed in the *Convivio*, and these changes result in a rather different conclusion. Compared to the *Convivio*, in the *Monarchia* he plays down the divine contribution to the achievement of the classical Romans and "humanizes" them. (Ironically, many of the virtues which he ascribes to the ancient Romans had been the strength and glory of the republic rather than of the empire). It is perhaps fair to say that in the *Convivio* he had gone a little further than is possible or necessary in "Christianizing" pagan Rome, and that in the *Monarchia* he restores the balance.

On the other hand, Dante earns his palm in being the first, as far as I know, who systematically links the pre-Christian empire to that of the Christian era. This continuity had always been assumed rather than worked out fully. Dante's effort to establish this continuity has had the result we have already described: he ends up with an empire having such a secular nature that its subjects are considered as having only secular needs. Apparently philosophy, like the sorcerer's broom, has assumed a function not intended by its user. For I have indicated that the result of this thinking seems to have dissatisfied Dante.

Nancy Lenkeith, in her very fine study on *Dante and the Legend of Rome,* points out quite rightly that even with the development of the view of the *Monarchia* beyond that of the *Convivio*, Dante was still unorthodox for, "according to the Christian doctrine, man has only one nature, and one ultimate end; it is necessary that human activity be entirely directed towards this one ultimate end."[20] Viewed in this light, the *Monarchia* appears as a stage in Dante's development towards the *Commedia* and so it is necessary to consider the language and content of his Latin works together as one does with regard to his vernacular writings. I find it hard to believe that the *Monarchia* was written after the *Paradiso,*[21] for if this were so it would indicate that Dante regressed intellectually towards the end of his life.

Lenkeith also points out that Dante, especially in the *Monarchia,* emerges as a humanist "to the extent that the dream of reviving Roman ways of life makes a humanist".[22] "There is", she continues, "no difference in Dante's mind between the Rome of the Caesars and the Rome which he yearns to see revived in his own day, except that the old Rome is now Christian."[23] We must be aware that this "except" carries an enormous weight, for it embodies the problem of the Renaissance, that inspiring and ultimately fatal marriage of things Christian and things pagan. In this light, it appears more apt to award Dante's *Monarchia* not the palm but rather the laurel wreath even if it means depriving Petrarch of this distinction.[24]

Notes

[1] I have used P. G. Ricci's ed. of the *Monarchia,* M. Simonelli's ed. of the *Convivio* and Dante's *Epistolae,* ed. Paget Toynbee, 2nd edition (Oxford, 1966). I also generally use the translations (emended where necessary) by D. Nicholl, *Dante: Monarchy and Three Political Letters* (London, 1954).

[2] *Mon.*I.xii.6 and see the extensive comment on pp. 158-9 there.

[3] There is some dispute over the reading of the text. Normally the reading is "aliquo", which would conform to *Mon.*III.i.5; Ricci prefers "alio", followed by a comma and justifies this by the cross-reference to *Mon.*III.xv.16, see pp. 136-7 a note to *Mon.*I.ii.3. I follow Ricci without, however, being completely convinced by his arguments.

[4] We are not thereby merely repeating the work of textual comparison done so excellently for the *opera Dantis.* Though these editions note parallels, they do not make it sufficiently clear where texts differ even when dealing with the same context. In addition we need to consider those passages in *Mon.* II and III which are not paralleled in the *Convivio* and the political letters. Only when textual and contextual analysis stand side by side will the full significance of the *Monarchia* as a work in its own right emerge.

[5] For Virgil as "divinus poeta noster" see *Mon.*II.iii.6; "noster vates" *Mon.*II.iii.12; "poeta noster" *Mon.*II.iii.8,10,11,14,15,16; II.iv.8; II.v.11,13; II.vi.9; II.vii.11; II.viii.11; II.ix.14. No epithet or possessive pronoun: *Mon.*I.xi.1; II.v.12.

[6] See also the stimulating study by U. Leo, "The Unfinished *Convivio* and Dante's Rereading of the *Aeneid*", *Mediaeval Studies* 13 (1951) 41-64.

[7] Commentators normally confine themselves to pointing out precedents for this

statement in Christian times, e.g. Ricci in his note to p. 186, as well as Toynbee in *The Letters of Dante,* note on pp. 49-50. H. Fichtenau, *Arenga. Spätantike und Mittelalter im Spiegel von Urkundenformeln* (Graz-Köln, 1957) p.42, shows that the statement is already found in the works of Valerius Maximus, *Factorum dictorumque memorabilium* liber V 6 ext. 2: "Dignitas et excellentia Romani imperii, que ab ipso pietatis fonte manavit".

[8]A. P. D'Entrèves, *Dante as a Political Thinker* (Oxford, 1952) p. 39.

[9]See above, note[7].

[10]See the note by the editor Ricci p. 239.

[11]"Imperator ex sola electione eorum ad quos pertinet electio verus efficitur imperator nec alicuius eget confirmatione seu approbatione", quoted from H. Mitteis, *Die deutsche Königswahl und ihre Rechtsgrundlagen bis zur goldenen Bulle,* 2nd edition (Brno, 1944) p. 218 and note 745. On Charlemagne's acclamation see *Handbuch der europäischen Geschichte* ed. T. Schieder, Volume 1 ed. T. Schieffer (Stuttgart, 1976) pp. 580-1. For more detail see C. R. Brühl, "Fränkischer Krönungsbrauch und das Problem der *Festkrönungen"*, *Historische Zeitschrift* 194 (1962) 265-326. I agree with Brühl as far as the acclamation of 800 goes and this interpretation has found acceptance subsequently. I do not however accept all the other points raised in the article, but these are of no concern to the present argument. The best discussion of the concept of the medieval empire available in English is that by Marc Bloch, "The empire and the idea of empire under the Hohenstaufen", in *Land and Work in Medieval Europe,* selected papers by Marc Bloch, translated by J. E. Anderson (London, 1967) pp. 1-43; on the title "Romanorum rex" see pp. 13-14.

[12]Charles T. Davis, *Dante and the Idea of Rome* (Oxford, 1957) p. 192.

[13]Davis (see note[12]) pp. 141-2.

[14]See T. Silverstein, "On the Genesis of *De Monarchia,* II, v" *Speculum* 13 (1938) 326-49.

[15]See e.g. *Mon.*I.iii.2,3; I.x.1; I.xiv.2; II.ii.2; III.ii.2,5; III.xiii.2. See also *Epistola* VI.2.

[16]Walter Ullmann, *Principles of Government and Politics in the Middle Ages,* 2nd edition (London, 1966) p. 260.

[17]E. H. Kantorowicz, *The King's Two Bodies: A Study in Mediaeval Political Theology* (Princeton, 1957) p. 463.

[18]Kantorowicz (see note[17]) p. 465.

[19]É. Gilson, "Philosophy in the *Monarchy"*, *Dante the Philosopher* (London, 1948) pp. 162-224 especially p. 180.

[20]N. Lenkeith, *Dante and the Legend of Rome: An Essay,* Mediaeval and Renaissance Studies, Supplement II (London, 1952) p. 148.

[21]See above note[2].

[22]Lenkeith (see note[20]) p. 176.

[23]Lenkeith p. 177.

[24]Since the completion of this paper the importance of the vernacular language and Latin in Dante's works has been discussed at some length by Robin Kirkpatrick *Dante's "Paradiso" and the Limitations of Modern Criticism* (Cambridge, 1978), especially pp. 61-76, 87-95. Dr Kirkpatrick does not however treat the issue raised in this paper, nor does he concern himself at any length with the *Monarchia.* I acknowledge with gratitude his comments on my paper when he was my colleague at University College Dublin, but I do not see any need to alter my text in the light of his published study.

Index